THE DESERTS OF BOHEMIA

The Deserts *of* Bohemia

CZECH FICTION AND ITS SOCIAL CONTEXT

PETER STEINER

CORNELL UNIVERSITY PRESS

ITHACA AND LONDON

First published 2000 by Cornell University Press

Printed in the United States of America

Library of Congress Cataloging-in-Publication Data

Steiner, Peter.
  The deserts of Bohemia : Czech fiction and its social context / Peter Steiner.
    p.   cm.
  Includes bibliographical references and index.
  ISBN 0-8014-3717-2 (cloth)
  1. Czech fiction—20th century—History and criticism.   2. Czech Republic—Civilization.
I. Title.
PG5011 .S74 2000
891.8'6305—dc21   99-055905

Cornell University Press strives to use environmentally responsible suppliers and materials to the fullest extent possible in the publishing of its books. Such materials include vegetable-based, low-VOC inks and acid-free papers that are recycled, totally chlorine-free, or partly composed of nonwood fibers. Books that bear the logo of the FSC (Forest Stewardship Council) use paper taken from forests that have been inspected and certified as meeting the highest standards for environmental and social responsibility. For further information, visit our website at www.cornellpress.cornell.edu.

Cloth printing   10 9 8 7 6 5 4 3 2 1

TO HENRY HOENIGSWALD

ANTIGONIUS: Thou art perfect, then, our ship hath touched upon
The deserts of Bohemia?

MARINER: Aye, my lord, and fear
We have landed in ill time. The skies look grimly
And threaten present blusters. In my conscience,
The Heavens with that we have in hand are angry
And frown upon's.

—William Shakespeare, *The Winter's Tale*

Contents

Acknowledgments

Writing a book about a relatively small culture far from the shores of the Delaware River is, of necessity, a collective undertaking. So it is a pleasure finally to be able to thank in print all of those without whose kind help my access to Czech materials would have been far too limited to carry out such a project: Jaromír Adamec, Libuše Benešová, Libuše Eliášová, Viktor Faktor, Pavel Mánek, Zuzana Nagy, Ivan Poledňák, Miroslav Procházka, Jan Rubeš, Michal Schonberg, Ivan Špirk, Zdeněk Starý, Pavel Vošický.

I am also grateful to the readers—Mike Holquist and Josef Škvorecký—for suggestions that improved the book, and to Bernhard Kendler, the executive editor of Cornell University Press, who made smooth sailing of "my voyage to Ithaca."

My special regard goes to Jean Gurley whose all-encompassing linguistic assistance combined with an indomitable patience helped to make the peculiar idiolect of mine more English-compatible.

Furthermore, I was exceptionally fortunate to receive the support necessary for my research from several grant-giving agencies: the Rockefeller Foundation and the National Endowment for the Humanities (during the early stages of my project); the American Council of Learned Societies (at its middle stages); and the Research Support Scheme of the Higher Education Support Program (whose travel grant No. 539/95 facilitated its conclusion). Without their generous financial aid, this book would never have come about.

P. S.

THE DESERTS OF BOHEMIA

Politics or Poetics

An Introduction

I'm regretting that I never studied the Czech language. Interestingly, it's
very close to Polish, plenty of archaic Russian words.

—Vladimir I. Lenin to his mother, March 2, 1901

This book grew out of an earlier preoccupation with Slavic literary theory, to the exploration of which I have dedicated a good deal of time and
energy. In the 1970s and the 1980s such a research agenda had its intellectual appeal. This was the period of *Sturm und Drang* in American literary
criticism, when traditional scholarly models were rejected and new ways
of reading and analyzing texts examined. In those heady days, Slavic poetics enjoyed a special status. Because of the peculiarities of its own history it had passed through a similar turmoil somewhat earlier—between
the two World Wars—and so it was able to participate actively in the theoretical dialogue of the day, to offer insights and stimuli that would be of
interest to non-Slavic specialists as well.

Yet I would not be telling the whole truth if I claimed that my forays
into formalism and structuralism were motivated only by intellectual curiosity. A detached "thirst for knowledge," I must admit, was just one part
of the story. What compelled me with equal force was the political aspect
of this enterprise. Such an assertion might strike American readers as
strange, to say the least. How could an explication or an application of
highly abstract critical concepts have political ramifications? Moreover,
these were the very theories that insisted on the autonomy of literature in
respect to all other fields of human endeavor, politics included. Dominated by the autotelic aesthetic function, the distinctive feature of verbal
art, according to the proponents of the formalist-structuralist matrix, was
its oblique or general mode of signification devoid of any practical relevance. It is not "what" the work means but "how" this meaning is orga-

1

nized that matters, they insisted. So what could have been political about intricate phonological patterns, syntactic parallelisms of various kinds, and/or narrative structures almost invisible to an eye bereft of such scholarly optics? Let me explain.

There are two main reasons why the Czechoslovak Communist Party watchdogs found such an overtly apolitical criticism subversive. Structuralism, first of all, as an interdisciplinary paradigm for the humanities and social sciences, offered a viable alternative to the official doctrine of Marxism-Leninism, thereby challenging its ideological hegemony—the *conditio sine qua non* of a Communist society. Second, though quite international in its composition, the Cercle linguistique de Prague was also very much rooted in local intellectual life. There were indeed very few Czech thinkers who in the twenty years of its existence did not, in one way or another, pass through its orbit. True, after the Communist revolution of 1948 the Circle disbanded itself "voluntarily" and its leaders publicly renounced previously held views. Yet the guardians of ideological purity knew well how difficult it is to eradicate entirely such a well-entrenched tradition. And there were good reasons for them to worry. Not all prominent members of the Circle actually underwent the humiliating post-1948 auto-da-fé. Roman Jakobson and René Wellek left Czechoslovakia in the late 1930s, eventually reaching the hospitable shores of the New World, where they resumed scholarly careers interrupted by Hitler's intervention. These two fugitives from "class justice" were instrumental in disseminating Prague School ideas around the globe.

Timing is all! This dictum applies equally to comedy acts and historical events. The conflict animating my story was hatched in the mid-1960s, when an unexpected convergence of Czechoslovak and international factors occurred. After a decade of Stalinist terror, the Communist Party's iron grip on the society began to loosen somewhat. And, not surprisingly, the young generation of scholars brought up on a bland Marxist diet of Leninist "reflection theory" were more than eager to taste the forbidden fruit of structuralism. This interest, however, was not merely the manifestation of nostalgia: as quaint as it is naive. Suddenly the structuralist paradigm became the dernier cri in Parisian intellectual circles and beyond. Even in the Soviet Union, researchers belonging to the so-called Moscow-Tartu School began to formulate ideas much more akin to the scholarly agenda of the Linguistic Circle than to what was considered Marxism proper. Thus, in a paradoxical turnabout, by looking back at the state of their discipline in the years between the wars, Czechoslovak theoreticians were able, at the same time, to catch up with the latest professional developments abroad.

Weathered Party apparatchiks, quick to recognize the direction of the prevailing winds, issued an urgent storm warning. In a monograph re-leased in 1966, the highest arbiter of Marxist literary taste, Ladislav Štoll, did not mince words in describing the reactionary *Weltanschauungen* that had spawned structuralism, and he fingered Jakobson as the chief instiga-tor of this appalling heresy.[1] But his were the words of a man crying out in the wilderness, for with the gradual liberalization of the Communist sys-tem, they no longer carried any real punch. So, two years later, with the advent of Prague Spring, the employees of the Institute of Czech and World Literature (a unit of the Academy of Science, emulating the Soviet model) unceremoniously kicked Štoll out of his directorship, electing instead the junior member of the Circle, Felix Vodička, as their new boss. The Sixth International Congress of Slavists, which by chance convened in Prague in August 1968, became an unabashed celebration of Prague Lin-guistic Circle achievements, presided over by the devil incarnate—Roman Jakobson himself. When the meeting ended, on the ominous thirteenth day of the month, none of the participants could have imagined that just a week later Warsaw Pact tanks would be rolling through the town.

It took the Soviets more than half a year to gain full control of the coun-try, but as of April 1969, a new and reliable Central Committee of the Communist Party of Czechoslovakia (CPCS) was ensconced in its job and "normalization" (an official euphemism for the process of re-totalitarian-ization of the society) had been launched. It would be futile to try to de-scribe the wholesale destruction of Czechoslovak culture that ensued. Louis Aragon's expressive sobriquet "the Biafra of spirit" is perhaps the best shorthand description of the barbarity that Moscow's compradors in-flicted on their own nation.[2] The reemergent structuralism and its practi-tioners were victims of this return to "normalcy." Dismissed from their academic positions and assigned to a variety of menial jobs, blacklisted, their works banned from the libraries, they were effectively made second-class citizens. Nor were the perfidious émigrés able to escape Štoll's wrath: the entire edition of Jakobson's selected essays on poetics (half of them written during his interwar years in Prague), ready for distribution, was turned into pulp by the watchful censor in 1969.[3] The list could go on,

---

[1] Ladislav Štoll, *O tvar a strukturu v slovesném umění: K metodologii a světonázorovým vý-chodiskům ruské formální školy a pražského literárního strukturalismu* (Prague, 1966).

[2] For a summary of the purges that followed the Soviet invasion of 1968, see Karel Ka-plan, *Political Persecution in Czechoslovakia, 1948–1972* (Cologne, 1983), pp. 27–40.

[3] Texts, however, are much more resilient than they might seem. Jakobson's friend, the Slovak poet Laco Novomeský, managed secretly to procure two copies of this "vanished" book and had them delivered to the author in the United States. Subsequently the volume was modified somewhat to avoid copyright problems and reprinted by Ladislav Matějka in his Michigan Slavic Contributions series under the title *Studies in Verbal Art: Texts in Czech and Slovak* (Ann Arbor, 1971).

and I could even add personal notes to it. But I mention these already half-forgotten facts with a single purpose in mind: to make the reader aware that a few decades ago involvement with Slavic literary theory was not merely a cerebral, scholastic undertaking. It implied a specific political commitment that infused this enterprise with an "arresting" extra-academic excitement.

The situation I have just described was, however, somewhat paradoxical. If forging the structuralist paradigm had a distinct political ring, its textual application could not have had; an approach that disassociates poetics from all other human activity is unable to account for literature's political role. Within the history of criticism such an intrinsic orientation may be seen as a useful heuristic device, a radical switch in the scholarly agenda that enabled philologists to focus on hitherto neglected properties of a text. Here lies the indisputable contribution of the formalist-structuralist legacy to the discipline. But outside this historical context, the application of its methods to contemporary material seems far less felicitous. One need not be a genius to reckon that what attracted readers to literature in post-1968 Czechoslovakia was not an intricate interplay of poetic devices or ingenious violations of aesthetic norms automatized through overuse. People did not risk their livelihood (or even personal freedom) to produce, copy, and distribute literary works just because of their artistic merit. These were read and appreciated, above all, as vehicles for dissenting political voices suppressed by a government installed by foreign intervention.

True, the counterargument might go, during this period Czech literature carried an unusually heavy political burden, attested to by the simple fact that it was a playwright who, after the demise of the Soviet Empire, became the first president of the Republic. But, a cautious voice might point out, the situation in the 1970s and 1980s was quite abnormal and therefore should not be taken as a reliable basis for any meaningful generalization about the social role of literature. I do not wish to engage here in a lengthy analysis of the term "normalcy." Its use by Czechoslovak Communists should be sufficient, I believe, to illustrate its considerable elasticity. Normal for whom?

Even leaving aside such semantic qualms, one would be hard put to decide which segment of modern Czechoslovak history could be considered "normal." Within a single century the inhabitants of a small territory in the middle of Europe experienced eight major political upheavals: (1) the national revolution of 1918 that liberated Czechs and Slovaks from the Habsburg Empire and enabled them to create a democratic republic; (2) the German invasion of 1938–39 which turned Czechia into the Protektorat Böhmen und Mähren and Slovakia into a Nazi puppet state; (3) the postwar experiment at becoming a neutral bridge between the East and the West which lasted for less than three years; (4) the Communist revolution of 1948 and the subsequent Stalinist terror; (5) the gradual erosion of totalitarianism in the mid-1960s, culminating in the short-lived Prague Spring of 1968; (6) the Soviet army's "fraternal aid" and the transformation of "Socialism with a human face" into "Socialism with gooseflesh" that followed the invasion; (7) the Velvet Revolution of 1989; and (8) the 1993 dissolution of Czechoslovakia into two successor states. What a roller coaster ride, with no regime lasting more than a generation or two! And how could literature remain on the sidelines of a struggle that sometimes touched the very existence of the nation—the same nation that literature to a considerable degree had helped to create!

Which brings me to the crux of the matter. It would be utterly wrong, I believe, to conceive of Czech literature as an aesthetically neutral institution dragged willy-nilly into the political arena by the vicissitudes of history. For the exact opposite seems to be the case. Upon its reinauguration in the early nineteenth century during the era of National Revival (after a prolonged period of decline), Czech literature entered the public sphere as a quintessentially political force. At this time, it should be recalled, no Slavic people (with the exception of the Russians) had their own state, and all were incorporated into several multinational imperia ruled by more powerful neighbors. The sustained drive to change the status quo was inspired by the notion of ethnic identity advanced by nascent Romanticism. Human perception, the adherents of this movement postulated, is by no means universal. Our most basic attitudes are, above all, products of a specific collective mentality. Who we are and how we act is determined by what we share with other members of our ethnic group: language, culture, history. Recognition of ethnic uniqueness had serious political ramifications, especially among groups (such as the Slavs) who perceived their social status as inferior. It provided them with an ideological platform from which to challenge foreign domination. Thus, initial consciousness-raising soon became augmented by political demands for self-governance, escalating eventually into territorial secession and the creation of nation-states that transformed formerly oppressed minorities into new ruling majorities.

This is in a nutshell the story of all the states that sprouted in East Central Europe from the ruins of the Austro-Hungarian, German, and Ottoman empires. But even though their overall developmental trajectories were quite similar, the agents of change differed from place to place, reflecting local conditions. In the Czech lands, whose native Protestant nobility was to a large extent replaced in the seventeenth century by Catholic foreigners allied with the victorious Habsburgs, a political elite capable of spearheading a nationalist drive was conspicuously lacking. In its absence, men and women of letters—the very initiators of the idea of Czechness: philologists, historians, writers—were invested with the political mantle of leadership in their nation's quest for self-determination.[4]

Of all professional groups involved in the National Revival, it was Czech writers who were able to forge the closest bond with the people. The reason for this, I believe, is above all linguistic. Though the founder of Slavistics, Josef Dobrovský, could write the trailblazing *Institutiones linguae slavicae dialecti veteris* in Latin, and the "Father of the Nation," František Palacký, could write most of his magisterial *Geschichte von Böhmen* in German to reach the widest audience possible, authors of fiction did not have this luxury of choice. For to be a Czech writer meant writing in the Czech language, despite the quantitative and qualitative limitations in readership that this choice inevitably entailed. To overcome this handicap, writers had to assume a special attitude toward their audience: to educate them, to bring them to the level at which they could fully participate in the literary process. This was a complex task that included not only the cultivation of a language atrophied during centuries of limited use, or the conveyance of cultural and intellectual values missing locally, but also the justification of the entire project of recreating a Czech nation whose ultimate utility was not entirely clear to many.

In so doing, Czech writers attained a status that no other professional group had had: that of pundits expected to proffer authoritative opinions on all relevant public matters. And throughout history their declarations often precipitated or endorsed important political events, for example, the May 1917 manifesto of Czech writers criticizing the pro-Austrian actions of Czech representatives at the Vienna Reichsrat and demanding national independence, or the Fourth Congress of the Czechoslovak Writers' Union of July 1967, which in an unprecedented move openly challenged the domestic and foreign policies of the Communist Party, setting the stage for the social experiment known as Prague Spring. Other campaigns involving writers may have been less illustrious, but they surely support my line of argument. I have in mind, for instance, a series of articles in the country's leading dailies throwing unqualified support behind the witch-hunt trial of General Secretary Rudolf Slánský and thirteen other high Party officials in November 1952. Penned by several prominent members of the literary profession, these contumelious pieces served a single purpose: to supply credence to politically motivated judicial murder. Whether these denunciations were written freely or under coercion is not

---

[4] For a conveniently brief overview of Czech nationalist thought, see Ernest Gellner, *Nationalism* (New York, 1997), pp. 96–101.

important here. What matters is that the Party propagandists who un-leashed the media blitz around this show trial had clearly recognized the value of writers' voices for influencing public opinion.

My thesis that there was an intimate relationship between Czech litera-ture and politics is not entirely original and has been proffered by others as well. What, in my opinion, sets me apart from them is the way that I ap-proach the issue. Let me take as an example A. French's *Czech Writers and Politics*, concerned with the post-World War II years up to the beginning of normalization.[5] It is a well-researched study that traces the minutest convolutions of Czech political life in the not-so-distant past and with skill and precision positions a plethora of writers within this sensitive process. There is very little for which one could reproach this work, with one important caveat. It does not really analyze what is considered the true domain of verbal art: the literary texts. This is not to say that French ignores the literature of the period he pursues. There are plenty of plot summaries and literary quotations in his book. But these are used primar-ily as indices of their authors' social commitments or illustrations of the ideological ambiance of the time. Writers are censored or arrested or be-come the regime's apologists. They make public statements and retrac-tions, they meet and pass pro- and anti-government resolutions. But their literary output is always secondary to these political undertakings. In French's account, literary works are either passive reflections of particular political circumstances or social commentaries that could equally have as-sumed other forms. I do not wish to be unduly harsh to French's book, if only because it was one of the original stimuli behind my own project. And its limitations directed my inquiry in a particular way: toward con-ceptualizing literature as an active voice within the polylogue that consti-tutes modern Czech society.

My search, however, proved to be frustrating in more than one respect. First of all, I was unable to find or advance a single explanatory model that could account for all the forms that the encounter between poetic texts and their political contexts can assume. By examining a variety of works and their recorded receptions, I soon realized that there are no fixed ground rules governing the interaction of these two spheres. Even the most esoteric poetic form can, in a particular situation, serve a political purpose, while political acts can be motivated to some extent by aesthetic considerations.[6] And even if one focuses only on texts, the historical flux further complicates the matter: allegories that were written with very spe-

5   A. French, *Czech Writers and Politics: 1945–1969* (Boulder, 1982).
6   In this connection critics usually quote Walter Benjamin's ad hoc remark about Fascism that renders politics aesthetic and Communism that politicizes art ("The Work of Art in the

cific social referents in mind might lose this dimension when separated from the situations to which they related in the first place. Or "innocent" literary works may be deliberately misread in an act of politically motivated *allegoresis*, imbued with a topical message unimaginable to their authors. And these are only the most obvious problems.

Trapped in this theoretical quicksand, I opted for the most commonsensical solution at hand. I selected a text whose artistic nature and political commitment were generally recognized and proceeded to analyze its social involvement. Václav Havel's version of *The Beggar's Opera* was an obvious choice for a number of reasons. First of all, both John Gay's original and its 1928 rendition by Bertolt Brecht were able to elicit not only great critical acclaim but also considerable political reaction. Second, since the signing of Charter 77,[7] the Czech playwright had become one of acknowledged leaders of the dissident movement and as such was jailed several times for activities that the Communist government deemed subversive. So this writer neatly combined artistic as well as political concerns. Finally, besides his plays, Havel also authored a number of essays that addressed with admirable perspicuity the social ills of normalized Czechoslovakia, thus providing some insight into the potential message of his artistic works.

My initial plan was to compare Gay's, Brecht's, and Havel's texts, mapping their convergences and divergences. This approach, however, soon proved to be too extensive for my purpose, yielding much too much material for a single chapter. But, by reading secondary sources about the reception of these three "versions" of the same play in quite dissimilar milieux, I was surprised to detect a pattern that led to a productive view of Havel's work. Simplifying the matter somewhat, one might argue that the main effect of *The Beggar's Opera* in all its versions derives from its satirical comparison of a ruling class to a criminal underworld. Both Sir Robert

Age of Mechanical Reproduction," in *Illuminations*, trans. H. Zohn [New York, 1968], p. 242). This catchy dichotomy is, in my opinion, off the mark. As I illustrate in my chapter on Fučík, the Communists, too, aestheticized politics. This should not come as a surprise, given the common Romantic origins of the two great totalitarian movements. For the German Romantics' (con)fusion of art and politics, see Carl Schmitt, *Political Romanticism*, trans. G. Oakes (Cambridge, Mass., 1986), pp. 123–27.

[7]   Charter 77's name was derived from a petition to the Czechoslovak government signed by some 250 citizens protesting its chronic violations of human rights. Before it could be mailed on January 6, 1977, however, it was seized by the police. By bringing together dissidents of different ideological orientations, Charter 77 became the focal point of local opposition; subsequently this label was used to designate a broadly based human rights movement that, until the revolution of 1989, regularly voiced its discontent with various forms of official abuse of power. For more information, see H. Gordon Skilling, *Charter 77 and Human Rights in Czechoslovakia* (London, 1981).

Walpole in 1728 and the German bourgeoisie in 1928 accepted this unflattering analogy but deflected its ethical implications by a double irony that William Empson termed "Comic Primness." Yes, the moral façade that high society projects is false, they admitted readily, but let's not worry about it, for that's the way the world has always been! The British lower classes, Empson reports, were very much pleased by Prime Minister Walpole's disarming "honesty." Thus, instead of polarizing his society, Gay's play functioned as a stimulus for national reconciliation. But not so in post–World War I Germany, where the Nazis, according to Hannah Arendt's recollection, took the bourgeoisie's admission of moral bankruptcy at face value. It served as a justification for their radical program to dismantle the corrupt Weimar Republic by force. The reaction of the Czechoslovak Communists to Havel's version of *The Beggar's Opera* was vastly different: they denied a priori any resemblance between their government and the play's characters, immediately banned any further productions, and punished the perpetrators of this mockery.

I would argue, however, that Havel's chief objective was not to make his government the target of an unfavorable analogy. Such comparison merely provided a background for his sustained inquiry into the issue of duplicity with which *The Beggar's Opera* confronted all holders of power. And their responses varied: some acquiesced to the charge, others denied it. But can either of these reactions be considered sincere? Empson's figure of comic primness indicates that, at least as far as Walpole is concerned, they cannot. Walpole acknowledged the immorality of his administration, but he did not relinquish office or the material benefits derived from it. So his "telling the truth" seems to have been merely a strategic ploy of pretense. The indignant response of the Czechoslovak Communist leaders to Havel's play, one of his essays suggests, had a similarly hollow ring. Though obviously brought to power by Soviet tanks, they legitimized their control over the country by appealing to Marxist-Leninist ideology. Far from their being the Kremlin's puppets, they insisted, their rule was the embodiment of the inexorable logic of history according to which Socialism must triumph over capitalism. Did they convince anyone? Most likely not, but this was not their primary goal anyway. Their recourse to ideology was merely a convenient device enabling the Party, in Havel's words, "to pretend that it pretends nothing." And the Party did not care whether the population seriously believed all its cabala. Pretending to do so was quite enough. A massive security apparatus made sure that nobody opted out of this game by speaking his or her mind.

The relation between those in power and the powerless in post-1968 Czechoslovakia resembles to a considerable degree the kind of coercive mechanism for which Gregory Bateson coined the term "double bind." Such a mental trap thrives, according to the British anthropologist, on a particular confusion generated by a discrepancy between utterances of different logical types: the object-linguistic and the meta-linguistic. A demand articulated at the primary level is contradicted by an equally authoritative counterdemand made at the secondary level. The logical paradox thus generated results in a serious communicative disorder (Bateson even speaks of schizophrenia). The interlocutors are paralyzed because they are unable to pin down correctly the logical type of the utterance to which they are to respond. Let me illustrate. As I mentioned earlier, the Czechoslovak government coerced its subjects to pretend that they freely supported the "proletarian dictatorship," while simultaneously prohibiting them from voicing in public their true feelings on the subject. So they did so in private—with a vengeance. To those they trusted, disgruntled citizens intimated that they were not the obedient cowards the authorities considered them to be, and they did not really pretend but rather *pretended* to be pretending while pursuing objectives at variance with official policies.[8] Thus, to reinforce behavioral rules, the authorities dispatched an armada of secret agents who, by pretending to pretend to pretend, were supposed to ferret out all those who stepped out of line. And as I illustrate in Chapter 6, the game of meta-pretending did not stop there. Under these circumstances it was virtually impossible to distinguish collaborators from heroes, supporters of the regime from its detractors. Almost every Czechoslovak was a bit of each—which suited the government just fine.

Now, how does Havel's text fit these particular social circumstances? In general, the play depicts the power struggle between the London police and the criminal underworld. But it narrows this theme by focusing on the discursive practices of the participants. And what a manipulative lot they are: incessantly cheating, lying, deceiving, and double-crossing one another to achieve their strategic targets! As the play unfolds, however, these targets become less and less clear. At every turn the audience wonders not only about who is gaining the upper hand in this tug-of-war but also, above all, about the very identity of the competitors. Are the cops pretending to be the robbers to uphold the law or vice versa? The surprising ending of the play does not eliminate the confusion. There can be no winners, Havel seems to suggest, in this self-delusional game. His *Beg-*

---

8   The concept of "meta-pretending" I am applying to Havel's text was developed by Gaston Bachelard in *La dialectique de la durée* (Paris, 1936), pp. 105–28. Havel knew Bachelard's work and regarded it highly enough to include the sixth chapter of *La dialectique*, "Les superpositions temporelles," which analyzes in detail the issue of "pretending to pretend" as it affects our perception of time, in the literary almanac he edited, *Podoby: Literární sborník* (Prague, 1967), pp. 193–207.

gar's Opera is a literary representation of the communicative disorder only too well known to his Czechoslovak audience from its everyday life.

But there is more to consider. Havel's text might be a skillful artistic representation of a particular discursive practice characteristic of "normalized" Czechoslovakia. But did his dramatic mimesis have social utility? The author's theoretical essay about the pitfalls of modernism provides, I believe, one plausible clue. Art, he asserted in his 1967 essay "The Vicious Circle," is rooted in the basic human instinct of playing. This activity, however, presents the very same logical paradox as Bateson's double bind. While playing, we are at one level performing specific actions while at a meta-level we signal that we do not mean what we are actually doing. Modernist aesthetics, Havel argues, escalates this clash to the point of absurdity. Art of this period aspired to be more than just play, and to achieve this goal it programmatically rejected all existing artistic conventions. But its success leads to paradoxical results. The modernist work becomes so utilitarian that it can no longer be judged by any artistic criteria, thus becoming something else: a piece of political propaganda, for example. This is the case of Julius Fučík's *Reportage: Written from the Gallows*, which I engage in Chapter 3. Or else its breaking of artistic norms is so sophisticated, so rarefied, that it becomes play merely for a few initiates, subverting de facto the very anti-ludic drive that generated it. Is there a way out of this self-defeating fallacy, Havel asks? Only via an act of reflection: the conscious bringing out into the open the contradictions that inform art and fuel the interminable gyrations of modernism that lead nowhere. True, he concedes, such analysis is not a panacea that will automatically abolish all future artistic self-mystifications. But it can surely help us not to repeat the mistakes of the past.

In my opinion, Havel's version of *The Beggar's Opera* transplants this theoretical stance into the realm of politics. As a drama it is a playlike representation of a particular discursive practice in which its Czechoslovak audience was well versed before it entered the theater or read the text. By communicating about a communicative disorder, the play is a meta-statement which reveals those inner contradictions of the primary communication and its utter futility, not obvious to the protagonists. Thus reframed, the double bind predicament is presented for examination to viewers trapped in it at the primary level. As such, *The Beggar's Opera* is not merely artistic free play but also a political gesture, an invitation to fellow citizens to step out of the vicious circle that regulates their behavior, to reflect on it critically, and, if displeased with what they see, to break out of this self-perpetuating spiral.

I have devoted so much space to the discussion of my analysis of Havel's play because it is paradigmatic of my approach in general. That was, after all, the first chapter I actually wrote, and therefore it *nolens volens* provided the theoretical impetus for the rest of the book. *The Beggar's Opera* is a representation of a particular discourse that, according to my observation, was highly characteristic of post-1968 Czechoslovak life. But its ambition was not just to imitate but to influence, to unlock the double bind that, in its author's mind, implicated everybody to some degree in a totalitarian system. So, given the vicissitudes of that country's history, I started to search for other texts that would, in a similarly active fashion, relate to particular social contexts of different periods. Ideally, I would be able to provide a sort of historical typology of discursive strategies through which literary texts of different periods effected interaction with the social milieux surrounding them.

This project, I was soon to learn, proved to be unduly idealistic. Literary history, first of all, need not keep in step with its social counterpart. Texts may be belated reactions to political events that have already transpired, or they might anticipate situations yet to come. Second, works are read again and again in contexts quite different from those that generated them. And it is often the case that a literary text assumes a distinctly political role during such a belated reception, which fact, needless to say, radically altered any preconceived idea about the neat linear progress that my presentation might have had. Finally, as I sieved through the myriad works that appeared potentially relevant for my project, I became acutely aware of how fuzzy the concept of literature is. Notoriously resistant to any analytical definition, this notion is a social construct that derives its existence from an implicit and ever-changing consensus among the members of a particular collectivity. Concerned primarily not with the aesthetic value of the texts being analyzed but with their political ramifications, I became quite leery of using the concept of literature as the exclusive distinctive feature of the subject matter of my book. The terminological crisis hit the proverbial fan when I decided to include in my presentation (for reasons that I will explain shortly) a text that could not be considered literary by any criteria imaginable. So, after prolonged soul searching and with a heavy heart, I decided to change my terminology. The subtitle of my book—"Czech Fiction and Its Social Context"—bears testimony to this conceptual switch.

I do not assume, however, that the notion of "fiction" is without its own problems. Scholars employing it systematically always point out its considerable semantic breadth. In common language "fiction" means something close to "fabrication," "invention," if not an outright falsehood. But in critical parlance it refers to a very specific speech act: pseudo-assertions that do not imply a speaker's commitment to the truth of what they affirm. To return to *The Beggar's Opera*, whatever we learn about Peachum

or Macheath has no truth-value because these characters are mere fig-
ments of Gay's fancy. Yet, it is important to point out, his "assertions" are
not lies (at least not in the ordinary sense of the word). The author makes
them not to deceive his audience for some obvious gain but to engage in a
socially sanctioned game called "creative writing." So we willingly suspend our disbelief about what we hear to partake joyfully in the fictitious
universe of discourse thus created.

Such an understanding of fiction, propounded in the 1970s by speech
act theorists, has its commonsensical appeal. But can the difference between fiction and nonfiction be maintained as rigorously as John Searle
and his followers believed? Is the boundary between truth, lie, and fiction
so absolute that simple logical criteria can sufficiently distinguish one
from another? Let me muddy the waters a bit. One can easily imagine that
in sixteenth-century Spain, for example, the assertion that "Ms. X is a
witch" complied with the four Searlean rules for nonfiction. The speaker
would have been committed to the truth of his proposition; he would
have been able to provide evidence to back up his claim; the assertion
would not have been obvious to the audience; and the speaker would
have believed firmly in the truth of his statement.[9] But since witches, as
we have known since our childhood, exist only in fairy tales, very few
today would classify such an utterance as nonfictional. How to account
for this discrepancy? So long as we belong to a particular group (whether
ethnic, social, or professional), we share with its other members a certain
worldview, a particular group psychology that skews, to some extent, our
perception of all that is around us. We see the world from a sui generis
vantage point. And though we might be totally sincere as to what we assert, and our statements might appear absolutely truthful to other insiders
with browsers having the same operating system as ours, to outsiders
outfitted with different receptors we might as well be fiction writers. The
situation can even turn malevolent if two groups enter a competitive situation. Under such circumstances the extrinsic *Weltanschauung* is no longer
seen as innocent self-delusion, an excusable error, but as something more
sinister. It is interpreted as an instrument of a political power game, a co-
herent set of mystifications foisted on others to further the interests of another group at their expense, an exculpatory mechanism supporting utterly illegitimate claims.

At first glance, my extension of the concept of fiction over the sphere of
ideology might seem forced. An "ideological" fiction, to be sure, is different from an "aesthetic" fiction in one important respect. Ideological fiction

9   See, for example, John Searle, "The Logical Status of Fictional Discourse," *New Literary
History* 6 (1975), 319–32.

is to a great extent spontaneous. We are inculcated with a specific world-view in the process of our acculturation. Ideology becomes second nature, and it is precisely because of this that we cannot see the idiosyncrasies of our own social habits. Aesthetic fiction, however, is clearly intentional. We deliberately suspend the signifying conventions valid in a nonfictional discourse to plunge into the realm of "as if," where anything is possible and nothing really matters. This is certainly true, and I do not wish to claim otherwise. The point I am trying to make is that the very license to engage in the game of non-serious illocutions is not natural but in and of itself ideological. It was quite alien to the European Middle Ages, as illustrated by the oft-quoted story about the incensed audience of a Passion play stoning the actor performing Judas. And the idea that writers enjoy a special "truth-exempt status" so that they might say whatever comes into their heads is clearly unacceptable in some modern societies as well. The 1965 trial of the two Soviet writers, Andrey Sinyavsky and Yuli Daniel, which dispatched the defendants to Siberian labor camps for slandering their homeland through their literary output, and Ayatollah Khomeini's *fatwa* issued in 1989 against Salman Rushdie, the author of the novelistic "blasphemy" *Satanic Verses*, are just two egregious examples of how relative, in fact, is the notion of fiction.

These complications are not advanced gratuitously. Considering what I have termed ideological fictions was an integral part of my project. The strongest and the most pervasive *Weltanschauung* known to the twentieth century generated some of the texts I deal with. A spiritual heir to German Romanticism, Marxism-Leninism always maintained that if facts contradict its grand sociohistorical scheme, they alone are to be blamed. This, of course, is not at all surprising for an intellectual tradition that self-avowedly entered the world not to interpret it but to change it. And, though quite resourceful in pointing out various biases and slants in social theories propagated by others, Marxism-Leninism turned a blind eye to its own follies, declaring itself to be not "a false consciousness" of one class but an all-embracing "objective" science. The "serious" Communist societies built on the basis of this doctrine never exhibited much sympathy toward the unrestrained free play of imagination, even if garbed as fiction. Within the grim confines of Socialist Realism, this notion would hardly make much sense anyway. The authors utilizing this creative method would probably have perceived it as a personal failure if their readers disbelieved what they wrote, and no subsequent suspension of this incredulity would have assuaged them. For the representation of concrete historical reality in its revolutionary transformation can only be truthful. Or else!

But can this observation about the primacy of ideology be extended to writings (and they constitute a clear majority in my book) that would qualify as fictions even in the restricted, Searlean sense of this word? Such works unfold in a possible rather than a real world, and because of their hypothetical modality, so the argument goes, they are exempt from the constraints of any ideological straitjacket. Pragmatically speaking, I am willing to concede that some texts under certain conditions are much less susceptible to a political reading than are others; for if everything were equally political, this category would be utterly useless. But, as I pointed out earlier, interpretation is above all an act of contextualization, and therefore the social function of any work is determined solely by the situation into which it is projected. Transportable to the extreme, one and the same text may be read in altogether different circumstances in a number of incompatible ways. So if Milan Kundera, for example, insists of late that *The Joke* is not a political novel at all but a love story, he may be right, but if so, his authorial intention was sorely misunderstood by all those who reviewed the novel in the 1960s.[10] Yet his might become—and why not?—the normative interpretation for future generations utterly confounded by the ironic avalanche rolling through the book.

In my own project, as its subtitle indicates, I am interested in the social ramifications of the texts at hand. This is not a frivolous choice. For as I have explained, since its rebirth some two hundred years ago, Czech literature has always been involved somehow in the game of politics. From this perspective, then, I take it for granted that any artistic fiction capable of swaying public opinion either for or against the societal status quo does so from some ideological standpoint. Persuading an audience implies— and let us be direct about it—nothing less than selling it a piece of ideological fiction. The monolithic and overarching doctrine of Marxism-Leninism is perhaps the most pronounced form that a collective belief system can assume. The "mental software" peddled by authors subscribing to less rigid types of worldviews is softer, consisting sometimes of mere intuitive axiological hierarchies or generalized attitudes. Such loosely knit cognitive structures may be less effective as direct mind-controlling mechanisms, but this does not make them ideology-free. And the same holds true for writers who, like Karel Čapek, attempted to avoid the trap of a singular ideology by conceiving of all human convictions as equally compelling. This relativist outlook explains Čapek's penchant for the technique of polyperspectival narrative which he employed innovatively in some of his novels. But in his *"fictions-engagés,"* such as his *Apocryphal Stories*, Čapek consistently promulgated, in a very special way, a

---

10 Milan Kundera, "Author's Preface," in *The Joke*, trans. M. H. Heim (London, 1982), p. xi.

partisan ideological and political agenda against the public views of others with whom he disagreed.

Like Caesar's Gaul, this book can be divided into three parts: the first two chapters dealing with Hašek's and Čapek's works from the interwar period; the middle three chapters analyzing texts relevant to the historical interval between the German occupation of 1938–39 and the Soviet invasion of 1968; and the final chapter on Havel's play focusing on the social role of fiction in the 1970s. Jaroslav Hašek's unfinished novel *The Good Soldier Švejk*, written between 1920 and 1923, is a text that occupies a highly prominent position in Czech culture. There are only a very few who would have not read it at all. Moreover, its plebeian protagonist with his robust dislike for lofty idealism and transcendental values of any kind is often perceived as the purest embodiment of the Czech national character. In my own reading, though, I discover a parallel between the good soldier and the Greek *kynik* philosopher Diogenes of Sinope. The two figures, I argue, are prototypal individualists who resist all attempts to mold them into collaborative members of their respective societies. This challenge to authority, however, is indirect, ludic. Instead of promoting political or philosophical claims of their own, they subvert the idea of power or truth through free play, a homonymic-synonymic slippage of verbal signs that turns same into different and different into same.

Given the considerable dissimilarity between the societies whose communal values these two heroes defied—fifth-century B.C. Athens and twentieth-century Austria-Hungary—the discursive strategies employed to thwart undesired social control could not be the same. Drawing upon H. P. Grice's logical approach to conversation, I sketch a distinction between Diogenes' and Švejk's semiotic self-defense. While both refuse to observe the cooperative principle of felicitous conversation, the former does so openly by "opting out" and "flouting" conversational maxims. Švejk, by contrast, does so surreptitiously, in a manner that makes his superiors wonder whether his violations of maxims are not caused by mental aberration rather than a conscious intent to sabotage their authority. This, combined with his insatiable appetite for narrating long stories only tangentially related to the speech situation in which they are told, makes him an unpredictable interlocutor virtually impervious to orders from his superiors.

The numerous commentaries on Hašek's novel usually agree about the historical circumstance that generated his antihero: the growing alienation of the Czech people from the Habsburg monarchy. If in 1848 František Palacký could still have foreseen the future of his country within a federalized Austrian Empire, the unresponsiveness of that government to Czech nationalist aspirations convinced his heirs that true autonomy could be achieved only outside Austria-Hungary. The unpopularity of World War I among the local population, who felt dragged into it against their will, only exacerbated this feeling of non-belonging. Thus, the "artful dodger" Švejk is seen by Czech interpreters as a personification of their nation's "passive" resistance to the centripetal etatist force represented by the hypertrophied civil and military bureaucracy that strove to keep Bohemia incorporated in the Habsburg-ruled state. This explanation, however, cannot account for Švejk's enormous popularity outside the work's original context. This figure, in my view, exceeded the moment of his birth because Švejk's antiauthoritarian stance provided a behavioral model to be emulated en masse by his countrymen after the 1940s, when totalitarian regimes—whether Nazi or Communist—gained the upper hand in their homeland. Švejk-derived discursive strategies proved handy for coping with unrelenting pressure to be co-opted into the service of a political system considered inimical by many.

If, within the context of Czech letters in the interwar period Hašek's novel represents the extreme pole of an individualistic, competitive value system, Karel Čapek's oeuvre was its most direct antipode. Though Hašek's junior by only seven years, Čapek belonged to the next generation of writers, whose careers came to full fruition after the Czechoslovak Republic was established in 1918. This culmination of a long-lasting political struggle for statehood, however, required more than the creation of effective organs of governance. A hitherto missing attitude of cooperation toward the state had to be fostered among its citizens for the new Republic to prosper. To this arduous task Čapek dedicated most of his talent and energy. From 1918 until his death in 1938, he was an ardent and vociferous supporter of the Czechoslovak government and the liberal democracy that it represented. I cannot enumerate here all the social actions and petitions he organized, or the polemics with ideologues of all colorations in which he engaged. The image of a man "who sought to rule by love and reason," crucified between "the hatred on the left [and] on the right" which Čapek evoked in one of his apocryphas, may be easily recognized as his own not-so-ironic self-portrayal.[11] Čapek never hesitated to wield his pen for public causes in which he believed. And *Apocryphal Stories*, straddling literary form and social activism, is an exemplary case of his endeavor.

Earlier I wrote about Čapek's decidedly pluralistic outlook, and I observed how it helped to shape the narrative mode of some of his novels. In general it might be said that for Čapek the distinctive quality of art rested in its curious axiological neutrality, its ability to portray all human values

---

[11] Karel Čapek, *Kniha apokryfů* (Prague, 1945), p. 126; *Apocryphal Stories*, trans. D. Round (London, 1949), p. 80.

as equipotent. This, of course, is not an entirely new insight but a paraphrase of the time-honored Kantian dictum about the disinterested nature of aesthetic judgment. Conceived this way, however, art would be a priori disqualified from any political involvement. In his *Apocryphal Stories*, Čapek evaded this injunction. But this is not the only reason why I decided to focus on the *Stories*. Equally striking to me was the fact that the political dimension of the apocryphas seems totally lost today. Contemporary readers perceive these minute texts solely as witty parodies of venerable texts from the Western cultural heritage, but remain unaware of another message. The reason for this is simple. The apocryphas carried out their political agenda indirectly, through analogy, a strategy that was possible because they were first published in a daily paper. Any discerning reader would have been able to make a connection between them and the news reported there. Though explicitly about such unworldly figures as Archimedes or Jesus, within their original context Čapek's apocryphas were implicated in the politics of the day, permitting the author to plead his point about topical public matters.

Despite its appeal, the ideal of a cooperative value system, promulgated by Čapek, has its practical limits. It can work only if others subscribe to it as well. Though a liberal state, the first Czechoslovak Republic was unable to solve to the satisfaction of all the problem of national minorities who became its citizens after the First World War. I have in mind, in particular, about 3 million Germans who never fully acquiesced to their new minority status. Whether their grievances could have been eventually accommodated remains moot. The political rise of the Nazi Party with its platform of extreme nationalism in the country next door was not helpful for diffusing the tension. And Hitler's coming to power in 1933 set Czechoslovak-German relations on a collision course. President Edvard Beneš—a skillful diplomat and a staunch proponent of a European collective security—based the defense of his country on a military alliance with the Western democracies (France in particular). When tested by Hitler's aggressive blackmail, however, the solidarity of the democratic allies proved to be merely superficial. The infamous Munich Conference of 1938, at which England and France sold Czechoslovakia to Nazi Germany for an utterly worthless promise of future peace, was the death knell for democracy in Čapek's homeland for the next half century.

Chapters 3 through 5 are dedicated to texts that sprang, so to speak, from the womb of Marxist-Leninist ideology. The Munich debacle radically transformed the Czechoslovak political scene, with the CPCS being the most direct beneficiary of this change. The shameful surrender to Hitler discredited in the eyes of many Czechs and Slovaks not only the hitherto ruling liberal political establishment and its Western allies but also the very idea of a democratic government. Suddenly—after a painful encounter with Nazi genocide—the Communist alternative, capable of effectively checking any future German expansionism, seemed an altogether reasonable option. This feeling was further boosted by the fact that most of Czechoslovakia was liberated at the end of World War II by the Red Army. Thus, where France and England had failed, the Communist Soviet Union had demonstrated that it alone had military power capable of guaranteeing the Republic's territorial integrity. And who could be better suited, in the public eye, to realign Czechoslovak foreign policy eastward than the CPCS, whose close relations with Moscow dated to its founding in 1921.

The flames of postwar infatuation with Communism were further fanned by an ambitious propaganda campaign launched by the CPCS. This brings me to the topic of my third chapter—Julius Fučík's *Reportage: Written from the Gallows*. This book, penned illicitly in the Prague Gestapo prison in 1942 and smuggled out to be published only after the liberation, has been the subject of heated controversy. Among the bones of contention have been the history of the manuscript (sanitized on the sly by the author's friend, the aforementioned Ladislav Štoll) and Fučík's behavior in German captivity before his execution in Berlin in 1943. *Reportage*, I believe, exemplifies well the gesture of artistic self-denial—so typical, according to Havel, of modernist aesthetics. Spurning the traditional literary mimesis whereby soft fancy substitutes for hard facts, Fučík deliberately stepped out of the realm of fiction. His book was a factography, a truthful account of self-sacrificial struggle against the Nazi invaders. And it was precisely its truth-claim that made *Reportage* so well suited for propagandistic use.

Earlier I insisted not only that the very opposition fiction / nonfiction is ideologically grounded but also that even the criteria for determining what is factual might differ substantially from one group to another. Fučík's own worldview, as he himself was more than happy to acknowledge, was Marxist-Leninist, and the robust skeleton of this ideology left its indelible impression on his prose. If viewed as a narrative, historical materialism's story about social evolution is emplotted very much in the genre of romance. It is a tale of lapse from bliss to misery but with a happy ending: the proletariat recognize their true identity and through revolution reestablish disrupted harmony. Fueled by the desire for justice pure and simple, the vision of the world that Marxism-Leninism projects is highly disjunctive, one in which the good guys separate from the bad like oil from water. Fučík's *Reportage* follows *summa genus* its ideological model. It is structured as a romance—but with one curious twist ignored by all commentators. Its first half approximates quite faithfully the most famous romantic story of the Western tradition: the crucifixion and resurrection of Jesus Christ. So, not surprisingly, whenever eyewitnesses or historians assail the veracity of Fučík's report, one can be sure that the author distorted the facts so as not to stray from the scriptural pattern that his "nonfiction" follows.

It may not have been only the atheistic bent of their ideology that made Party propagandists inhospitable to the Christological parallel in *Reportage*. For their specific purpose, Fučík's sacrificial death was to be linked to an altogether different myth: that characterized by a British critic as the peculiar belief of the Czechs that throughout their history martyrdom was the only way to preserve their national identity.[12] From this perspective then, *Reportage* grafted remarkably well the Marxist-Leninist romance about the ultimate proletarian victory onto the very domestic mythological tradition of sacrificing one's life to save Mother Czechia from the German peril. Read this way, *Reportage* can be seen, indeed, as Fučík's application to join the benevolent association of Czech national martyrs founded in the tenth century by good old King Wenceslas. But it added a significantly new ideological spin to the old game. Julius was not just a lonely patriot bravely confronting a numerically superior foreign power but the personification of the Communist movement fighting a rear-guard battle after the cowardly bourgeoisie had delivered the nation into the Nazi yoke. Given the paucity of deeds (the level of anti-Nazi resistance in Czech lands across the political spectrum was not very high), Fučík's words provided an invaluable support for the CPCS's efforts to legitimize its grab for power by portraying itself as the only political force always ready to defend the nation's independence to the last drop of blood.[13] Within the context of Marxist-Leninist ideology, *Reportage* represents the thesis, the pole of absolute positivity. Fučík's life and death set the supreme example for Communist youth, and his book was the ultimate inspiration for Communist writers such as Milan Kundera, whose 1955 panegyric, *The Last May*, fancifully magnified a minute scene from *Reportage* into a thirty-page poem. But this is only half of the ideological enchilada.

The wonderful world of romance must be inhabited not only by larger-than-life heroes but by despicable-beyond-the-pale villains as well. Party propagandists knew well the rules of their genre. But given their distaste for the mendaciousness of literary mimesis, no representation of evil could have

---

12   Robert R. Pynsent, *Questions of Identity: Czech and Slovak Ideas of Nationality and Personality* (Budapest, 1994), pp. 147–210.
13   The subtitle of Vojtěch Mastný's monograph *The Czechs under Nazi Rule: The Failure of National Resistance, 1939–1942* (New York, 1971) accurately characterizes the dismal state of the Czech anti-Nazi underground to which Fučík belonged.

been good enough for them. The scoundrels had to be real, or, preferably, more real than real. And the infamous political trials carefully staged by the security apparatus delivered what was needed. In Chapter 4 I analyze perhaps the most spectacular of all Czechoslovak ideological fictions: the 1952 trial of Rudolf Slánský and his thirteen "accomplices" which resulted in a whopping eleven death sentences. But I do so from a very particular angle. What interests me about this case is its poiesis, or how this text was made. Given the "projectional" nature of such trials, it is not the semantic aspect of mimesis that I investigate but its *pragma*. Rather than probing the original-copy relationship, I focus on the mimetic rivalry among the members of the Communist movement which, I suspect, generated such witch-hunts. Following René Girard's lead, I therefore approach the Slánský case as an instance of the panhuman ritual of scapegoating and describe various stages of this process (the selection of victims, their appointed characteristics, the final disposal of them, etc.) as well its social functions. From an overall generic perspective, then, such trials appear as sui generis "demonographies," collections of maximally negative characterizations—the antithesis of the Communist heroes' hagiographies—a stick ready to be used against anybody deviating, if ever so slightly, from the Party line.

What most observers find especially disturbing about these judicial murders is the uncanny lack of any clear attributable guilt—as if everybody and, at the same time, nobody was directly responsible for what happened. In this way they often suggest a parallel with the macabre universe of Kafka's prose, where justice follows an equally inscrutable course. It is this intuitive insight that I attempt to substantiate in the last part of the chapter. Drawing on linguistically oriented Kafka scholarship, I point to several levels of similarity between the famous Prague author's style and the public rhetoric surrounding the Prague trial. In tropological terms, the figure of prolepsis plays a cardinal role in both. It is as if the accused were sentenced at the very moment of their arrest, and the intermediary judicial proceedings were totally superfluous. This collapse of linguistic cause and effect can also be approached from a speech act perspective. For a locution to secure an upshot in the real world, it must conform to specific linguistic conventions. One cannot, for instance, promise things that are outside one's control because such a promise would not carry an illocutionary force; it would be empty. The resolutions of "angry" Czechoslovak workers—too numerous to be counted—demanding, from the outset of the trial, the ultimate punishment for the "traitors" are good instantiations of such pseudo-illocutions that should not have a perlocutionary effect. But they did, and eleven death penalties were meted out. Was it a case of judges yielding to the vox populi, or were they following the Politburo's orders, or did they believe, as some later claimed, the self-accusatory confessions of the defendants? Taboo for over a decade, these and similar questions were still exceedingly difficult to sort out even when, in the mid-1960s, the veil of secrecy surrounding the trial was finally lifted.

The Slánský case, together with other trials of Communist functionaries from the early 1950s, played an important role in the intra-Party fights triggered by the generational change a decade later. For young reformists (who rallied eventually behind Alexander Dubček), the trial was a handy tool for dislodging the old leadership, many of whose members were deeply implicated in the wrongful death of their comrades. But it was Milan Kundera's novel *The Joke* that in 1967 managed to vent in public the suppressed guilt of the past with unprecedented force. As some reviewers pointed out, this is a book about the destruction of ideologies. All four of its main narrators identify fully with well-defined social utopias supportive of, if not directly instrumental in, the Communist revolution of 1948. By the 1960s, however, youthful dreams of a just world had become hopelessly muddled, out of sync with the new reality. The respective belief systems that had endowed the protagonists' lives with meaning crumbled away. Bereft of any transindividual guidance, they floundered, dying symbolically in the middle of their lives. One hero, however, escapes this predicament: the Communist student Ludvík. Because of an innocent joke he was dismissed from the Party and sent, as a soldier in a penal battalion, to work in the coal mines. Alienated from his former comrades and their utopia, he tries to retaliate against the chief instigator of his suffering. But his revenge backfires, turning into just another joke. The intervening years have thoroughly reshuffled the makeup of Czechoslovak society, and in the new environment Ludvík's long-delayed vengeance turns utterly ridiculous.

On the surface, it might seem, the message proposed by *The Joke* is simple: the torts of the past are beyond retribution. Since what has been done cannot be undone, sinking into historical oblivion (as Ludvík does at the end of the book) is the only sensible solution. This, however, is not Kundera's own position. His novel, I argue, accepts the challenge of history's endless irony, playing, in fact, a joke on history itself. In writing the book, Kundera actually returned to his own past, if only textually. *The Joke* recapitulates a number of motifs from his lyrical poetry of the 1950s—well steeped in the utopian ideological spirit of the era. Such a repetition serves a very specific purpose, though: it enables Kundera-the-prosaist to destroy some of the myths that Kundera-the-poet had helped to create. The image of Fučík that appears in several crucial passages of *The Joke* is a good example of this deconstructivist technique. I have already alluded to Kundera's 1955 poem eulogizing the Communist martyr. In his novelistic rendition, however, not only is Fučík presented as a symbol of Stalinist terror and, by proxy, an accomplice to Ludvík's calvary, but also his actions are subjected to fierce scrutiny. Rather than a hero, the Fučík of *The Joke* is an insecure narcissist ready to endanger the lives of others just to be able to pass on to posterity his self-aggrandizing portrait. Kundera transforms his own previous ideological delusions into the material for a novel about the folly of all ideologies.

The thirty thousand copies of *The Joke* that were initially distributed made a hefty contribution to the painful soul-searching that dominated Czechoslovak political discourse in the mid-1960s. The victory in January 1968 of the reformist Party wing headed by Dubček led to the abolition of censorship, which step made the media available, for the first time since 1948, to people other than Communists. It is impossible to present here succinctly the plethora of conflicting voices that suddenly burst into the open. At stake was how far the rejuvenated CPCS would be willing to go to heal the wounds of the past. For by now it was clear that the victims of Stalinist terror were not just its own rank and file but, above all, the "class enemy," the scores of innocent bystanders notwithstanding. Would the Party suppress the memory of its shameful acts, relegating them to oblivion? Or would it learn a historical lesson, relinquish its political hegemony, and compete for office in a free election along with others? Evidently eight months did not suffice for the internally torn CPCS to make up its mind. But this hesitation proved fatal when it was confronted by the Warsaw Pact invasion of August 21, 1968. Arrested by the Soviets and taken to Moscow, Dubček's leadership, in a suicidal gesture, agreed to the "temporary" stationing of Red Army troops on Czechoslovak territory. Reformed socialism fell on its "human face," never to get up off it again.

The decision to close this book with Havel's play was, to a large degree, arbitrary. My manuscript was getting too long for its own good. Had I more space at my disposal, I would have take into account more recent works as well. Ludvík Vaculík's novel *The Czech Dream-book*, published first in the early 1980s in the samizdat Edition Padlock, is a truly outstanding specimen of the spurious category "fictional nonfiction" which I find so intriguing.[14] Produced by a leading Prague dissident, the book looks very much like Vaculík's own diary, with rather intimate personal information included. The author—a man under tight state security surveillance—is (we learn from the text) regularly summoned to police headquarters to be questioned about his anti-government activities, but he steadfastly refuses to talk. Does this diary/novel, the reader might ask, contain the information that Vaculík is withholding from the authorities, or is it a clever fiction that would provide little if any incriminating evidence against the author and his fellow dissidents when eventually brought out? Vaculík's monthly

---

[14] Ludvík Vaculík, *Český snář* (Toronto, 1983).

feuilletons—often caustic but always witty commentaries about the major and not-so-major events of the season which appeared in various underground periodicals—would undoubtedly have furnished my project with yet another challenging topic. I only hope to have enough stamina to return to these texts in the not so distant future.[15]

The period after the Velvet Revolution of 1989 seems far less hospitable to my project. It is clear that the political function of literature is now in decline. The basic reasons for this are rather obvious. The ideological battles of today are fought in Czechia on the floor of Parliament rather than in the pages of books. And the actual scorekeeping carried out daily in every newspaper is, with a few notable exceptions, devoid of any literary interest. This unprecedented divorce of poetics from politics reflects to some degree the peculiar nature of the Velvet Revolution as a social change born from the total exhaustion of the Communist utopia rather than from any new and stimulating ideological fiction of its own. At the same time, the capitalist economy that it helped to reconstitute has turned books into a commodity. For market-driven publishing, a high profit margin is the main criterion of success. Books appealing to the broadest possible audience—sensational nonfiction, do-it-yourself manuals of various kinds, popular thrillers—constitute, it seems, the staples of reading materials today. Serious literary periodicals are the prime victims of this change in taste. A prestigious weekly, *Literary Newspaper*, once upon a time the major platform for the interaction between poetics and politics, which during its heyday could have boasted a circulation of over a quarter million, has fallen to about 5 percent of this figure, with the Damocles' sword of bankruptcy dangling uncomfortably low above its head. But most important, literature is losing steadily to its most serious competitor—the visual media. As every concerned parent knows only too well, watching TV is more fun than reading. And this holds true nearly as much for Europe as for the United States. So what does the future look like? Can Czech literature, against all these odds, regain its privileged status and turn once again into a social institution of great authority? Or are we, instead, witnessing its ultimate decline, the product of the gradual disintegration of the "Gutenberg galaxy" at which Marshall McLuhan was hinting some forty years ago?[16] This is not just a rhetorical question. I myself wish I knew.

[15] A small selection of Vaculík's feuilletons is available in English, as *A Cup of Coffee with My Interrogator: The Prague Chronicles of Ludvík Vaculík*, trans. G. Theiner (London, 1987).
[16] Marshall McLuhan, *The Gutenberg Galaxy: The Making of Typographic Man* (Toronto, 1962), pp. 278–79.

1

Tropos Kynikos

The Good Soldier Švejk by Jaroslav Hašek

Freedom's just another word for nothing left to lose.

—Kris Kristofferson/Janis Joplin, "Me and Bobby McGee"

In his celebrated essay "Hašek and Kafka," Karel Kosík wrote:

> [Josef] Švejk's "odyssey under the honorable escort of two soldiers with bayonets" takes him from the Hradčany garrison jail along Neruda Street to Malá Strana and over Charles Bridge to Karlín. It is an interesting group of three people: two guards escorting a delinquent. From the opposite direction over Charles Bridge and up to Strahov, another trio makes its way. This is the threesome from Kafka's *Trial*: two guards leading a "delinquent," the bank clerk Josef K., to the Strahov quarries, where one of them will "thrust a knife into his heart." Both groups pass through the same places, but meeting each other is impossible.[1]

But had they met, the Czech Marxist philosopher continues his flight of imagination, one to be set free, the other executed, could the two Josefs have understood each other? Would they have discerned any trace of affinity in their plights?

This is a provocative question, and Kosík is fully aware of it. In Czech letters Kafka's and Hašek' s oeuvres (for which J. K. and J. Š. stand here as shorthand) have always enjoyed quite incompatible reputations. "Kafka," Kosík opined, "is read to be interpreted, while Hašek is read to make

[1] Karel Kosík, "Hašek a Kafka neboli groteskní svět," *Plamen*, no. 6 (1963), 96. Quoted from "Hašek and Kafka: 1883–1922/23," trans. A. Hopkins, *Cross Currents* 2 (1983), 127. Further references will be given in the text; the first number in parentheses refers to the Czech original and the second to the English translation (sometimes slightly modified).

people laugh. There exist dozens, even hundreds of interpretations of Kafka. His work is perceived and accepted as full of problems and problematic, as enigmatic, puzzle-like and cryptic, accessible only through decoding—in other words, through interpretation. Hašek's work, on the other hand, seems completely clear and understandable to everybody; his work is naturally transparent, provoking laughter and nothing more" (96; 127). Kosík, I would stress, did not pose his provocative question out of intellectual curiosity alone. By equating Hašek and Kafka, by arguing that "these two Prague authors . . . described two human types that at first glance seem far apart and contradictory, but which in reality complement each other" (102; 136), Kosík engaged in something more egregious than a revision of the socially sanctioned distinction between highbrow and lowbrow literature. His revisionism was political, verging on what Communist Party ideologues used to call "opportunism," that is, "an affirmation of Marxism in words but voiding it of its revolutionary content."[2] I must elucidate this remark.

Jaroslav Hašek is, without doubt, the most controversial figure in modern Czech letters. Bigamist, closet homosexual, chronic alcoholic, disciplined revolutionary, intellectual parasite, mentor of the venerable Suke Bator, who was the Mongolian Lenin—these are a few of the many labels attached to his name.[3] Although he was a prolific author (a recent edition of his selected works comprises five hefty volumes), Hašek's claim to literary fame rests on a single unfinished novel written and published in weekly installments (his main source of income) during the last two years of his life. Predictably, the critical responses that it elicited were highly discordant: according to Max Brod (the first to comment on Švejk in print), "Hašek's is a first-rate achievement," while for René Wellek, "the book is not much of a work of art, as it is full of low humor and cheap propaganda," to mention just two.[4] This clash of opinions indicates that the Hašek controversy is more than a matter of literary taste. Švejk is a truly transgressive work whose vulgar language, bawdy humor, and thorough debunking of all lofty ideals (whether heroism, loyalty, or justice) sharply

2 "Revizionismus," in *Malý encyklopedický slovník* (Prague, 1972), p. 1000.
3 For Hašek's lofty reputation in Mongolia, see Owen Lattimore's letter to the *Times Literary Supplement*, April 14, 1978, p. 417; or František Cinger's interview with L. Tüdev, "Nemám důvod měnit své názory," *Rudé právo*, January 21, 1989, p. 5. In his letter of September 17, 1920, from Irkutsk, Hašek wrote that, among his other duties in the Red Army was the editorship of three journals, one of them in Mongolian (reprinted in Zdeněk Ančík, *O Životě Jaroslava Haška* [Prague, 1953], pp. 83–85). It is most likely that Hašek met Suke Bator in this capacity.
4 Max Brod, "Zwei Prager Volkstypen: Szenen von E. E. Kisch und J. Hašek im 'Kleinen Theater Adria,' " *Prager Abendblatt*, November 7, 1921, p. 6; René Wellek, "Twenty Years of Czech Literature: 1918–1938," in *Essays on Czech Literature* (The Hague, 1963), p. 41.

polarized its readership along ideological lines. The "good" soldier Švejk prompted supporters of the traditional social order to jeer and the revolutionaries to cheer; in short, Hašek's novel became a convenient arena in which the representatives of the right and the left could settle scores. Such a political reading of the novel was further facilitated by two extratextual circumstances: the emergence of Švejk as a behavioral model and Hašek's conduct during World War I.

From the very beginning, reviewers of the book have proclaimed that its protagonist is an original literary type. The Communist writer, and Hašek's erstwhile friend, Ivan Olbracht, observed in 1921: "In world literature Švejk is an entirely new type: human *phlegma* captured from a new aspect. . . . a man pleasantly at contrast with the bothersome type of 'problematic characters' who 'are dissatisfied with every situation because they were created for none.' For Švejk is satisfied with any situation and prevails in each one of them. A smart idiot, perhaps an *idiot savant*, who through his stupid but cunning good nature must win everywhere because it is impossible for him not to win: this is Švejk." Olbracht's description of Hašek's figure is quite sensible, I believe, but he should have stopped there. To explain Švejk's popular appeal, however, he conceived of "Švejkism" as a specific human trait, which, moreover, "could not have been noticed earlier or with such clarity anywhere but in the Czech lands, with their strange attitude toward state authority and the War."[5] Hence, the archetype of Švejk as an embodiment of the Czech national character was born.

It would, however, be unfair to blame Olbracht alone for this crude conflation of art and social psychology. Švejk, it seems, stepped out of the literary realm prior to his review. As Hašek himself witnessed and recorded in the "Epilogue to Part I" of his novel, even before the first volume was finished, the proper name of its protagonist had ceased to be a rigid designator and had become a general lexical item. "I do not know whether I will succeed in achieving my purpose with this book," Hašek complained fastidiously. "The fact that I have already heard one man swear at another and say 'You are as stupid as Švejk' suggests that I have not. But if the word 'Švejk' becomes a new curse in the already florid garland of execration, I must be content with this enrichment of the Czech language."[6] And

---

[5] Ivan Olbracht, *"Osudy dobrého vojáka Švejka za světové války,"* *Rudé právo*, November 15, 1921, pp. 3–4.
[6] Jaroslav Hašek, *Osudy dobrého vojáka Švejka za světové války*, ed. Z. Ančík et al. (Prague, 1954), p. 234. The English translation of the novel is taken, with some minor changes, from *The Good Soldier Švejk and his Fortunes in the World War*, trans. C. Parrott (London, 1973), p. 216. Further references will be given in the text; the first number in parentheses refers to the Czech original and the second to the English translation.

it is not important whether this story is true or not because the word "Švejk" (and its derivatives such as the intransitive verb *švejkovat*) has entered modern Czech usage, though with a meaning quite different from that reported by Hašek. "Švejk," according to a standard dictionary, designates: (1) "a man who with feigned naïveté and zeal submits to official authorities but does so only formally with an intent to ridicule" ; (2) "a wag"; and (3) "a (sly) dodger [*ulejvák*]."[7] One might argue that such an interpretation unduly flattens a complex literary figure, but this is how the "good soldier" has entered Czech political discourse.

Because of their sheer quantity, it would be futile to attempt to provide here a representative sampling of charges leveled against Hašek's book by the Czech political right. The instances I will mention should suffice to illustrate their heterogeneity and overall contradictoriness. An early full-fledged polemic against the novel was launched in 1928 after a conservative writer and politician, the staunch Czech nationalist Viktor Dyk, lambasted Švejk as a threat to national security. Dismayed by the popularity of the "hero dodger [*hrdina ulejvák*]" among his compatriots, Dyk pondered aloud about the deleterious effects this protagonist might have on the fighting morale of the Czechoslovak army. Superordinating a moral readiness to fight over mere physical preparedness, he wrote, "Moral readiness requires that a soldier not consider war waggery [*psina*]; moral readiness presupposes a sense of duty and discipline."[8] Would the many admirers of this pathological wag, Dyk asked darkly, risk their lives if the nation's existence were threatened? And referring to the revered Czech theologian of the fifteenth century, an apostle of nonviolent ethics, Dyk concluded, "For us, the nation of Chelčický, it is dangerous to have Švejk as our hero."[9]

One might wonder whether it was the spirit of Švejk that made Czechoslovak President Beneš accept the Munich agreement ten years later, ceding Sudetenland to Hitler without a fight. If so, it is curious, then, that Emanuel Moravec, minister of education in the Berlin-sponsored Protektorat Böhmen und Mähren and infamous quisling, singled out the unfortunate Czech *švejkism* as the main barrier to a fruitful collaboration of his people with the Third Reich. Angered, after the assassination of acting Reichsprotektor Reinhard Heydrich at Beneš's order in May 1942, by the lack of popular support for the Gestapo's investigation of the incident,

---

7   *Slovník spisovného jazyka českého*, ed. B. Havránek et al., vol. 3 (Prague, 1966), p. 747.

8   The words *psina* and *psinařství* which Dyk applies to Švejk's behavior are derived from the noun *pes* (dog). This is a curious semantic calque that unites the connotation of fun with that of baseness and vileness. It was Dyk's essay that directed my attention to the affinity between Švejk and the Greek kyniks, discussed later in this chapter.

9   Viktor Dyk, "Hrdina Švejk," *Národní listy*, April 15, 1928, pp. 1–2.

Moravec berated his countrymen: "I have spoken to the Czech people on the radio as a military retiree. . . . I have spoken to the Czech people as a [Protectorate] minister. I have written, exhorted. But of late I lack words that might unlock the door to the Czech mind. The intelligence of a philosopher but the character of a bootlegger. The diligence of an ant but the horizon of a slug. These are the facets of our unhappy national peculiarity which culminate in the disgusting figure of a calculating sloth and a titular idiot Švejk."[10] The Czechs had better stop disingenuously affecting zealous submission to German rule and turn in the attackers, Moravec warned, or else!

If, according to Moravec, it was their Švejk-like psyches that prevented the Czechs from finding their proper place in the Hitlerite "new Europe," some fifty years later the émigré scholar Peter Hrubý would condemn with equal conviction the very same Czech mindset for the ease with which the Czechs succumbed to the Communist yoke. "The Czech predilection for Švejk then became an important part of the gradual, though unintentional Soviet re-education of the masses into cheaters, pretenders and characterless cowards. . . . The Švejkian attitude of spineless roguery became an almost national norm. T. G. Masaryk's fight for the nation's soul appears to have been lost by decades of exposure to systematic degradation and clever oppression by both foreign and domestic lumpenproletariat and lumpen-intelligentsia in power."[11] A single book had ruined the destiny of a noble nation! Alas, the power of the printed word in the land of Kafka seems boundless.

Earlier I mentioned that Švejk fared much better with the leftist critics who drafted him (despite his rheumatism) into their people's liberation army. To make him fit for the ultimate battle, however, they had to modify his image: in the 1928 polemics with Dyk, a young Communist journalist—future martyr of the anti-Nazi resistance and "National Hero" — Julius Fučík, wrapped "the good soldier" in the flag of proletarian internationalism. "Švejk," he argued *contra* Dyk (but also against his comrade-in-arms Olbracht), "belongs to the Czech nation only ethnically." This is, of course, not very important. What matters is that "he is an *international* type, *the soldier of all imperialist armies*." Švejk is not a revolution-

10   Emanuel Moravec, "Chvíle vyzrála do zoufalé osudovosti," in *V hodině dvanácté: Soubor projevů státního presidenta a členů vlády Protektorátu Čechy a Morava po 27. květnu 1942*, ed. V. Fiala (Prague, 1942), p. 37. Moravec's interpretation of Hašek's work might be idiosyncratic, but it betrays his deep knowledge. To mention a text whose first few chapters make light of Franz Ferdinand's assassination in the aftermath of a similar assault on Heydrich is either a case of "švejkism" par excellence or a subconscious slip by somebody well steeped in the novel.
11   Peter Hrubý, *Daydreams and Nightmares: Czech Communist and Ex-Communist Literature, 1917–1987* (New York, 1990), p. 146.

ary, as Fučík assessed this cadre, but a "semi-proletarianized petit bourgeois." Yet he is useful for the cause because of his ability to undermine
the imperialist army from within—through his stolid passivity. In this he
is a real social type, and "because of these characteristics," Fučík predicted slyly, "*The Good Soldier Švejk* will become a school text on which
history teachers will demonstrate the decay of the bourgeois class and of
its last triumph—the military."[12]

A similar line of reasoning was offered at the First Congress of Soviet
Writers in 1934 by one of the Czechoslovak delegation's speakers, the
long-forgotten Vladimír Borin. Seconded by a Dane, Martin Anderson
Nexø, and a German, Theodor Plivier, Borin elevated Švejk to a symbol of
anti-militarism at this forum, which also forged the concept of Socialist
Realism as proletarian literature's sole creative method.[13] But only a year
later the good soldier's fortune changed. After the Seventh Congress of
the Comintern, the Communists no longer welcomed Švejk's blatant anti-
militarism. Faced with the rise of Hitler, they realized that the military
preparedness of bourgeois armies was an important asset in the struggle
against Fascism in the united front, which they suddenly decided to create. A delegation of Soviet journalists who visited Prague in the fall of that
year drove this point home (to the great glee of the conservative newspapers) after attending a dramatization of Hašek's novel at an avant-garde
theater. The response: "Žižka [a fierce fundamentalist warrior of early fif-
teenth-century Bohemia], not Švejk," allegedly made by a member of the
Soviet delegation after the performance, was perceived in some quarters
as a clear vindication of Dyk and his view of Hašek's work.[14]

Fučík's 1939 essay about Hašek's novel is a good illustration of this shift
in hermeneutic focus. His reassessment of the text is overtly motivated by
the simple fact (which had not bothered Fučík previously) that "Hašek . . .
did not finish his *Švejk*, which hinders many from comprehending the
[human and literary] type of Švejk fully, in its totality." From such a holis-

---

[12] Julius Fučík, "Válka se Švejkem," in *Stati o literatuře (Dílo Julia Fučíka*, vol. 6), 1st ed.
(Prague, 1951), pp. 122–23.

[13] *Pervyy vsesoyuznyy s"ezd sovetskikh pisateley 1934: Stenograficheskiy otchet* (Moscow,
1934), pp. 349, 320, and 363.

[14] For opposing views in this controversy, see, e.g., Ferdinand Kahánek, "Od Švejka zpět
k Žižkovi," *Venkov*, October 27, 1935, pp. 3–4; and Marie Bergmanová, "Kolem návštěvy
sovětských žurnalistů," *Haló noviny*, October 27, 1935, p. 3. Moscow's change of heart on
Švejk had repercussions outside Czechoslovakia as well. Arthur Koestler recalls in his
memoirs that in the summer of 1935 he "wrote about half of a satirical novel called *The
Good Soldier Schweik Goes to War Again*. . . . It had been commissioned by Willy Münzen-
berg [the Comintern's chief propagandist in the West] . . . but was vetoed by the Party on
the grounds of the book's 'pacifist errors' " (*The Invisible Writing: An Autobiography by
Arthur Koestler* [New York, 1954], p. 283).

tic view, the stolid passivity of this figure is purposive adaptation (Fučík goes so far as to compare it to the camouflage of a tiger), a façade hiding from the authorities his future readiness to act. Anticipating the afterword, never written, Fučík argues that Švejk's "development, reminiscent of Hašek's own, tends toward complete self-recognition, and one feels directly how Švejk becomes serious at a certain point. He might not stop joking, but when the situation gets tough, he will fight seriously and tenaciously."[15] From this interpretive prolepsis it is only a small step to the fabrication of evidence that would make Švejk a closet revolutionary who, alas, did not have time to come out into the open. Thus in the 1950s Hašek's official biographer and the editor of his oeuvre, Zdeněk Ančík, insisted that "according to Ivan Olbracht's testimony[?] Švejk . . . , a POW in Russia, after the Great October Socialist Revolution, was supposed to join the people . . . and together with them participate in the struggle for the liberation of China."[16]

These creative misprisions, it might be observed, share one feature: to fill in the *Unbestimmtheitstellen* of Hašek's text they draw on its author's biography. Which brings me to the second circumstance mentioned earlier as contributing to the political readings of *The Good Soldier Švejk*: Hašek's conduct during World War I. Drafted in 1915, he was dispatched with his regiment to the Carpathian front, where he soon defected to the Russians. After some time in a POW camp, he joined the deserters who were to form the Czechoslovak Legions—the military wing of Masaryk's resistance abroad to the Habsburg monarchy—and in June 1917 participated in the historic Battle of Zborów, where the Legions engaged the Austro-German forces. But when the Communist revolution erupted some four months later, Hašek went AWOL from his unit (a warrant for his arrest was issued). He enlisted with the Reds and became a member of the Russian Communist Party. After a distinguished career (he was a propagandist attached to Frunze's Fifth Army), in 1920 Hašek returned to the newly formed Czechoslovak Republic (as an agent of the Comintern, according to some). It was not just the waving of the red flag in front of the bourgeoisie that made Hašek the target of attacks from the right. He was also accused of high treason for deserting from the Czechoslovak Legions and joining the Red Army. Since the Legions were on their way through Siberia to fight the Communist forces during the Russian Civil War, he was guilty in the eyes of many of abetting the enemy. And given the fact that members of

---

[15] Julius Fučík, "Čehona a Švejk, dva typy z české literatury i života," in *Milujeme svůj národ: Poslední články a úvahy (Dílo Julia Fučíka,* vol. 3), 4th ed. (Prague, 1951), pp. 110–11.
[16] Ančík, *O životě Jaroslava Haška,* p. 107.

the Legions enjoyed privileged positions in the newly created Czechoslovak Republic, becoming to a large extent the backbone of its military and civil service, such a charge was hardly a laughing matter

What was a stigma for the right, however, the left saw as a badge of honor. The Czech Communists (the Party was founded in 1921) conveniently expunged from their memory the fact that after his return to Prague, Hašek eschewed all political activities, resuming instead his old dissolute lifestyle; they mythologized him according to their own image. Thus, "Comrade Gashek" (the Russian transliteration of his name) was born—a dedicated revolutionary ready to sacrifice his life for the liberation of the proletariat. The Communist takeover of 1948 marked the beginning of a new stage in Hašek's posthumous life. Elevated to the pantheon of immortals in 1959, he was made the patron saint of socialist humor and satire, and a yearly festival dedicated to this genre was established in his name in Lipnice, the little town in southeastern Bohemia where Hašek is buried. One must not forget to mention that in 1963, during the international festivities celebrating the eightieth anniversary of his birth, a feature-length movie about Hašek's life was released in the Soviet Union and a street in Moscow was named after him. What more could a Marxist-Leninist ask for?

After this lengthy digression, it is obvious that the parallel between Hašek and Kafka that Kosík drew in 1963 is not altogether innocent. Why would a Marxist philosopher seriously compare two writers with such different ideological profiles, likening a *politruk* of the Red Army with a decadent bourgeois who, as Howard Fast put it with Lenin-like bluntness, sits "very near the top of . . . the 'cultural dung heap of reaction,' . . . one of the major Olympians in that curious shrine the so-called 'new critics' and their Trotskyite colleagues have erected"?[17] But Kosík's marriage of the two Prague writers did not take place in a social vacuum, and politics do make strange bedfellows. The union was part of a well-orchestrated campaign to rehabilitate Kafka, or, more precisely, to use him in the intra-Party struggle between the Stalinist establishment and the Communist reformists in the early 1960s. This in itself is an excellent example of how fiction can function politically in a one-party society.

In May 1963, Liblice Castle near Prague provided an appropriate setting for an international scholarly conference whose explicit aim, according to its organizer, Eduard Goldstücker, was to become the "basis of a future, well-founded Marxist view of Kafka."[18] This is not to say that

---

[17] Howard Fast, *Literature and Reality* (New York, 1950), p. 9.
[18] Eduard Goldstücker, "O Franzi Kafkovi z pražské perspektivy 1963," in *Franz Kafka: Liblická konference, 1963*, ed. E. Goldstücker et al. (Prague, 1963), p. 23.

previously all Marxist critics had treated Kafka as Fast did. Some of them had seen in his absurd, tragic stories a veiled attempt at a critique of a de-humanizing capitalist society or, as did Brecht, the prophecy of a doom yet to come: "Fascist dictatorship was ingrained, so to speak, in the blood of the bourgeois democracies, and Kafka described with wonderful imagination future concentration camps, the uncertainty of the law, the growing absolutism of the state system, the bleak life of many individuals governed by forces inadequate to this task."[19] But this was not exactly what most of the conferees gathered at Liblice had in mind. They sought to establish the relevancy of Kafka for their own time and the Socialist society with which they identified.

This was a tall order, and the participants reacted to it as they saw fit. The East German scholars rejected it on principle. Roger Garaudy's answer was highly abstract: this member of the French Communist Party Presidium argued that Kafka's three unfinished novels, precisely in their openness, "are the image of our life: they are runways toward infinity, toward the attainment of truly human dimensions for man, the infinite dimensions of his history, the making of which has no boundaries. And this is," Garaudy concluded, "Kafka's message to us Communists."[20] A member of the Austrian Communist Party Central Committee, Ernst Fischer, by contrast, assessed Kafka's value for the movement in more pragmatic terms:

> The alienation of the human being, which [Kafka] depicted with maximal intensity, is reaching a terrifying scope in the capitalist world. But it is a long way from being overcome in the Socialist world as well. To overcome it step by step in the struggle against dogmatism and bureaucracy, in the struggle for Socialist democracy, initiative, and responsibility is a lengthy process and a great task. Reading works such as *The Trial* and *The Castle* can help us to fulfill it. A Socialist reader will find in them some facets of his own problems, and a Socialist official will be forced to argue many issues more thoroughly and with nuance.[21]

Aside from the occasional dissent, a few scholarly papers (which gave this meeting a thin academic veneer), and minor variations in interpretive emphasis, the conference's political message was clear if muted: rather than a paradise on earth, contemporary Socialist society bears a striking resem-

---

19 Quoted by Werner Mittenzwei in "Brecht a Kafka," ibid., p. 118.
20 Roger Garaudy, "Kafka, moderní umění a my," ibid., p. 201.
21 Ernst Fischer, "Kafkovská konference," ibid., p. 151. An English translation of the six most important papers from this conference can be found in *Franz Kafka: Anthology of Marxist Criticism*, ed. K. Hughes (Hanover, N. H, 1981), pp. 53–122.

blance to Kafka's traumatic nightmares and something should be done about it.

Seasoned Party apparatchiks got this message immediately and fought back. Replying to Garaudy's report on the conference which appeared in *Les Lettres françaises* under the title "Kafka and Prague Spring," Alfred Kurella, the venerable secretary of the poetry section of the Berlin Academy of Arts, did not mince words. "It is inappropriate," he declared authoritatively, "to use Kafka's name in an argument that openly opposes genuine Marxist analysis and that, by ostensibly making Kafka contemporaneous, pursues explicitly political goals."[22] I shall not reiterate here the charges of revisionism, falsification of Marxism, and the other heinous apostasies that Kurella leveled against the conference, nor repeat Fischer's, Garaudy's, and Goldstücker's protestations to the contrary. From the vantage point of today one might concur with Kurt Zimmermann's conclusion, drawn in the GDR Party's daily *Neues Deutschland* in September 1968 after the Warsaw Pact tanks crushed the short-lived Czechoslovak experiment in non-Kafkaesque Socialism, about the close spiritual connection between the Liblice event and the subsequent counterrevolution of 1968. "The Kafka conference," he assessed correctly, "was an important milestone in the growth of the influence of revisionist and bourgeois ideology" because "on this occasion revisionism appeared in Czechoslovakia for the first time massively and openly."[23] Was it not, after all, Garaudy's article in *Les Lettres françaises* that gave Prague Spring its name?

This introduction of the various political responses to the oeuvres of the two Prague writers is necessary to provide the historical background for Kosík's essay. Yet—and this must be stressed—"Hašek and Kafka" cannot be reduced to a mere commentary on the ideological strife surrounding its origin. Compared to the Liblice conference papers, which today appear quaint if not downright superannuated, Kosík's text has retained its intellectual punch even though the juxtaposition of the two writers does reflect a particular political struggle of the day. Through the sheer power of proximity, it might have made Kafka more palatable than before to the Party's ideological watchdogs. But, at the same time, it rendered Hašek a new author: a sophisticated *penseur* projecting a novelistic universe as multivalent and aporetic as Kafka's. The difference between them, Kosík insisted, is a function of their inverse perspectives on the world. And here lies the political effect of *Švejk*. "Kafka's man is walled into a labyrinth of petrified possibilities, alienated relationships, and the materialism of

[22]   Alfred Kurella, "Jaro, vlaštovky a Franz Kafka," *Literární noviny*, October 5, 1963, p. 8.
[23]   Quoted in Eduard Goldstücker, "Ten Years after the Kafka Symposium of Liblice," *European Judaism*, no. 2 (1974), 24.

daily life, all these growing to supernaturally phantasmagoric dimensions, while he constantly and with unrelenting passion searches for the truth. Kafka's man is condemned to live in a world in which the only human dignity is *the interpretation of that world*; while other forces, beyond the control of any individual, determine the course of *world's change*." Kafka's antipode, "Hašek, through his work, shows that man, even in a reified form, is still man, and that man is both the object and the producer of reification. He is *above* his own reification. Man cannot be reduced to an object, he is *more* than a system" (102; 136).

Kosík's essay has continued to weld together Kafka and Hašek. Their image as Siamese twins breech-delivered is still very much in vogue. It is used abundantly, for example, by Kosík's friend Milan Kundera in his probes into the common core of the Central European novelistic tradition.[24] "The world according to Kafka: the bureaucratized universe. The office not merely as one kind of social phenomenon among many but as the essence of the world," Hašek's universe, Kundera asserts, contrary to its appearance, is not altogether different. "Like Kafka's Court, Hašek's army is nothing but an immense bureaucratic institution, an army-administration in which the old military virtues (courage, perseverance, skill) no longer matter." What separates Kafka's and Hašek's characters, according to Kundera, is their antithetical attitude toward this universe. Adding a Kosíkian twist to the cherished critical platitude about the immense mimetic power of the two Prague writers, Kundera remarks parenthetically:

> Those of us who have experienced the totalitarian Communist version of the modern world know that these two attitudes—seemingly artificial, literary, exaggerated—are only too real; we've lived in the realm bounded on one side by K.'s possibility, on the other by Švejk's; which is to say: in the realm where one pole is the identification with power, to the point where the victim develops solidarity with his own executioner, and the other pole the nonacceptance of power through the refusal to take seriously anything at all; which is to say: in the realm between the absolute of the serious— K.—and the absolute of the nonserious—Švejk.[25]

[24] Karel Kosík is the eloquently unnamed "famous Czech philosopher" with whom Kundera strolled through the streets of Prague one morning in the early 1970s after the secret police confiscated the only existing copy of Kosík's manuscript—the fruit of ten years of scholarly labor. Not surprisingly, the "Dichter und Denker" walked along the route of the two Josefs (from Prague Castle to Old Town), but, as if in a sudden brainstorm, just before Charles Bridge they turned left and crossed the river via the next bridge (Milan Kundera, "A Kidnapped West or Culture Bows Out," *Granta*, no. 11 [1984], 114).

[25] Milan Kundera, "Notes Inspired by 'The Sleepwalkers,' " in *The Art of the Novel*, trans. L. Asher (New York, 1986), pp. 48–49. For another parallel between Kafka and Hašek, see, e.g., Kundera, "The Czech Wager," *New York Review of Books*, January 22, 1981, p. 21.

Kundera's readings of Kafka and Hašek, however, do not merely regurgitate Kosík's analogy. Some of them shed surprising new light on the relationship of J. K. and J. Š., for example, Kundera's succinct observation about the ontic primacy of simulacrum over reality in Kafka's fictions. "In the Kafkan world, the file takes on the role of a Platonic idea. It represents true reality, whereas man's physical existence is only a shadow cast on the screen of illusion."[26] And this brings us back to the question underlying the hypothetical encounter between J. K. and J. Š.: Why was the former executed and the latter released from his stockade prison? A close reading of Hašek's novel yields an uncanny answer supporting Kundera's assertion: J. Š. was released in a case of mistaken identity, of military courts running amok because of a faulty filing system. The documents charging Švejk with treasonous intent were inadvertently placed in the files of somebody else whose initials, J. K., look only too familiar. And, as if this were not sufficient, Josef K.'s files bear the ominous sign of death. "The papers on Švejk," we learn from the omniscient narrator, "were not found until after the war. They were in the archives of the Army Legal Department and were minuted: 'Planned to throw off his hypocritical mask and come out publicly against our ruler and the state.' The papers had been placed in files dealing with a certain Josef Koudela. On the file cover was a cross and underneath it 'Case closed' with the date" (119–20; 92). In a world where one's existence is a mere shadow of a bundle of legal documents bearing one's initials, a man can be easily "arrested one fine morning," to be sure, even without someone "telling lies about him."

So far I have been concerned primarily with the hermeneutic uses and abuses to which Hašek (and Kafka) were subjected in their homeland. Let me now join the fray myself, using as a stepping-stone Kosík's piece on which I have hitherto relied extensively. Given the opposing trajectories of Josef K.'s and Josef Š.'s journeys, which Kosík traced with meticulous precision, it seems appropriate to read *The Trial* and *The Good Soldier* in an antistrophic manner, to compare, so to speak, heads and tails, the end of one text with the beginning of the other.

The closure of Kafka's novel is all too well known. Watching the knife being plunged into his heart, Josef K. utters his last sentence: " 'Like a dog!' he said; it was as if the shame of it must outlive him."[27] *Švejk* opens with an equally violent act, albeit only a reported one—the assassination of Archduke Franz Ferdinand: " 'And so they've killed our Ferdinand,'

---

[26]   Milan Kundera, "Somewhere Behind," in *The Art of Novel*, p. 102.
[27]   Franz Kafka, *The Trial*, trans. W. and E. Muir (New York, 1956), p. 229. Further references will be given in the text.

said the charwoman to Mr. Švejk, who had left military service years before, after having been finally certified by an army medical board as an imbecile, and now lived by selling dogs—ugly, mongrel monstrosities whose pedigrees he forged" (41; 3). There are a number of similarities and differences in these two passages that could be discussed. What intrigues me, however, is the image of a dog repeated in both. "Wie ein Hund," says Josef K., and the shame overwhelms him. It is this linkage of a dog with shame that distances Kafka from Hašek: while for Josef K. the animal signifies his ultimate humiliation, for Josef Š. dogs are part of his everyday milieu, the source of his livelihood. And these are not even ordinary dogs, as the text makes clear, but dogs' dogs, "ugly mongrel monstrosities" whose pedigrees Švejk brazenly doctors.

It is not only among English speakers that the word "dog" is charged with contemptuous connotations. "Shamelessness," a classical scholar tells us, "was the peculiar characteristic of the dog, according to the Greek view."[28] And the adjectival form of *kyon* provided a handy appellation, joyfully appropriated by those to which it was applied, for a distinct philosophical trend that in doglike fashion flouted the social norms considered sacrosanct by the Athenians of the fourth century B.C. "Kynism," as this intellectual strain has been called ever since, became personified for posterity by the eccentric figure Diogenes of Sinope—the philosopher-dog par excellence. The importance of the kynik tradition for European fiction seems to be twofold. On the one hand, it is the *spiritus movens* of the Menippean satire (named after the kynik Menippos, its putative originator), the genre that, according to Mikhail Bakhtin and Northrop Frye, informs the works of writers such as Petronius, Rabelais, Swift, and Dostoyevsky.[29] On the other hand, Diogenes furnished the literary imagination with a prototype of a new hero, appearing in numerous texts either under his own name (in Lucianus, Comenius, Wieland) or transmogrified as Sancho Panza, Mephistopheles, and the Grand Inquisitor.[30] Hašek's novel, I believe strongly, could be profitably analyzed in terms of Menippean satire. But since the political reading of this text, which is what concerns me here, conceives of the novel, above all, in terms of its main character, I focus on the good soldier Švejk as a twentieth-century version of the kynik hero—*Diogenes Cynicus redivivus*—to recycle the title of Comenius' play about this famous figure.

[28] Donald R. Dudley, *A History of Cynicism from Diogenes to the Sixth Century A.D.* (London, 1937), p. 29.

[29] For a convenient overview of Bakhtin's and Frye's theories, see H. K. Riikonen, *Menippean Satire as a Literary Genre: With Special Reference to Seneca's Apocolocyntosis*, Societas Scientiarum Fennica, Commentationes Humanorum Litterarum, no. 83 (1987).

[30] See, e.g., Heinrich Niehues-Pröbsting, *Der Kynismus des Diogenes und der Begriff des Zynismus* (Munich, 1979), pp. 195–243; Peter Sloterdijk, *Critique of Cynical Reason*, trans. M. Eldred (Minneapolis, 1987), pp. 155–95.

At this point discerning readers might begin to question the somewhat jagged trajectory of my argument. Is it not an unwarranted leap (so the argument could go) to classify Švejk as a Diogenes for our time just because of his mongrel-mongering? Such an objection could be countered in two ways. First of all, Švejk's close association with dogs, highlighted in the opening sentence of the novel, is not the only textual allusion to a kynik heritage. Equally important, though more veiled, is the mention of Švejk's forging of dogs' pedigrees. One of Diogenes' most infamous deeds, for which he eventually had to emigrate to Athens, was the adulteration of coinage (*paracharaxai to nomisma*) in his native Sinope. In his *Lives of Eminent Philosophers*, our basic source of information on kyniks, Diogenes Laertius (hereafter D. L.) provides four versions of this event.[31] By the same token, Švejk's imbecility, certified by the army medical board, parallels the similar assessment of Diogenes' mental incompetence, declared by the man whose authority in the science of Being surpasses even that of military doctors. When asked his opinion of Diogenes, we read in D. L.s' *Lives*, Plato replied, "A Socrates gone mad" (55).

It is, however, Hašek's "Preface" to his novel that provides the most explicit link between Švejk and Diogenes. "Great times call for great men," he ventures. "If you analyzed their character you would find that it eclipsed even the glory of Alexander the Great." One of these unsung heroes is, of course, "a shabbily dressed man in the streets of Prague," who "if you asked him his name would answer you simply and unassumingly: 'I am Švejk' " (37; 1). By juxtaposing Švejk to Alexander, Hašek follows closely the model established by the biographers of Diogenes: in a number of anecdotes from his life, the shabbily clad kynik is confronted with Alexander the Great—the symbol of political power.[32] In these emblematic duels the obvious underdog does not yield ground to the mighty ruler. "Alexander," we read in D. L., "once came and stood opposite him, and said 'I am Alexander the great king.' 'And I,' said he, 'am Diogenes the Kynic' " (63). Their parity was acknowledged by Alexander himself, who, as the *Lives* records, apparently said after one such encounter, "Had I not been Alexander I should have liked to be Diogenes" (35). The subtext for the comparison of Švejk and Alexander entertained in the "Preface" seems to be yet another chreia from the life of the great kynik reported by D. L.: "When he [Diogenes] was sunning himself in the Craneum, Alexander came and stood over him and said, 'Ask of me any boon you like.' To

---

[31] Diogenes Laertius, *Lives and Opinions of Eminent Philosophers in Ten Books*, trans. R. D. Hicks (London, 1925), 2:23. Further references will be given in the text. Diogenes' crime is translated variously as "reminting the coinage," "falsifying currency," "restamping mintage," and so on; see Paul Elmer More, *Hellenistic Philosophies* (Princeton, 1923), p. 260. I will return to this term later.

[32] The other frequent counterpart of Diogenes is Plato, the representative of truth.

which he replied, 'Stand out of my light' " (41). Hašek's text, one might argue, metaphorically reverses the role of the kynik hero vis-à-vis Alexander: now it is the famous warrior who is basking in the sun of historical glory while Švejk's presence is obscuring the source of light.

Are all of these textual parallels convincing evidence of a close kinship between Diogenes and Švejk? Or ought one to jump through hoops proving that Hašek must have been familiar with the Greek kynik—either because of his father, a high school professor of history, or because of his voracious reading habits and photographic memory? Whatever the case, I find that a historical linkage is not important to my discussion. The kinship I wish to establish between these two figures is not genealogical but topological. Despite their great spatiotemporal distance, what Diogenes and Švejk share is a specific stratagem for extracting oneself effectively from social constraints of any kind. And what interests me is the essential underpinning of Diogenes' and Švejk's ploy, captured with the most remarkable brevity by the line from Janis Joplin's famous song, which is an epigraph to this chapter. In what follows I hope to substantiate why this particular attitude deserves the attribute "kynikal."

Kynik philosophy evolved in a period of intense axiological readjustment of Greek society: what Arthur Adkins strikingly termed the transition from a competitive to a cooperative system of values. In the world of Homer, men's *arete* (usually rendered as "virtue") was identified with the ability to "protect their families and followers, their *oikos*."[33] Any means could be justifiably employed to further one's own interests (as we learn from perusing the *Iliad*). Greek gods are in this respect as amoral as mortals are, and it is precisely through an excess of *arete* that men can approximate them. Around the fifth century B.C., however, the rise in commerce and the growth of cities required of Greek males new behavioral patterns. The warlike essence of the traditional *arete* had to be amended to include quiet, cooperative values (such as moderation and justice). Plato's defense of Socrates, Adkins illustrates well, is an exercise in this axiological shift. Whereas from the standpoint of Homeric tradition Socrates' inability to defend himself legally and his compliance with the death sentence would be considered shameful (*aischron;* here Josef K.'s fate comes to mind), Plato praises Socrates highly for this decision to subordinate individual interest to the law of the *polis*.

Although through their spiritual lineage the kyniks are considered by most to be the offspring of Socrates, they did not share with him his supreme loyalty to communal authority (which, after all, cost him his life). Their robust aversion to anything smacking even vaguely of the common good stemmed in part from their low social standing. Émigrés and descendants of slaves, the kyniks were not considered full-fledged Athenian

---

[33]   Arthur Adkins, *Merit and Responsibility: A Study in Greek Values* (Oxford, 1960), p. 35.

citizens and were thus marginalized. Whether it is true, as Theodor Gomperz asserts, that the force of kynism springs from "the contrast between a well-founded self-esteem and a mean situation" is secondary.[34] What matters is that this strain of thought offered an original strategy by which a lonely outsider might defend himself against an inhospitable society. The kyniks' one-against-all attitude very much affirmed the Homeric sense of *arete*. Yet, one might wonder, how could these bizarre thinkers with no arms or military training compete with warlords like Achilles and Hector? Only by changing the rules of engagement. And this is precisely what the *kynikos tropos* is all about. A victory, the example of Pyrrhus teaches us, consists of two complementary aspects: the vanquishing of the enemy and the minimizing of casualties on one's own side. It was the latter facet of the contest on which the kyniks concentrated exclusively. By decreasing, in a zero-sum game, the sum to another zero, the kyniks made themselves invincible: neither had they anything to lose nor had anybody else any incentive to compete with them.

Autarkeia, or self-sufficiency, is the ultimate *arete* for which the kyniks strove in their conflict with society.[35] If the insuperability of the Greek gods derives from their lack of needs, to emulate them requires of the kynik the radical suppression of all needs to the barest minimum. And since it is those values acquired in the process of socialization that tie one most closely to the collectivity, these should be jettisoned first. A human being, in fact, ought to be reduced to his or her physiological substratum. Thus, in a surprising twist, to become godlike a kynik must turn animal-like, similar to "a mouse running around . . . not looking for a place to lie down in, not afraid of the dark, not seeking any of the things which are considered to be dainties," from which D. L. points out Diogenes "discovered the means of adapting himself to circumstances" (25).

The tenets of kynism are paradoxical not only in the logical but also in the etymological sense of this word. The equation of obvious opposites which kynik argumentation displayed flew strongly in the face of the received opinion of ordinary Athenians. But, precisely because of this, I very much suspect that kynik pronouncements and behavior cannot be taken at face value as sincere statements or spontaneous acts. All Diogenes' pointed attacks against the reasoning of his fellow philosophers, his defense of strange cultural practices (such as cannibalism), all his public masturbations and other curious "biographical" items appear in their

---

[34] Theodor Gomperz, *Greek Thinkers: A History of Ancient Philosophy,* trans. G. G. Berry (London 1905), 2:149.
[35] See Audrey N. M. Rich, "The Cynic Concept of *Aytarkeia,*" in *Die Kyniker in der modern Forschung: Aufsätze mit Einführung und Bibliographie,* ed. M. Billberbeck (Amsterdam, 1991), pp. 233–39.

deliberate ostentatiousness like well-choreographed performances destined to shock his audiences. One of these staged events, reported in *Lives*,
sums up well Diogenes' perception of his social role: "He was going into a
theatre, meeting face to face those who were coming out, and being asked
why, 'This,' he said, 'is what I practice doing all my life' " (67).

It would be unwise, however, to conceive of Diogenes as a simple con-
trarian, as a mirror image of Plato or Alexander the Great. He undermines
their authority not directly but by an oblique gesture. In opposing them
he does not advance a competing philosophical system or a political claim
of his own, but, in a lateral move, he renders suspect the very idea of truth
or desire for power within the confines of which philosophers and politicians operate. He counters serious efforts with the freedom of play. The
avatars of etatism could not accept Diogenes' ludic challenge for several
reasons. The word "play" is, first of all, semantically linked to the notion
of game as contest (*agon*), and therefore it echoes an individualistic,
Homeric code of honor. Second, the engine of play is driven not by quiet,
cooperative values such as rational interest but instead by subliminal passions. To allow individuals to satisfy their libidinal drives through unbridled play with and/or against others is the last idea that comes to the
mind of any social engineer. And for advocates of law and order there is
an uncanny similarity between play and the adulteration of coinage: Diogenes' original sin that made him an exile and a philosopher. Both of these
activities entail splitting into two what the believers in Truth and Justice
consider an essential oneness. Like a fake bill, play represents reality as
something other than what it pretends to be. The realm of play is that of
"funny money"—of illusion, inauthenticity, fabrication.[36] And if monetary forgery undermines the government by stripping it of its economic
power, play devalues the concept of truth, the currency of intellectual
rulers.

The suspicion of the authoritarians regarding Diogenes' scurrilous duplicity is, I must concede, fully warranted. By a sleight of hand the cunning felon turns malfeasance into play—or wordplay, to be more precise.
The phrase *paracharattein to nomisma*, experts tell us, is a pun based on the
homonymity of *nomisma*, which originally signified anything sanctioned
by law or convention and only through a subsequent extension was applied to money as legal tender. This etymological exercise imbues the incriminating passage in *Lives* with an additional meaning: figuratively, it
refers to Diogenes' radical project of "revaluation of all values" rather

[36] I have derived most of my information about the Greek view of play from Mihai I.
Spariosu, *God of Many Names: Play, Poetry, and Power in Hellenic Thought from Homer to Aris-
totle* (Durham, 1991).

than to the minting of two-drachma coins in his garage.[37] Through this rhetorical loophole the rascal beats the legal rap!

But how do we know, an agelast will ask, that the non-serious (metaphorical) reading of this anecdote is correct? This question points to the heart of the ludic matter. We will never know, because play unfolds in the name of chance, forgoing the comfortable security of decidable truth. The reiterations of signs in the Diogenes chreiai are therefore governed not by the principle of identity as utter self-sameness, as a faithful imitation of the original, but by exigencies of an ever-changing context. These are playful remintings of the "same" as different (homonymity of *nomisma*) and, at another level, of the "different" as same (synonymity of counterfeiting and transvaluation). What such permutations of analogies and divergencies strive for is not the approximation of an ideal that is measurable by the yardstick of veracity but the nebulous joys of probing, laughing, and challenging (or whatever motivations for playing there might be). And their outcome is as secure as that of any other wager. Others might view what is for some Diogenes' brilliant display of ludic prowess as the proof of his ignorance, his madness, or, in the case of forged money, his moral turpitude.

Let me illustrate Diogenes' ludic challenge to the authority of truth and power with two examples. Kierkegaard's essay on repetition opens (as everyone knows) with a repetition. "When the Eleatics denied motion," reads its first line, "Diogenes, as everyone knows, came forward as an opponent. He literally did come forward, because he did not say a word but merely paced back and forth a few times, thereby assuming that he had sufficiently refuted them."[38] What intrigued Kierkegaard in this story is, I believe, its amusing ambiguity. For is it the repetition that creates motion (a unidirectional walk by Diogenes would most likely have been interpreted as his retreat, not as an instantiation of the concept), or is it motion that creates repetition (Diogenes' coming forward to repeat in deed what Parmenides or Zeno had negated verbally)? Moreover, by doing what he did, did Diogenes intend to refute the Eleatic doctrine (as Kierkegaard intimates, *Lives* is silent on this issue) or something else? In other words, was his walking around an assertion of the existence of motion or merely an imitation of it—a pantomimic jab at those who predicated its nonexistence? Diogenes' performance—and this is the only thing we can say with

---

[37] For an extensive discussion of this theme, see Pröbsting, *Der Kynismus des Diogenes*, pp. 43–77.
[38] Søren Kierkegaard, *Fear and Trembling. Repetition*, ed. and trans. H. V. and E. H. Hong (Princeton, 1983), p. 131. In *Lives* this event is recorded as follows: "In like manner, when somebody declared that there is no such thing as motion, he [Diogenes] got up and walked about" (41).

some certainty—did not prompt Kirkegaard's Eleatics to endorse Heraclitus but made them look, to be sure, rather silly.

The encounter between Alexander and Diogenes mentioned earlier is another token of such a non-identical repetition, in this case, toying with the social hierarchy. The dialogic exchange "I am Alexander the great king, and I am Diogenes the Kynic" has, at first glance, the appearance of a temporal series of two successive speech acts: "A-then-B." If we take it this way, the actual sequencing of the interlocutors is not important. We could hypothetically reverse the order and let Diogenes introduce himself first. But if we do so, we realize immediately the asymmetry of A and B. The actual word order is an icon not of temporal succession but of worldly success: first the great king, then the philosopher-dog. The aporetic quality of this chreia derives from the dual function of "and" in it (as a connective between two consecutive events and a coordinate conjunction between two equal terms). Grammatical parallelism, one might argue, serves here to level the usual pecking order: the different is presented as a replica of the same, and the power of the sovereign is relativized while the prestige of the outcast is boosted. All of this, of course, the chreia hints at but does not say.

The semantic openness of the individual anecdotes is further enhanced by their overall combination into Diogenes' "biography" as presented by D. L. I use quotation marks around this word because, apart from beginning with his origins and concluding (more or less) with his death, it contains virtually no history of Diogenes' life. It is a mosaic of apophthegmata, chreiai, and mini-stories drawn from different sources, some identified by the author, some apocryphal. A number of these segments are repeated or retold from different perspectives; others are anonymous insertions by later scribes. The provisional, incomplete nature of his account is underscored by the narrator himself when he writes, "Many other sayings are attributed to him [Diogenes], which it would take long to enumerate" (71). From this textual medley rises the often inconsistent, sometimes contradictory, but always playful figure of a protean Diogenes who, through a series of antagonistic contests with the surrounding world, reaffirms again and again his right to free speech (*parresia*) and individual liberty, thus defying any form of societal control.

It is not difficult to demonstrate that the figure of Švejk shares many characteristics with the great kynik. Like Diogenes, Švejk lingers at the margins of an unfriendly society against which he is defending his independent existence. This is not to say, however, that Austria-Hungary was like ancient Greece, where one could dwell in a tub and freely match wits with monarchs and philosophers. The institutions that Western civilization has developed in the more than two millennia since Diogenes to secure the acceptance of cooperative values among its citizenry have made an individual much more vulnerable to social pressure than at that time. And the tragic fate of Josef K., who sought justice within the impenetrable jungle of a bureaucratic legal system, suggests that even conformity with communal laws cannot guarantee happiness. The existence of coercive mechanisms such as the secret police, mental institutions, and jails requires that a latter-day kynik moderate his voice and seek more insidious weapons of self-protection than his Athenian predecessor. But at the psychological level, defense mechanisms have remained virtually the same.

If a poll were taken of the Czech population to find out what they consider the most dominant trait of Švejk's personality, equanimity, I am sure, would be first on the list. From my youth I remember vividly that nearly every pub in Prague was adorned with a picture of Švejk and the inscription "Take it easy!" (supplemented often with a secondary admonition: "And keep your feet warm!"). This perception of Švejk is obviously rooted in his overwhelming adaptability to inhospitable circumstances. Whenever faced with hardship, the good soldier finds his conditions more than tolerable and never fails to exteriorize his feelings. It suffices to read just the first eight chapters of the novel, in which Švejk manages to get himself incarcerated successively at Prague police headquarters, at a psychiatric clinic, at the police station in Salmova Street, and in a sick ward at the military stockade, to recognize a pattern:

[*Police headquarters*:] "Nowadays it's fun being locked up," Švejk continued with relish. "There's no quartering, no Spanish boots. We've got bunks, a table, a bench. We're not all squashed together; we get soup; they give us bread and bring us a jug of water. We've got our latrines right under our snouts. You can see progress in everything." (58; 21)

[*A psychiatric clinic*:] When Švejk subsequently described life in the lunatic asylum, he did so in exceptionally eulogistic terms: "I really don't know why those loonies get angry when they are kept there. You can crawl naked on the floor, howl like a jackal, rage and bite. If anyone did this anywhere on the promenade people would be astonished, but there it's the most common or garden thing to do. There's a freedom there which not even Socialists have ever dreamed of." (66; 31)

[*The police station*:] "It's not too bad here," Švejk continued, "the wood of this plank-bed has a finished surface." (73; 37)

[*A sick ward*:] "Don't spare me," he [Švejk] invited the myrmidon who was giving him the enema. . . . "Try hard to think that Austria rests on these enemas and victory is ours."

The next day on his round Dr. Grünstein asked Švejk how he was enjoying being in the military hospital.

Švejk answered that it was a fair and sublime institution. In reward he received the same treatment/punishment as the day before and, in addition to it, aspirin and three quinine pills which they dissolved into water so that he should drink at once. And not even Socrates drank his hemlock bowl with such composure as did Švejk his quinine, when Dr. Grünstein was trying out on him all his various degrees of torture. (100; 69)

Impervious to the punishment meted out to him, Švejk is always either quickly released or transferred to another coercive institution, where the story repeats itself.

If society cannot manipulate Švejk with a stick, neither will it succeed with a carrot. He is a bachelor without any relatives and with no strong proclivities to attend to. His trading in dogs, as far as the text tells us, is rather irregular and not exactly profitable. And even the switch from civilian to military status does not affect him. He proves his supreme self-sufficiency on a number of occasions, most spectacularly during his "Budějovice anabasis"—a grueling journey on foot for three nights and two and a half days that he undertakes equipped merely with "a packet of army tobacco and an army loaf" (255; 239)—seeking his sustenance in a truly kynik way, through the charity of others. The trek might have lasted much longer had the police not arrested Švejk as a suspected Russian spy. At the police station, "when they made a thorough search of Švejk's person and found nothing except a pipe and some matches, the sergeant asked Švejk: 'Tell me, why do you have absolutely nothing on you?' " Švejk's answer, "Because I don't need anything" (268; 254), would undoubtedly have made Diogenes proud of him.

In my zeal to project a kynik-like attitude toward pleasure on Švejk's part, I have so far treated his words as straightforward utterances. This is, however, a mere heuristic device on my part. We must not forget that, as was the case with his Greek predecessors, our hero's use of language is performative, employing words not to tell but to dis-play. His bidding the male nurse at the sick ward of the military prison where he is sent as a malingerer (a "simulant" in Czech) not to spare him has as much referential value as, let us say, Diogenes' answer to the question why he begs alms of a statue: "To get practice in being refused" (51). But, precisely because of this usage, the meaning of words is not at all easy to pin down.

Švejk goads the enema-dispensing myrmidon to be cruel to him with this argument: "Try hard to think," he urges his tormentor, "that Austria rests on these enemas and victory is ours." Its logic seems lucid if morally flawed. Torturing malingerers, Švejk suggests, might be unpalatable, but if it makes them fight for Austrian victory, it is worth it. This patriotic fervor coincides fully with that enthusiasm for serving the monarchy that Švejk demonstrates so abundantly upon receiving his draft notice in the preceding chapter. One might find it strange, though, to hear an "Austria first" cry from somebody who is being forced into a patriotic mold through a pain in his ass. To which observation the *good* soldier would probably reply, as he has done earlier in the novel under similar circumstances: "And if a man, even in such a difficult moment as that, does not forget what he ought to do when there's a war on, I think he's not so bad after all" (79; 45).

Yet, at second glance, we might detect a certain awkwardness in the wording of Švejk's sentence. By saying "Austria rests on these enemas," he is somehow, infelicitously, substituting cause for effect. If Austria rests, so to speak, on anything, it is the soldiers fighting for it at the front rather than the enemas which have propelled them there. This logical lapse inevitably tinges the patriotic message with irony. Like Musil's imaginary Kakania, it injects the idea of monarchy with scatological connotations. And from an anal vantage point the implication of Švejk's argument changes considerably. For is he not implying that "Austria rests on these enemas" because the population's war efforts are not spontaneous and that victory is, above all, a function of various pumping devices capable of imbuing them with bellicose spirit? If so, then Švejk is a *bad* soldier who deserves all the enemas he gets, and his plea to be "sodomized" must be seen as a provocation, a glove thrown in the face of his tormentor to deny him the pleasure of seeing his victim squirming at his hands.

At the same time, however, Hašek makes sure that his readers know that, in contrast to all the other malingerers in Dr. Grünstein's care (perhaps with the exception of the man without a leg and another suffering from genuine bone decay), Švejk is sick indeed. But next to the "real" diseases (anemia, deafness, epilepsy) of the real malingerers, his rheumatism looks very much like a convenient excuse to avoid the wartime draft. And it is perceived as such by both the staff and fellow inmates in the sick ward of the military prison. Moreover, Švejk would be hard put to convince anybody of his disability because its symptoms—swollen knees— have disappeared during his transfer to the ward. Perched precariously between sadists playing the role of doctors and masochists impersonating patients, the *poor* soldier Švejk's desperate "Don't spare me" might also be the cry of a man who has nothing to hide and welcomes torture as the ultimate litmus test of his sincerity.

A patriot, a rebel, an innocent victim of the military machinery—these are the three incarnations of Švejk that I was able to tease out of just one scene of a lengthy (and unfinished) novel. They show that an overall, totalizing interpretation of the good soldier is impossible. This impossibility could be explained in a positivistic fashion by calling attention to the archaeology of the text (the novel actually compacts several earlier and discordant images of Švejk) and the history of its production (Hašek apparently wrote the novel from memory, without recourse to earlier, already serialized chapters). But this is not, I believe, the point. If the figure of Švejk lacks overall unity it is not just because of the hazardous circumstances of his birth, but above all because he was born under the star of chance. Hašek made this clear when he called this patchwork quilt account of Švejk's adventures *Fortunes* to underline the capricious, play-like nature of his novel. It is always luck, whether good or bad, that makes the story unfold.

The trajectory of Švejk's adventures is thus a chain of somewhat improbable happenings linked in a quasi-causal way. Actions do have effects, but these cannot be fully calculated in advance: they are always coincidences of several random events. Let us look, for example, at the circumstances of Švejk's release from the Hradčany military stockade. It was not his playing the role of a reformed sinner during Chaplain Katz's sermon that got Švejk released but his "frank" admission to Katz that he cried just to amuse everybody. My quotation marks are meant to indicate that the surprising answer to the chaplain's prodding, "Confess that you only blubbed for fun, you sod," was not motivated entirely by Švejk's candor but was a wager of a sort: " 'Humbly report, sir,' said Švejk *deliberately, staking everything on a single card* [emphasis mine] . . . that I was really only blubbing for fun' " (116; 88). Luckily for him, this was the sixty-four-dollar answer. Yet, if the indictments against him had not been misfiled with the papers pertaining to Josef Koudela's case, Švejk would not have regained his freedom and a comfortable position working with the erratic chaplain.

To simplify matters somewhat, I could say that the unpredictable nature of Hašek's novelistic universe is generated by the interaction of two forces. There are, on the one hand, the machinations of hostile social institutions which, from an individual's perspective, are utterly arbitrary (the haphazard nature of the legal system in the story just cited). This perception of the world, Kosík shrewdly observed, makes Hašek akin to Kafka. The second source of randomness is Švejk's free play (or that of characters such as Katz). His "catholic" principles (for example, crying for fun during mass and confessing to it) add by their capriciousness another layer of unpredictability to the world he inhabits. But here lies the difference between Kafka and Hašek. Seeking desperately to cooperate with the enigmatic system and through unshakable logic to defend himself against the unfounded charges, Josef K. ends up dead. By matching the illogic of the system with his own idiosyncrasies, Josef Š. stays alive.

This behavior does not make for a harmonious relationship with the authorities, and Švejk is tossed from one coercive institution to another. Yet, by multiplying the confusion inherent in the system itself, he disrupts the faltering mechanism and paralyzes the deadly grip it exercises over an individual. Kosík is correct when he writes that through his work Hašek shows that even under conditions of extreme alienation man can transcend a system. But this is too general a statement to make about Švejk. His ability to push the limits of a system derives from the fact that he is a crystallization of a very specific and essential trait of human nature—our ability to play. Like Diogenes, Švejk is a representative not of the genus *Homo* as such, but of its small subgroup *Homo ludens*.[39]

Earlier I noted that Diogenes' play derives its existence from his ability to duplicate signs, to fold them in upon themselves in a way that highlights their nonidentical sameness and/or tautologous otherness. Švejk's play can be traced to a similar skill. The reinscription of formulaic expressions charged with a definite set of values into a nonstandard context is the most obvious example of a ludic challenge to authority. Thus, the patriotic greeting by which Švejk addresses the commission of psychiatrists that was to judge his legal sanity elicits the following comment in their report: "The undersigned medical experts insist upon the complete mental feebleness and congenital idiocy of Josef Švejk, who appeared before the aforesaid commission and expressed himself in terms such as: 'Long live our Emperor Franz Joseph I,' which utterance is sufficient to illuminate the state of mind of Josef Švejk as that of patent imbecile" (65; 30). Upon noticing the just-published declaration of war, the arrested Švejk utters an equally patriotic exclamation on his way to police headquarters, "God save our Franz Joseph! We shall win this war! (71; 43), which causes a minor mob scene and is interpreted by the police official as seditious irony.

The formulaic expressions repeated more or less out of context by Švejk need not be explicitly ideological to have ludic force; the only condition they must meet is that they must be appropriate only in certain situations and not in others. Švejk's social gesture of maintaining temporal order, politely extended to a fellow cellmate in the holding cell of the police station, is a case in point: "In the passage energetic steps could be heard, the key grated in the lock, the door opened and a policeman called Švejk's name. 'Excuse me,' said Švejk chivalrously, I've only been here since twelve noon, but this gentleman has been here since six o'clock in the morning. I'm not in any hurry anyway' " (76; 42). Another case is Švejk's concern (after admitting all legal charges against him at police headquarters) not to be late for his transfer to criminal court next morning: "In the morning you'll be taken off to the criminal court," the interrogating officer tells Švejk. "At what time, your worship?" he asks, "so I don't oversleep,

---

[39]   The ludic aspect of Hašek's novel is treated extensively in Hana Gaifman, "Švejk—the *Homo Ludens*," in *Language and Literary Theory: In Honor of Ladislav Matejka*, ed. B. Stolz et al. (Ann Arbor, 1984), pp. 307–22. Although Gaifman's concept of play is different from the one I am applying here, I am indebted to her essay for its many insightful observations.

for Christ's sake" (59; 22). Occasional "misapplications" by Švejk of standard military commands (such as calling to attention soldiers on the latrine because a general is in the vicinity) also belong in this category.

It is, in fact, their inability to alter the identity of reiterated signs that distinguishes the bad guys from the good in Hašek's novel. The epitome of the first group is Colonel Friedrich Kraus von Zillergut, whose discourse consists primarily of agglutinated tautologies such as: "A book, gentlemen, is a number of squares of paper cut in different ways and of varying format which are printed on and put together, bound and gummed. Yes. Well, do you know, gentlemen, what gum is? Gum is adhesive material." Poetic justice for this type of repetitiveness is swift in *Švejk*: the Colonel is run over when he attempts to demonstrate (in a fashion that mimics Diogenes) his definition of "the rear part of the house" as the part "we cannot see . . . from the pavement," which we may "prove to ourselves by stepping into the driveway" (221–22; 201). His counterparts are characters such as the one-year volunteer Marek whose creative forays into zoological taxonomy published in the journal *The Animal World*, of which he was editor, drove the partisans of science into fury, or Army Chaplain Katz—the noncanonical performer of Catholic rituals.

One of the most striking stylistic features of Hašek's text is the abundance of stories narrated by Švejk and other characters. In this respect, the novel differs significantly from D. L.'s account of Diogenes' life, in which narrativity is kept to the bare minimum. Švejk's stories serve several functions in the book, some of which I will return to later. But, as a commentary on or a paraphrase of what was said previously by other characters, they are also a recontextualizing device. Typical in this respect is Švejk's reply to the news from his charwoman, Mrs. Müller, "And so they've killed our Ferdinand," with which the novel begins. " 'Which Ferdinand, Mrs. Müller?' he asked . . . 'I know two Ferdinands. One is a messenger at Průša's, the chemist's, and once by mistake he drank a bottle of hair oil there. And the other is Ferdinand Kokoška who collects dog shitties. Neither of them is any loss' " (41; 3–4). Ostensibly, Švejk's misunderstanding is evoked by Mrs. Müller's use of the so-called possessive dative, "our Ferdinand," which in Czech implies both a strong identification with the Archduke Franz Ferdinand (her meaning) and a close familiarity with somebody called Ferdinand (his interpretation of it). But regardless of what prompts it, Švejk's question creates an analogy whose rhetorical effect can be compared to that of the kynik anecdote about Diogenes introducing himself immediately after Alexander the Great.

I could list many more instances of such nonidentical repetitions in Švejk's utterances (his chronic misunderstanding of rhetorical questions comes immediately to mind), but it would not add much to what I have already said. Instead, I will illustrate how this ludic device, as utilized in Hašek's novel, strikes at the core of the social system and eliminates even the possibility of co-opting the good soldier into its structure. Resisting the lure of cooperative values, I must stress, is a greater problem for the latter-day kynik than for his Greek ancestor. By declaring himself "a citizen of the world [*kosmopolitos*]" (65), Diogenes clearly opted out of Athenian society; and his choice, it seems, was respected by the *polis*. While his was definitely not normative behavior, D. L. does not mention any strong measures taken by the Athenians to modify it. The modern state, as I argued earlier, is incomparably more jealous of its subjects, and it maintains a number of establishments whose only function is to recast an uncooperative individual into an obedient citizen. This is not always a smooth process, to say the least, but one often resulting in split personalities among those exposed to it, in the opening of gaps in their psyches between their social and private identities.

The tension between these two identities is palpable throughout Hašek's novel. The state is always watchful of its citizenry for potential disloyalty to the crown, for the evasion of the draft through malingering, or even for abetting the enemy. In a gesture that mirrors the unhappy consciousness of its subjects, it dispatches an armada of undercover policemen to find out the truth. This is most likely the source of the popular perception of Švejk among the Czechs as a master of double identity: a sly dodger in the guise of a zealous patriot. But this reading of Hašek's text, despite its widespread popularity, is not persuasive for at least two reasons. It obliterates, first of all, the fine line between cynicism and kynism, between the immoral, profit-motivated juggling of the private and public norms of behavior and the amoral, nonnormative free play whose purpose is difficult to define. Furthermore, and more important, an unequivocal interpretation kills this text. At the moment when we are able to solve the enigma of its protagonist's identity, the novel will go flat. For as *Homo ludens* Švejk, by his very existence, defies the principle of a simple identity, or, to repeat myself, displaces it with an infinite series of nonidentical substitutions.

From this perspective, therefore, Hašek's novel reads like a never-ending story of mistaken identity: the hero is being constantly taken for somebody else. It would be tedious to recapitulate here all of Švejk's transfigurations. It is perhaps enough just to mention his totally gratuitous reply to the question of the two soldiers escorting him from the Hradčany garrison to Katz's apartment as to why they are taking him to the chaplain: " 'For confession,' said Švejk nonchalantly. 'Tomorrow they're going to hang me. This is what they always do on these occasions and they call it spiritual consolation' " (126; 100). His escort, needless to say, believes him fully. This conversation may perhaps add yet another layer of meaning to Kosík's tale of the two Josefs meeting on Charles Bridge, one to be executed, the other mimicking the first one's fate. But from a practical point of view, Švejk's claim does not make any sense at all. There is no profit to be gained from his putting on a false front, save the pure pleasure of fooling around. This example, to be sure, hovers somewhere between being a private joke and an interference with the system. The military escort is an arm of the state, but by inquiring about Švejk's private affairs, the soldiers transgress their duty. Once this has happened, they succumb easily to Švejk's temptations to indulge in intoxicating substances, and because of their inebriation while on duty, they lose their official status.

But there are other scenes in the novel where the uncertainty about Švejk's affiliation with a specific group frays the very warp of the social fabric. Memorable in this respect is Švejk's mission to find billeting for his military unit on its way to the front, which mission ends in his being captured by Austrian troops:

> In the afternoon Švejk came to a small lake where he ran into an escaped Russian prisoner who was bathing there. At the sight of Švejk he immediately ran away as naked as he was when he came out of the water.
>
> His Russian uniform was lying underneath the willows and Švejk was curious to know how it would suit him, so he took off his own and put on the uniform worn by the unfortunate naked prisoner, who had escaped from a transport which had been billeted in a village behind the wood. Švejk wanted to see his reflection in the water and so he walked such a long way along the dam of the lake that he was caught by a patrol of field gendarmerie, who were looking for the escaped Russian prisoner. (637; 666–67)

Since these are Hungarians, they cannot understand Švejk's explanations and so take him "back" to the transport for the Russian POWs. If the garment makes the man, Švejk, for all practical purposes, joins the enemy force. Were he a true draft dodger, he would maintain his Russian identity and wait out the end of the war in a POW camp. Instead, Švejk stubbornly insists that he is an Austrian soldier. He even develops a story according to which he "had heard that the uniform of fallen enemies could be used at the front for purposes of espionage, and so as an experiment he put on that cast-off uniform" (645; 677). The officer to whom he presents this tale is, however, dead drunk and therefore unresponsive. But after he is finally able to persuade his captors that he is an Austrian subject, the story is reversed and the unauthorized change of identity is judged to be high treason: the willful act of an AWOL who (like Hašek himself) enlisted voluntarily in the Russian army to fight for the liberation of the Czech lands from Habsburg rule. Švejk is court-martialed, and only a timely telegram from brigade headquarters saves him from being hanged.

As this story illustrates, because it is easily detached from its bearer a uniform is far from an unequivocal sign of group affiliation. It can serve not only as its marker but also as a deceptive disguise. Costume parties and masquerades of all sorts (but not the military) are the socially sanctioned forums where we can satisfy our ludic instinct for doubling our appearance. To separate the quotidian from the carnivalesque, however, the state has designed a number of tight semiotic bindings that tether us to a single identity or that make a change of identity difficult. Two that figure most prominently in Hašek's novel are personal IDs and the oath of allegiance, whose binding power seems always somehow circumvented by the good soldier. Švejk's "Budějovice anabasis," to provide just one example, is both launched and terminated by the fact that his personal documents are in the possession of his superior officer, Lieutenant Lukáš. Without them he is unable to obtain a train ticket (to which every soldier with a military ID is entitled) and thus is forced to walk to his unit, only to be arrested eventually as a Russian spy in an Austrian uniform.

A military oath is perhaps one of the most pronounced semiotic devices for superimposing a unitary identity on disparate subjects, and in this respect it is an act utterly inimical to the anarchic free play of the kyniks. It consists of a ritualized ceremony during which men (usually) abjure most of their individual rights, promising loyalty and obedience to an institution that can put them in harm's way, and that they often do not wish to join at all. Even more important, taking an oath is a unique act in the sense that unless the armed force to which the original allegiance is pledged ceases to exist or the oath is revoked by a legal authority, it cannot be repeated with any other army short of severe punishment. It is, therefore, not entirely accidental that Hašek's text remains quite ambiguous on the issue of Švejk's oath. At a certain moment Lukáš recalls that "when the whole battalion took the oath, the good soldier Švejk did not take part, because at that time he was under arrest at the divisional court" (416; 422), and this makes him laugh hysterically. But after being accused of high treason for wearing the Russian uniform, Švejk argues that he could not have committed such a crime because he has "sworn an oath of loyalty to His Imperial Majesty" and, quoting a line from Smetana's famous opera, "in loyalty my vow I have fulfilled" (655; 688). We do not know whether Švejk is referring to his prewar military service, prior to which he most likely had sworn an oath, and we will never know whether his being "certified by an army medical board as an imbecile" has de jure abrogated such a contract.

Yet Hašek's text contains an instance of another legal act—in many respects very much like an oath—that by its nature ought to have stopped Švejk's unfettered play with identity. This is the signing of his confession in Chapter 2, "Švejk at Police Headquarters" :

"Do you confess to everything?"

Švejk fixed his good blue eyes on the ruthless man and said softly:

"If you want me to confess, your worship, I shall. It cannot do me any harm. But if you say: 'Švejk, don't confess to anything,' I'll wriggle and wriggle out of it until there isn't a breath left in my body."

The severe gentleman wrote something on the file and handing Švejk a pen invited him to sign it.

And Švejk signed Bretschneider's [the arresting plainclothes policeman] deposition with the following addition:

All the above-mentioned accusations against me are based on fact.

Josef Švejk

When he had signed, he turned to the severe gentleman:

"Have I got to sign anything else? Or am I to come back in the morning?"

"In the morning you'll be taken off to the criminal court" was the answer. (58; 22)

What does the signing of a confession represent? In broadest terms, we can speak of the volitional and semiotic ramifications of such an act. If breaking the law manifests a strong preference for competitive values on the part of the criminal, voluntary cooperation with the police (which the signature appended to a confession indicates) clearly marks the willingness to move in the opposite direction. An admission of guilt is the first signal to the authorities of an individual's readiness to reenter society, even at the cost of punishment. From a semiotic perspective, the signing of a police deposition is (like an oath) an unrepeatable event tethering the signer to the evidence in a singular, legally binding fashion, one that discredits any subsequent renditions of facts. And the evidence is authenticated because a signature is the unfalsifiable index of a unique individual which, because of its attachment to a confession itself, implies actual physical contact between the document and the signatory.

This is the normative function that a signature effects in a society, and Švejk, we learn from another scene in the novel, is well aware of it. During his prewar service Švejk is regularly harassed by one of his NCOs, Sergeant-Major Schreiter. The opportunity for revenge occurs when Švejk, on sentry duty, notices on a nearby wall the inscription "Old sweat Schreiter is an oaf." Since this coincides fully with his own sentiments on the subject, he places his signature under it. This does not escape the attention of the hostile NCO, but the investigation he initiates reveals something more serious: Švejk's signature is also in proximity to another inscription that has a blatantly pacifist message. Švejk is immediately taken to the regional court, and handwriting experts begin to collect evidence as to which of the two inscriptions Švejk actually has written and authorized by his signature. "They sent all the material to Vienna and in the end," Švejk recalls some three years later, "the result was that as far as those inscriptions were concerned it was not my handwriting, but that the signature was mine as I confessed to it. So I was sentenced to six weeks because I had signed it while on sentry duty and they said I couldn't be properly on guard at the time that I was doing it" (342; 337).

Švejk gets off the hook in this instance only because his signature falls, so to speak, into the crack between the two writings on the wall. Because of this crack the authorities are unable to decide whether his signature was intended to defame the NCO or to endorse draft resistance or both or neither. Švejk's signing the police deposition on the dotted line, however, closes the loophole and makes it seem inevitable that he will now face prosecution for his antisocial behavior. Yet the concept of signature is far from being as unproblematic as is commonly assumed. In his polemics with Austin, Derrida argues convincingly that "in order to function, that is, to be readable, a signature must have a repeatable, iterable, imitable form; it must be able to be detached from the present and singular intention of its production."[40] Put differently, so long as the signature remains a sign, its connection to what it stands for cannot be completely transparent. Not only is it made with different purposes in mind, but also, because of its written form, a signature always exceeds the immediate context that generates it and thus obfuscates the originary intention behind it. With this caveat in mind, let us return to Hašek's text.

What strikes us when we read Švejk's exchange with the police inspector is the patent inappropriateness of the good soldier's behavior. Even societies based on Plato's ideals sanction a judicial process as an agonistic situation in which an individual is encouraged to prove (within the bounds of the law) his or her competitive mettle. Yet, in an unpredictable fashion, Švejk turns a contest into cooperation, or better, straightforward submission. If Josef K. did the same, The Trial would be a short story accommodating in a single chapter a morning arrest and an evening execution. Thus, treating the inspector as the highest authority, Švejk asks his only question: To confess or not to confess? And when handed a pen he readily signs the deposition, offering, moreover, to replicate his signature on any other document the policeman might deem appropriate. But is

[40] Jacques Derrida, "Signature Event Context," Glyph: Johns Hopkins Textual Studies, no. 1 (1971), 194.

Švejk's signing the confession tantamount to his acquiescing to crimes such as high treason, abuse of His Majesty and the members of the imperial family, approval of the murder of the Archduke Ferdinand, or the incitement (57; 20) for which he is charged? The answer, as the novel illustrates, depends entirely on context. As far as the inspector at police headquarters is concerned Švejk clearly confirms the evidence. The magistrate at the criminal court who sees the signature "detached from the present and singular intention of its production" is not so sure. One of the first questions he asks is whether anybody coerced Švejk to confess. The candid answer puzzles him: "Why, of course not, Your Worship. I asked them myself if I had to sign it, and when they told me to do so I obeyed. After all, I wouldn't want to quarrel with them just because of my own signature, would I? It wouldn't do me any good at all. There must be law and order" (61; 25). Švejk's intention, if this category still makes sense, in paraphing the deposition is not to authorize the document but to protect law and order, he says. Yet, by so doing he manages to subvert due process. This again brings Švejk close to Diogenes—the adulterator of coinage. For Švejk's autograph is a fraud of a forgery as well; a counterfeit of his own signature that renders it legally worthless. Like Diogenes, Švejk gets away with proverbial murder. After listening to him for a while, the magistrate concludes that Švejk is not responsible for his actions on the grounds of insanity, and instead of jail the good soldier ends up in a psychiatric hospital.

To draw a final analogy with the Greek kynik, it is wordplay that once more becomes an instrument of eluding the law. In trying to make up his mind about Švejk's mental condition, the magistrate inquires, "And you don't occasionally feel run down by any chance?" "Oh no, sir," answers Švejk, "I was only once nearly run down by a car on Charles Square but that was many years ago" (61–62; 26). This is the last question asked. Only a deranged creature could make such a bad pun, the magistrate decides, calling in medical experts.[41] And with the benefit of hindsight we might recall that Švejk predicted such an outcome when he told the police inspector that a confession could do him no harm. Indeed, it did not!

I have so far attempted to illustrate a strong affinity between the figure of Švejk and that of his Greek predecessor Diogenes. I have argued that adherence to the principle of self-sufficiency is a kynik hero's chief ploy

---

[41] This pun is so bad in Czech that the translator decided to fudge it. What the magistrate actually asks Švejk was whether he suffers from occasional seizures (*záchvaty*), only to learn that years before he was almost seized (*zachvátit*) by a car. In Czech, as in English, one is usually not seized by cars. About difficulties in translating this text, see František Daneš, "The Language and Style of Hašek's Novel *The Good Soldier Švejk* from the Viewpoint of Translation," in *Studies in Functional Stylistics*, ed. Jan Chloupek et al. (Amsterdam, 1993), pp. 223–47.

for withstanding the pressure of being co-opted by society. Furthermore, I have maintained that the kynik challenge to authority and order proceeds from a ludic stance whose unlimited play subverts the principle of identity as a simple self-sameness. But I also have cautioned that the analogy between Diogenes and Švejk is not absolute. Modern society has refined the tools for coercing its citizens to be cooperative, and the latter-day kynik must negotiate his or her unimpeded passage through a hostile world with rhetorical strategies that his Greek ancestors could comfortably forgo. I will elaborate on this point in the final part of this chapter.

J. P. Stern's comparison of Hašek's novel with Joseph Heller's *Catch-22* poses an interesting question: why did "the Prague *Cercle linguistique*, famous for its concern with all sorts of out-of-the-way literary matters, totally ignore [Švejk] (as it ignored the writings of Hašek's Prague contemporaries, Kafka and Rilke)?"[42] The reason rests, I believe, in the overall scholarly orientation of the group. The Prague structuralists were concerned above all with the grammatical aspects of language (whether phonology, morphology, or syntax), from which perspective Švejk's verbal behavior is quite ordinary. Only in recent years did students of language begin to change the theoretical optics of their field to focus not on grammatical forms per se but rather on how these are exploited in an actual speech situation. The "linguistics of use," as this disciplinary matrix is often called, is a widely diversified movement with many complementary branches, some of whose analytical tools have already been successfully applied to the literary texts mentioned by Stern.[43] I will ground my attempt to draw a line between Diogenes' and Švejk's uses of language in the logical approach to conversation advanced by the British philosopher H. P. Grice.

According to Grice, all verbal exchanges in which participants engage because they recognize "in them, to some extent, a common purpose or set of purposes, or at least a mutually accepted direction," are governed by the "Cooperative Principle" (CP): "Make your conversational contribution such as is required, at the stage at which it occurs, by the accepted purpose or direction of the talk exchange in which you are engaged."[44] To

---

[42] J. P. Stern, "War and the Comic Muse," in *The Heart of Europe: Essays on Literature and Ideology* (Oxford, 1992), p. 119.

[43] See, e.g., Clayton Koelb's skillful use of speech act theory in *Kafka's Rhetoric: The Passion of Reading* (Ithaca, 1989), pp. 40–65.

[44] H. P. Grice, "Logic and Conversation," in *Syntax and Semantics*, ed. P. Cole et al. (New York, 1975), 3:45. Further references will be given in the text. Since its publication, Grice's theory has been scrutinized from many perspectives. For its most comprehensive critique, see Dan Sperber and Deirdre Wilson, *Relevance: Communication and Cognition* (Cambridge, Mass., 1986).

render the CP operative, interlocutors should observe four general conversational maxims:

Quantity (M.Qn.)	1. Make your contribution as informative as is required (for the current purpose of exchange).
	2. Do not make your contribution more informative than is required.
Quality (M.Ql.)	1. Do not say what you believe is false.
	2. Do not say that for which you lack adequate evidence.
Relation (M.R.)	1. Be relevant.
Manner (M.M.)	1. Avoid obscurity of expression.
	2. Avoid ambiguity.
	3. Be brief (avoid unnecessary prolixity).
	4. Be orderly. (45–46)

Grice is extremely careful to avoid the impression that his "maxims of felicitous conversation" are either exhaustive or all-inclusive. He allows that in a conversation some other maxims might be observed (aesthetic, social, moral) to implement a specific goal toward which the talk is directed. Furthermore, not all conversations, he concedes, are dedicated totally to the most effective passage of information, and so these maxims will have to be broadened to accommodate various strategic uses of language. Finally, not every instance of nonfulfillment of the four maxims necessarily entails the abandonment of the CP. Grice lists four ways in which a speaker might fail to observe a maxim:

1. He may quietly and unostentatiously VIOLATE a maxim; if so, in some cases he will be liable to mislead.
2. He may OPT OUT from the operation both of the maxim and the CP; he may say, indicate, or allow it to become plain that he is unwilling to cooperate in the way the maxim requires. . . .
3. He might be faced by a CLASH: He may be unable, for example, to fulfill the first maxim of Quantity (Be as informative as is required) without violating the second maxim of Quality (Have adequate evidence for what you say).
4. He may FLOUT a maxim; that is may BLATANTLY fail to fulfill it. On the assumption that the speaker is able to fulfill the maxim and to do so without violating another maxim (because of a clash), is not opting out, and is not, in view of the blatancy of his performance, trying to mislead, the hearer is faced with a minor problem: How can his saying what he did say be reconciled with the supposition that he is observing the overall

CP? This situation is one that characteristically gives rise to a conversational implicature; and when a conversational implicature is generated in this way, I shall say that a maxim is being EXPLOITED. (49–50)

There is, I believe, an important difference between the first two and the last two forms of breaching a maxim in relation to the CP. Whereas violation abrogates the CP in an inconspicuous way, opting out does so in plain view. Clashing and flouting, however, tend to maintain the CP. The inability on the part of the speaker to fulfill one maxim is dictated by his or her steadfast adherence to another. The case of flouting a maxim does not at all entail, from the Gricean perspective, the end of communication but instead provides for its continuation through other means. The message that a speaker tries to pass on to his or her listener consists not of what the utterance says but of what it implies. Irony is a case in point, Grice argues. If A says of a close associate X, who has just committed a disloyal act, to an audience aware of this fact, "X is a fine friend," listeners will surmise that "A must be trying to get across some other proposition than the one he purports to be putting forward. This must be some obviously related proposition; the most obviously related proposition is the contradictory of the one he purports to be putting forward" (53). And those versed in rhetoric will recognize in A's words the figure of litotes, which expresses the negative through the affirmative and vice versa.

The Gricean model of conversation is implicated in a rationalist and purposive outlook on human behavior in general. He makes this explicit when he writes: "I would like to be able to show that observance of the CP and maxims is reasonable (rational) along the following lines: that anyone who cares about the goals that are central to conversation/communication (e.g., giving and receiving information, influencing and being influenced by others) must be expected to have an interest, given suitable circumstances, in participation in talk exchanges that will be profitable only on the assumption that they are conducted in general accordance with the CP and the maxims" (49). The overall picture, however, becomes less transparent if interlocutors enter a speech situation with intentions that are not as constructive or direct as those outlined by Grice. Let us take, for example, the case of irony that Grice analyzes as a propositional trope, an exploitation of a conversational maxim. Some thinkers have argued convincingly that irony is not so much a figure of speech as a specific, radically skeptical attitude toward the world. This is, of course, the point Kierkegaard made in his dissertation on Socrates. But what are the goals central to skeptics' engagements in talk exchanges, and does their discourse profit from the observance of the CP and conversational maxims?

David Holdcroft's insightful essay "Irony as a Trope, and Irony as a Discourse" (with constant references to Grice) attempts to answer this

question. It proceeds from Kierkegaard's assertion about the sheer negativity of Socratic dialectics, which as a rule undermines all the arguments
of the counterlocutors without any commitment to a position of its own.
Juxtaposing Grice's concept of irony, as the full reversal of what the utterance says and what it implies, with Socrates' subversive use of it,
Holdcroft writes: "Given a choice between P and 'not-P' our ironist refuses to opt for either, but contents himself with pointing out the inade-
quacies of his opponent's argument for P."[45] In so doing, Socrates might
occasionally exploit a conversational maxim, but this, according to Hold-
craft, does not make his discourse ironic. Instead, the source of Socratic
irony is the gap between the patent fulfillment of the maxims and the latent disregard for the overall CP as to the possibility of a meaningful and
mutually profitable outcome of conversation. "But since an undeclared
non-adherence to the spirit of CP," Holdcroft concludes, "may at the
same time be accompanied by a strict adherence to the maxims that regu-
late the relations of successive contributions to each other—since destructive questioning is one of the ironist's most powerful weapons—the
fact that he does not adhere to the spirit of CP may be very difficult to detect. That is why it can be at the same time both subversive, destructive,
and infuriating" (511).

The relevance of Holdcroft's analysis for my essay is quite obvious.
The kyniks, it seems, radicalized Socratic skepticism by stripping it of its
polite veneer. The champions of competitive *arete* saw no reason to conceal their aversion toward cooperative exchanges (whether verbal or
nonverbal). It is even doubtful whether the sharp apophthegmata and
chreiai of our philosopher-dog qualify as exchanges at all. They are snip-
ing remarks out of left field, usually not very congenial to those at whom
they are directed. And Diogenes' praises of "those who were about to
marry and refrained, those who intending to go a voyage never set sail,
those who thinking to engage in politics do no such thing" (31) are nothing but antirationalist celebrations of playlike, openly aimless behavior.
Since observance of the CP is not what makes kynik interlocutors talk,
they are free to break the conversational maxims any way they wish. But
a closer scrutiny of D. L.'s profile of Diogenes suggests a certain selectiv-
ity in this respect, which, as I will argue later, distinguishes the Greek
prototype from his Czech variant. Given his great skill "at pouring scorn
on his contemporaries" (27), it is not surprising that Diogenes did not
bother to violate the maxims, quietly and unostentatiously. Nor did his
talk display clashes of several maxims because this would presuppose
his adherence to one of them. Thus, opting out and flouting are the two

---

[45] David Holdcroft, "Irony as a Trope, and Irony as a Discourse," *Poetics Today*, no. 4
(1983), 510. Further references will be given in the text.

basic reasons why Diogenes' conversations might be considered, from a Gricean perspective, infelicitous.

The implicatures that Diogenes' exploitations of the maxims generate are of a special kind. Let us recall the anecdote about the encounter between the kynik and Alexander the Great, who (with a generosity so sorely lacking among modern politicians) bade Diogenes ask of him any boon he would like. The reply, "Stand out of my light," flouts the M.R. because it is a clear nonsequitur to the ruler's proposition. What it implies, however, is the philosopher's desire to opt out not only from the conversation but also from the very power structure that Alexander represented. A simple answer, such as "Leave me alone, I do not care about you or your boons," would surely have been more to the point, but it would hardly have attained the same notoriety. This example of flouting that conceals an actual opting out from the CP is not unique at all. In fact, most such conversational implicatures are merely indirect insults aimed either at particular individuals or at the Athenians as a group. And they serve a dual function. On the one hand, they debase all Diogenes' contemporaries as unworthy beings or inferior intellects. On the other hand, because of their incisive wit and verbal brilliance, they stand as monuments to the kynik's towering presence in a pygmy world. One famous chreia repeated in D. L.'s *Lives* in several variants well typifies this discursive strategy: one day Diogenes "lit a lamp in broad daylight and said, as he went about, 'I am looking for a man' " (43). Needless to say, this utterance blatantly fails to fulfill the M.Ql. But its implicature is clear from Plato's response: "How much pride you expose to view, Diogenes, by seeming not to be proud" (29).[46]

To get back to Hašek's novel, it is clear that Švejk's verbal behavior is more complex and therefore more difficult to analyze than that of his Greek predecessor. Offhand, I would say that the good soldier virtually never opts out from the operation of a maxim. The only instance of such a breach I could find is Švejk's resistance to providing incriminating evidence against Lieutenant Lukáš at his divisional court-martial: He "refused to write the sentences dictated to him [for the sake of comparing his and Lukáš's handwriting], claiming that overnight he had forgotten how to write" (377; 375). Cases of clash are more frequent in the text, but they

---

[46]   Here are some mutations of this anecdote from D. L. (the pronoun "he" refers to Diogenes): "Being asked where in Greece he saw good men, he replied, 'Good men nowhere, but good boys at Lacedaemon' " (29); "One day he shouted out for men, and when people collected, hit out at them with his stick, saying, 'It was men I called for, not scoundrels' " (35); "As he was leaving the public baths, somebody inquired if many men were bathing. He said, No. But to another who asked if there was a great crowd of bathers, he said, Yes" (43).

seem to involve more than the simple problem of observing one conversational maxim without breaking another. The conclusion of the Russian uniform episode to which I have already devoted some attention vividly illustrates this point. After a telegram from brigade headquarters attests to his Austro-Hungarian identity, Švejk is asked to tell the court-martial what actually happened. He explains his predicament:

> When afterwards the major asked him why he had not stated [that he put on the enemy uniform only out of curiosity] under cross-examination before the court, Švejk answered that no one had in fact asked him how he got into Russian uniform and that all the questions had been: "Do you admit that you voluntarily and without pressure put on an enemy uniform?" Since that was true he could not say anything else but: "Of course—yes—certainly—it was like that—undoubtedly." This was why he had rejected with indignation the accusation made in the court that he betrayed His Imperial Majesty.
>
> "The fellow is a complete imbecile," said the general to the major. (681; 715–16)

Švejk's answers in court violate the M.R. because it clashes with the M.Qn. ("Do not make your contribution more informative than is required"), which he observed. But is this reasonable behavior? The general's remark to the major suggests that it is not. Yet, if Švejk is mentally handicapped, we perhaps should speak not of a clash of maxims in his speech but, instead, of his inability to realize what was relevant for his trial. This is the point that Mary Louise Pratt raised some years ago when she argued that Grice's list of the conversational infelicities is too limiting for literary analysis; she proposed to amend it with a fifth type which she termed an "unintentional failure."[47] The crux of the matter is that Hašek's text does not furnish enough clues to judge whether the good soldier's imbecility is genuine or whether it is just one of his many ludic identities.[48] Readers find themselves in the same position as the

---

[47] Mary Louise Pratt, *Toward a Speech Act Theory of Literary Discourse* (Bloomington, 1977), pp. 182–91. Further references will be given in the text.

[48] It is not easy to draw a precise line between criminal culpability and insanity outside the novelistic universe either. Psychiatric textbooks describe the so-called Ganser syndrome, which "develops only after a commission of a crime and, therefore, tells nothing about the patient's mental state when he committed the offense. In this syndrome, the patient, being under charges from which he would be exonerated were he irresponsible, begins, without being aware of the fact, to appear irresponsible. He appears stupid and unable to comprehend questions or instructions accurately. His replies are vaguely relevant to the query but absurd in content. He performs various uncomplicated, familiar tasks in an absurd manner, or gives approximate replies to simple questions" (Thomas S.

doctors called in by Dr. Grünstein, "half of whom insisted that Švejk was *'ein blöder Kerl,'* while the other half insisted he was a scoundrel who was trying to make fun of the war" (104; 76). Or, put differently, they and we are unable to pin down Švejk's nonfulfillment of conversational maxims as unintentional failures or as unostentatious violations intended to mislead.

The following two examples demarcate, in my view, the boundaries of the field in which Švejk's breaches of the conversational maxims operate: ignorance and deception. The first comes during the good soldier's psychiatric examination, which consists of a series of questions: "You don't know the maximum depth of the Pacific Ocean?" a psychiatrist asked. " 'No, please sir, I don't,' was the answer, 'but I think that it must be definitely deeper than the Vltava below the rock of Vyšehrad' " (64; 29). Common sense tells me that this reply betrays the deficiencies of Švejk's education, but as a "sophisticated" literary critic I cannot resist seeing in it a sneaky violation of the M.Qn—a substitution of a comparative value for a quantitative concept. The other breach occurs in the aftermath of one of the many confrontations between Švejk and his nemesis, Lieutenant Dub—a high school history teacher in civilian life: "Lieutenant Dub went away murmuring to himself: 'I will see thee at Philippi.' 'What did he say to you?' Jurajda asked Švejk. 'We've only arranged a meeting at "Philip's." These smart gentlemen are generally queers' " (535; 553). Although it is quite plausible that Švejk was ignorant of Roman history, his "mistake" was strained, to say the least. Švejk's failure to report correctly the purport of Dub's remark seems less an unintentional failure than a sneaky violation of the M.Ql. ("Do not say what you believe is false") intended to cast aspersions on the lieutenant's sexual orientation.

As far as flouting is concerned, predictably, this is the most frequent type of infringement of the maxims in Švejk's speech. The sheer number of these blatant conversational failures and the variety of implicatures which they give rise to precludes my dealing with this topic here. I will therefore limit my comments to two observations. First of all, though on a few occasions the good soldier exploits the maxims in order to deliver an indirect insult or threat, this is not very characteristic of his style; and this absence clearly sets him apart from the aggressive Diogenes. Second, some of the conversational implicatures that Švejk's conversations generate seem to transcend the discursive universe of this character. So far I have treated the good soldier as an independent figure, not as a part of a

Szasz, *The Myth of Mental Illness: Foundations of a Theory of Personal Conduct* [New York, 1974], p. 239). This description of a patient afflicted by the Ganser syndrome fits Švejk's behavior quite well.

larger novelistic structure. But it would be naive not to see that Švejk's discourse often conveys the narrator's point of view. The exploitation of implicatures is one of these ventriloquist techniques. Let me introduce just one example. When parting with his friend Sapper Vodička, Švejk urges him to seek him out after the war at his habitual pub, "At the Chalice." " 'Very well, then, at six o'clock in the evening when the war's over!' shouted Vodička from below. 'Better if you come at half-past six, in case I should be held up somewhere,' answered Švejk. And then Vodička's voice could be heard again this time from a great distance: 'Can't you come at six?' 'Very well then, I'll come at six,' Vodička heard his retreating friend reply" (393; 395). The incongruity of these meticulous arrangements with the semantics of the word "war" is quite obvious. Vodička and Švejk ostentatiously fail to fulfill the M.Ql., for neither of them can be reasonably sure that he will be at "At the Chalice" at exactly 6:00 P.M. when the war has ended. Yet it seems to me that the interlocutors do not exploit the flouted maxim; rather, what this specific breach implies is the narrator's attitude toward war. Through this linguistic device Hašek strips war of any metaphysical significance or meaning, reducing it to a trifling social event of limited duration (like a soccer game), after which the spectators adjourn to their favorite pub to enjoy beer and a good chat.

There is yet another discursive strategy exploited by Švejk that inconspicuously violates the normal relations among participants in conversation: his insatiable propensity for telling stories. As Pratt points out, by being able to control the floor for an indefinite period of time, a narrator enjoys an enormous advantage over his listeners. "In ratifying a speaker's request to tell a story we (the hearers) . . . waive our right to preempt the floor until the storyteller himself offers to give it up (with his narrative coda). . . . More than nearly any other speech act," she continues, "narratives, once begun, are immune to control by other participants in a conversation" (103–4).

Earlier I argued that Švejk's stories have a number of functions in the book; dominating the floor is one of them. And storytelling is perhaps the good soldier's most powerful ploy for disrupting the flow of information and orders toward him. We should notice, first of all, that his reasons for starting a narrative are usually quite weak ("it reminds me of . . . ," "as a friend of mine used to say . . . ," "there was a case like this in Táborská Street . . ."). Second, some of his stories are not very tellable (i.e., interesting to the audience), and Švejk proffers them simply to prevent conversational turn-taking. In some cases they function like this exchange with Dub: "They remained standing in front of each other and Lieutenant Dub was thinking hard what frightful thing he could say to him. But Švejk cut in: 'Humbly report, sir, if only the weather would keep. It's not very hot in the daytime and the nights are really quite pleasant so that this is the most suitable time for warfare' " (579; 602). At the extreme, Švejk's tales are weapons capable of inflicting injury on unfriendly listeners. For example, our hero tells a story about an absent-minded engine driver to Sergeant-Major Nasáklo, who is subjecting him to a punitive rifle drill. The story is so convoluted and takes so long to tell that poor Nasáklo, involuntarily absorbed by the narrative, eventually collapses with what is diagnosed by a doctor as "a case of sunstroke or acute meningitis" (540; 558).

From the Gricean standpoint, Švejk's narratives clearly clash with all the maxims except the M.Ql., which does not apply here (a story can be fictitious). But, once again, this nonfulfillment relates in a peculiar way to the overall CP. It might be described as the inversion of opting out—the termination of a conversation by a unilateral shutting down of the channel. Logorrhea accomplishes the same end through opposite means: one-sided overloading of the channel. Yet while such a radical "opting in" is similar in effect to opting out, it differs from the latter in that it does not break contact between the participants in a speech situation. The compulsive storyteller seems exceedingly interested in verbal intercourse—he keeps talking and talking to the listener—though, paradoxically, the very demonstration of this desire makes a genuine exchange impossible. The semblance of cooperation is, furthermore, perpetuated through Švejk's concern for his listener: "Wasn't that story perhaps a little long, sir?" (552; 570), he asks Lieutenant Lukáš when he finishes a tale extending over two printed pages.

My limited discussion of Diogenes' and Švejk's uses of language suggests a significant difference between the two kynik heroes. While neither makes the CP operative in his respective discourse, each tends to disrupt it in different ways: Diogenes by openly opting out of the conversational maxims (and the CP), Švejk by violating the maxims in a surreptitious manner which often makes his interlocutor wonder whether the detectable failure is not an unintentional consequence of mental defect rather than evidence of Švejk's unwillingness to engage in a reasonable exchange. This impression is further enhanced by the polite behavior of our good soldier, bordering sometimes on obsequiousness, his invariable habit of addressing his military superiors with the phrase "humbly report, sir," and his amiable countenance ("the tender blue eyes," "the gaze of a pure and innocent lamb"). These all signal Švejk's eagerness to cooperate, but this gesture is always somehow subverted, left unrealized because of circumstances that seem to be beyond his control.

Švejk's compulsive storytelling adds another dimension to this confusion. It subverts communication by communication: words are used as a protective shield against alien, hostile words. And though an outright refusal to engage verbally with those in power would be self-destructive, the structure of Švejk's discourse—the formal affirmation of the CP that obscures the actual breaking of the appurtenant maxims—seems to pacify the authorities. Thus, the good soldier sails unscathed through all the snares that society lays in his path. Whether this is the sheer luck of a babbling idiot or the brilliant stratagem of a calculating mind we will never know. But neither will the authorities—the *conditio sine qua non* of Švejk's success.

Throughout my study of Hašek's protagonist I stumbled across many political readings of this figure, and I have presented them in all their contradictoriness. In so doing, however, I do not mean to impugn their validity. Such interpretations, as I argued in my introduction to this book, are partial by their very nature, for they actualize the text in a highly particular context. Yet what sets *The Good Soldier* apart from the rest of Czech fiction is both the intensity of its political effect and its permanence, that is, the book's capacity to be projected against a great variety of social settings.

To explain this quality of Hašek's text one must take into account, first of all, its disjointed, episodic organization, which makes it especially inviting to a political reading. It is quite easy to extract a detail or a phrase from the book only to apply it to the situation at hand. And, given the fundamental ambiguity of *Švejk*, it is not surprising that it has been utilized for many different and often contradictory purposes. But there is yet another feature of Hašek's book that guarantees its exceptional status in modern Czech letters: its memorability. Among Czechs this novel has become a modern *epos* (in the original sense of this genre—*ta epe*, a composition set for oral delivery).[49] Most of them know it by heart, and they quote from it liberally at pregnant moments. It is this "epic" quality which has made Švejk a symbolic figure in his homeland—a recognizable *locus communis* charged with many cultural values.

But in assessing the social role of the novel, one should not lose sight of the thematic aspect of *Švejk*. It is about an event whose significance for modern European civilization can hardly be overestimated. World War I determined, the Czech philosopher Jan Patočka argued, the entire character of our century: "It was this war which demonstrated that the transformation of the world into a laboratory actualizing reserves of energy which had been accumulating for ages *had to* be achieved only through a war. It signified a definitive breakthrough of the understanding of being inaugu-

---

[49]   For a discussion of this genre, see Northrop Frye, *Anatomy of Criticism: Four Essays* (Princeton, 1957), esp. pp. 248–49.

rated in the seventeenth century by the rise of mechanistic natural science and by the removal of all 'conventions' hampering this release of power—the transvaluation of all values in the name of power."[50] The essential novelty of the war lies, according to Patočka, in its *total* character. If the nineteenth century could still differentiate between war and peace (in both space and time), the twentieth century erased this comfortable division. In order to manage, in a time of conflict, its finite resources most efficiently (along the lines of industrial production), the state was transformed into a huge monofunctional machine designed for an exclusive end: to vanquish the enemy. Entire populations were marshaled to participate in the war effort; and the generation on the home front of all the products necessary for the successful conduct of warfare became as important for strategists as the fighting itself. This in turn justified the targeting of civilian populations as legitimate objects of military action.

Military hostilities might have ended on the fields of Europe in 1918, but the war did not, Patočka argues. The traumas of the previous four years gave rise to grandiose political projects that were meant to organize society in ways that would eradicate all future conflict. Yet this "struggle for peace," as the term intimates, was engendered by the same bellicose spirit as the phenomenon it aimed to eradicate: the will to destroy the foes of peace by any means and at any cost. The two twentieth-century European experiments with totalitarianism give vivid testimony to this mentality. We should not forget that it was its nonnegotiable demand to stop the war immediately that gained the Communist Party many supporters in Russia in 1917. And, by the same token, it was the Nazis' quest for a "just peace" (rectifying the "diktat" of Versailles) in the 1920s that made them popular among the German population. The social engineering that appeared in Europe on a grand scale after World War I was obviously inspired by the new management of military affairs. States were conceived of as bulwarks of a single, apodictic *Weltanschauung*, and they were organized to guarantee their success in competition with other states and ideologies. This entailed, among other things, a strictly hierarchical chain of command with an extensive bureaucracy transmitting orders from the leadership to the masses, compulsory loyalty to the state reinforced by a strong repressive apparatus, a bipolar division of the world into allies and enemies, and the reduction of the citizenry to a mere dispensable materiel for achieving the state's strategic objectives.

The novelistic universe of Hašek's text, born from its author's involvement in the war and (as Kosík asserts) the Communist revolution, con-

---

[50]   Jan Potočka, *Kacířské eseje o filozofii dějin* (Munich, 1980), p. 122; *Heretical Essays in the Philosophy of History*, trans. E. Kohák (Chicago, 1996), p. 124.

tains in a more or less inchoate form all the etatist tendencies that came to fruition in the twentieth century.[51] And the stock of its protagonist, resisting successfully his incorporation into the state system, was rising as totalitarian trends gradually became actualized in Czech political life. Thus, in the year of Hašek's death, the popularity of his novel was seen as a purely generational infatuation. "After ten years," the two court-appointed assessors estimating the monetary value of Švejk wrote in 1923, "the content of this writing will be incomprehensible to the new generation and the book will find few readers."[52] They were wrong, of course, yet though the novel's audience did not diminish in the decades that followed, its political function was markedly different in the 1930s than it would be some ten years later. While the democratic atmosphere of the First Republic generated many discussions about the perils and benefits of Švejk as a potential role model, the German invasion of 1939, according to one commentator, rendered him such. "The verb 'to *švejk*' appeared just at the turn of the 1920s in military slang," asserts Josef Jedlička, "most likely as a curse in the mouths of COs and NCOs. Civilians began to *švejk* only during the [German] Protectorate and only toward its end did *švejk-ing* and *švejkism* become a conscious attitude. At the same time *švejking* as a strategy was transplanted into the 'strife' of [high school] students with their professors, and *švejkism* as a possible interpretation of reality entered the horizon of the younger generation."[53] For once, students learned something practical in school! After the victory of Socialism *à la Russe* in Czechoslovakia in 1948, they could have put this Švejk-inspired interpretation of reality to good use. But now, in a paradoxical twist, Hašek became an officially sanctioned author despite the patent fact that the ludic spirit of his protagonist was anything but congenial to the earnest seriousness of those revolutionary times. The pictures of Švejk displayed in Prague pubs in the 1950s and 1960s with the message "Take it easy!" were unmistakably the popular reply to the omnipresent Communist propaganda posters urging the populace to heroic deeds of various kinds. And it was precisely during the short period of decreased totalitarianism in the mid-1960s that Czech intellectuals such as Kosík formulated their positive political readings of *Švejk*.

In the world dominated by power, Švejk is an underdog, the object of manipulation and coercion by inimical social forces that constantly threaten his very existence. Yet, despite the tremendous odds against him,

51   Karel Kosík, "Švejk a Bugulma neboli zrození velkého humoru," *Nedělní Lidové noviny,* July 31, 1993, pp. viii–ix.
52   Quoted from *Lidský profil Jaroslava Haška: Korespondence a dokumenty,* ed. R. Pytlík (Prague, 1979), p. 257.
53   Josef Jedlička, *České typy aneb Poptávka po našem hrdinovy* (Prague, 1992), p. 78.

he passes through all the dangers unharmed. Švejk's mythical invincibility makes him a modern "epic hero" with whom his compatriots identify and of whose exploits they talk because they see in him "a modern Saint George, the hero of a saga of a single mind's triumph over the hydra of Authority, Regime, and System—of the mind disguised as feeblemindedness in the war with Absurdity in the guise of Wisdom and Dignity—the sense of Nonsense against the nonsense of Sense."[54] And though, to an outsider, next to the spectacular stunts of ancient heroes Švejk's feat—his survival achieved through his own doing, without any embarrassing compromises with those in power—might seem rather trifling, the historical experience of a small nation sandwiched between Germany and Russia suggests to a Czech reader that it also might be an absolute miracle.

[54]   Jiří Voskovec, *Klobouk ve křoví: Výbor z veršů V+W* (Prague, 1965), p. 29.

2

Radical Liberalism

Apocryphal Stories by Karel Čapek

KING: What do you call this play?
HAMLET: *The Mousetrap*. Marry how? Tropically. This play is the image
of a murder done in Vienna. Gonzago is the Duke's name, his wife,
Baptista. You shall see anon. 'Tis a knavish piece of work, but what o'
that? Your Majesty, and we that have free souls, it touches us not. Let
the galled jade wince, our withers are unwrung.

—William Shakespeare, *The Tragedy of Hamlet, Prince of Denmark*

The word "apocrypha," to venture into the deceptive realm of etymology, derives from the Greek verb *kryptein*, 'to hide." So its occurrence in
the title of Čapek's collection of stories, which has apparently been well
hidden from the prying eye of literary scholars, seems more than appropriate. It must be stressed, however, that such critical neglect is not entirely fortuitous. First, the collection is composed of twenty-nine baf-
flingly heterogeneous, tiny texts written between 1920 and 1938, mainly
as newspaper columns for the popular daily *Lidové noviny*, where Čapek
worked. Most are dialogues of various types, but there is also a letter, a
philosophical lecture, and a fragment of a play written in blank verse.
Thematically, the stories range from ancient myths and legends to
episodes from the Old and New Testaments and Shakespearean plays,
and contain an unlikely combination of heroes: a prehistorical man
named Janeček, Saint Francis of Assisi, Don Juan, Napoleon Bonaparte.
Given the discrepancy between the scope of this historical mosaic and the
trifling size of the stories themselves (the average length is about a thousand words), it is not surprising that most specialists regard the *Apocryphal Stories* as a simple exercise in journalistic entertainment inferior to
Čapek's heftier and more complex novels and plays.

Furthermore, the collection is also apocryphal in the sense in which this word is understood today, that is, of being somehow illegitimate, of dubious origin. Čapek certainly wrote all the texts and in 1932 even published a volume of five biblical stories titled *Apocryphas*.[1] But *Apocryphal Stories* did not appear until 1945, seven years after his death, and the editor, Miroslav Halík, admits that he took some liberties with its contents.[2] The fact that the composition of this collection may have more to do with editorial convenience than a unified artistic intent proves frustrating for critics. And though the individual texts are similar to one another, they are so in the manner of a Wittgensteinian family resemblance, in which all members of the set share no single trait. There seems to be no meaningful generalization about this collection that would apply to all the stories.

Last but not least, Čapek's stories are written, so to speak, in the margins of the great tales that constitute the Western cultural heritage. And they are apocryphal because they retell this tradition from a new, non-canonic vantage point. Evident in this technique is a variant on the polyperspectival narrative that Čapek introduced to Czech literature in his famous novels, whereby a single event is presented successively by several characters in different, incompatible ways. Unlike his novels, which openly display the clash of contradictory points of view, the *Apocryphal Stories* merely suggest disparity, portraying the European past from a heterodox perspective. The difference between the explicit polyvocality of Čapek's novels and the implicit polyvocality of the *Apocryphal Stories* affects their critical evaluation. While critics hail the novels as pioneering experiments with narrative technique, the stories are perceived merely as playful travesties of venerable texts, very much in the mold of traditional parodies. Most commentaries on this book deal primarily with other practitioners of this genre who might have influenced Čapek: Voltaire, Lemaître, Anatole France.

In what follows I challenge the traditional critical response to this collection and attempt to release it from its apocryphal obscurity. I hope to illustrate that this text, better than any other, reveals the stylistic traits characteristic of Čapek's writing and the epistemological underpinnings of his intellectual program. Far from being peripheral to his output, the *Apocryphal Stories* embody Čapek's creative method.

Anybody who has ever plowed through Čapek's oeuvre has realized his remarkable versatility. There is hardly a genre of writing that he did not try. Well known as a novelist and playwright, he was also an early practitioner of science fiction and a skillful essayist. Less famous, espe-

[1]   Karel Čapek, *Apokryfy* (Prague, 1932).
[2]   Miroslav Halík, "Poznámka vydavatelova," in Karel Čapek, *Kniha apokryfů* (Prague, 1945), p. 250.

cially abroad, are his philosophical treatises, tales for children, detective stories, and aphorisms. And virtually overlooked are his forays into verse and verse theory, despite their signal value for Czech poetry and poetics. Čapek's translation of Apollinaire's "Zone" established the linguistic basis for subsequent experiments of the Czech avant-garde, while his insight into the linkages between poetic rhythm and meaning helped stimulate the structuralists' interest in the semantics of meter.[3] This formal diversity had its thematic counterpart. The subjects that Čapek touched upon are too many to enumerate. He authored several volumes of conversations with the venerable president of Czechoslovakia, T. G. Masaryk, and a book about his puppy Dášenka. He wrote with equal ease and skill on the sociology of literature, city gardening, and the mission of intellectuals in the modern world. This ability, combined with Čapek's apparent interest in everything, explains why he settled for a journalistic career, despite its less than reputable image. Thus, the heterogeneity of the *Apocryphal Stories* is not at all unusual or particular to this collection. The brevity of the texts is equally typical. Throughout his career Čapek considered it important to defend the short story as an integral part of his creation, in no way inferior to longer genres. In a 1936 reply to an opinion poll on the provocative question "Why does nobody in our country write short stories?" Čapek points to the critic as the primary cause of this deficiency: "Criticism views short stories with mild contempt. It regards them as a trifling, applied art that cannot be treated as seriously or reflectively as a thick novel. A short story is considered 'small change,' 'a minuscule task,' or something that, in short, involves neither 'great form-giving effort' nor 'higher intellectual synthesis.' " Critics are wrong, he insists, because "for an author the short story will always remain one of the most attractive problems in both form and content."[4]

These remarks are important for our understanding of Čapek's poetics. He was, above all, a master of short literary forms: his larger pieces are often composed of smaller segments fused together with framing devices of various kinds. The play *From the Life of Insects*, for example, is a series of skits linked by a character called the Hobo who comments on them. The novel *Meteor* consists of four shorter narratives framed by the fact that they all describe the same event. In this respect, the *Apocryphal Stories* do not deviate significantly from these larger texts, with one important exception: there is no explicit reason for bringing the stories together. The

---

[3] See Vítězslav Nezval, *Moderní básnické směry*, 4th ed. (Prague, 1973), p. 32; and Roman Jakobson, "K popisu Máchova verše," in *Torso a tajemství Máchova díla: Sborník pojednání Pražského lingvistického kroužku*, ed. J. Mukařovský (Prague, 1938), pp. 245–46.

[4] Karel Čapek, "[Příspěvek v anketě] Proč se u nás nepíší povídky," in *O umění a kultuře*, vol. 3 (*Spisy*, vol. 19) (Prague, 1986), p. 706.

collection lays bare its discrete structure, and the apocryphas are presented as isolated fragments from the history of Western civilization. The contiguous pieces of *Apocryphal Stories* are incongruous formally, thematically, and tonally. Each narrative is concerned with a different problem; each proceeds from a different vantage point. Some tales are philosophical or quasi-philosophical; some cast well-known events or personalities in a deliberately commonsensical, antiheroic light; some seem didactic. And though the individual apocryphas may indeed be seen as variations on the literary device of polyperspectival narrative, as a collection they are diametrically different in technique. Instead of exploiting the fact that different people account for the same event in dissimilar ways, the *Apocryphal Stories* foreground heterogeneity within a single observer. Čapek presents not only different events but also different attitudes toward them. In a manner of speaking, this collection could have been authored by many.

At a surface level the unsettling changeability of the *Apocryphal Stories* might be explained quite simply as the result of an intrusion of one sequential order into another—the represented events and the presenting subject. Although in the book itself the stories follow one another according to the historical sequence in which they supposedly occurred (from antiquity to the nineteenth century), the subjective chronology of their actual origin is quite different. The one Čapek wrote first, in 1920, "Pilate's Creed," falls eighteenth in the collection, while "The Punishment of Prometheus," with which *Apocryphal Stories* opens, was written in 1932 after Čapek had already published thirteen other apocryphas. It is obvious that in the eighteen years it took to produce all the texts, the author changed both personally and in respect to his ever-evolving sociopolitical context. Thus, the historical sequencing of the collection necessarily scrambles the original biographical connections among the stories and brings into proximity texts from quite different periods of Čapek's career. It would be wrong, however, to blame this rearrangement on sloppy editorial work or the publisher's desire to create attractive packaging for a bunch of leftover stories. As Miroslav Halík, the man ultimately responsible for this book, insists, the original design of *Apocryphal Stories* is the author's.

I believe, therefore, that in planning this collection Čapek was experimenting with a problem that had occupied him in the 1930s and that he had exploited in his novel *Ordinary Life*: how to present one's own past. In *Ordinary Life* the protagonist decides to write his autobiography but realizes midway that it is an impossible task. A conventional autobiography cannot do justice to its author because it proceeds from false assumptions about human existence. It seeks to define personal identity where there is

none and to superimpose narrative order where there is only randomness. The hero's painful self-scrutiny reveals the utter relativity of his own
ego: under close introspection he dissolves into a myriad of different
selves. What at any moment he considers his real self turns out to be just
one of many which, for the time being, happens to have gained the upper
hand. But at no point in his life can he predict his future, know what his
next identity will be, or detect any order in his personal metamorphoses.
Confronted with the virtually unlimited potential of this protean ego,
which resists neat streamlining into a single narrative line, the hapless au-
tobiographer resigns himself to generating story after story, each bringing
to light a hitherto concealed aspect of his life, until death mercifully termi-
nates his endless project. The lesson to be learned from the "failure" of *Ordinary Life* is clear: one cannot narrate his or her past without distorting it.

But there are modes other than conventional narrative for capturing
one's history. The *Apocryphal Stories* presents one such alternative. They
are an oblique record of eighteen years of Čapek's career as a writer; and
as the author of *Ordinary Life*, one might emphasize, he could not have
been unaware of this fact. By arranging the volume in a nonbiographical
manner, it seems, he was deliberately presenting himself as an instantiation of his concept of human existence in general. By starting in the middle and moving back and forth, he emphasized the nonlinear, discontinu-
ous nature of his biography. Like images in a kaleidoscope, each
apocrypha reveals a different Karel Čapek—patriot, playwright and poet,
political activist, philosopher, to mention just a few. These partial configurations, convergences, and divergences of near and distant patterns, the
constant intermingling of past and future all enable the reader to recognize the haphazardness of Čapek's life story, its inner indeterminacy, the
fact that at any moment it could have taken many different courses. Thus,
by disassembling his biography in *Apocryphal Stories*, Čapek produced an
autobiographical account of his creative career, one that encompasses his
polymorphousness and presents it dynamically, as a process of becoming.

As a collection, therefore, the *Apocryphal Stories* are more concerned
with Čapek's own past than with Western civilization. But even if one dis-
regards their autobiographical aspect, these texts are still not ordinary historical tales using bygone events as material for artistic reproduction.
What the reader finds significant in them, as I insisted earlier, is not
simple *re*presentation but *mis*presentation. Čapek's stories clash too obviously with what we know about our own cultural patrimony to be taken
at face value. But neither are they parodies that create a discrepancy between two semantic planes in order to debunk values that the author considers obsolete. This would be too nihilistic a game for Čapek, who always maintained that no axiological system can be dismissed just because

we happen to disagree with it. The paradox that the *Apocryphal Stories* create, therefore, has not a dogmatic but an aporetic function: it strives not to establish a single apodictic truth to the detriment of all others but to relativize this very notion. The collection therefore reinscribes in historical material the leitmotif of all Čapek's writings: "In my entire oeuvre," the author observed in 1922, "I regurgitate *ad nauseam* two half-moral, half-epistemological themes. The first is negative, Pilate's: What is truth? The second is positive: Everyone has [his own] truth."[5]

Yet this reference to Pilate should not mislead us as to the intellectual underpinnings of Čapek's position. Its source was not the Bible but contemporary philosophy, and, more precisely, American Pragmatism, whose theories Čapek expounded to his Czech audience in considerable depth in his 1918 monograph devoted to this school.[6] It would take me too far from my present task to discuss how closely the Czech *penseur* followed the theories of James, Dewey, and others in his own writings. For my purpose it suffices to point out that Pragmatist pluralism had aesthetic and political consequences which the *Apocryphal Stories* attempted to negotiate.

Let me begin with the artistic concerns. In an impassioned essay of 1934 about the crisis of the modern world, Čapek turned to Sophocles' *Antigone* to make his point. The plot of this tragedy, generated by the moral conflict between individual conscience and the law of the supraindividual state, enabled him to raise once again his favorite question, Who is right here?: Antigone, burying her brother in violation of the king's injunction, or Creon, punishing her for this illegal act? It is easy, Čapek argues, to take sides in this conflict, to condemn either Antigone in the name of the state or Creon in the name of common human decency. But would either reflect a proper attitude toward Sophocles' drama? "If you opt for one of these positions," he cautions, "it is the end of tragedy, the end of human grandeur, the end of moral shock." The aesthetic force of the play stems from the simultaneous presence of opposing standpoints that are equally compelling, equally inevitable. "None of the clashing values is denied or denigrated; the tragic nobility of this case lies in the fact that majestic collides with majestic, upright with upright."[7]

Čapek's analysis of the aesthetic effect of *Antigone* can be applied, mutatis mutandis, to his *Apocryphal Stories* as well. They depict characters and events that conflict with the traditional understanding of the past. Yet neither the orthodox nor the revisionist view of history is dismissed. De-

---

5   Karel Čapek, "Musím dále," ibid., vol. 2 (*Spisy*, vol. 18) (Prague, 1985), p. 415.
6   Karel Čapek, *Pragmatismus čili filosofie praktického života* (Prague, 1918).
7   Karel Čapek, "Kapitola o hodnotách," in *O umění a kultuře*, 3: 577–78.

spite his irony or sarcasm, Čapek strives to present beliefs as comprehensible (if not justifiable), whether for sentimental, economic, or strategic reasons. In this axiological *isostheneia,* one may locate the aesthetic quality of the *Apocryphal Stories.*

Although one can understand how this recognition of opposite points of view contributes to the aesthetic effect of Čapek's writings, it is not entirely clear how it could foster political goals. Social action would seem to be predicated on bias, a preference for particular values over others. Čapek could adhere to his Pragmatist relativism so long as he wished the *Apocryphal Stories* to remain a purely aesthetic exercise. But if he wanted them to have a specific political effect, so the argument goes, he would have to give up disinterested impartiality, identify fully with some position, join one party in its struggle against others. But this is precisely the conception of political involvement which Čapek always abhorred: a blind war among mutually biased foes.

By saying this, however, I do not wish to imply that Čapek would deny that every political stance, including his own, is prejudiced. As a proponent of Pragmatism he knew only too well that our commitments reflect not ideals or truths but only limited human interests. At the same time, this does not mean that for Čapek social activism was nothing more than one-sided partisanship, blind to anything but its immediate political objectives. The shortcoming of this type of behavior, in his opinion, was not that it is partial but that it is not partial enough, or, more precisely, that it does not recognize the relativity of its own position, the arbitrariness of its preferences. By not being able to see beyond the confines of its own agenda, it reduces social life to a mere power game, a competition among incompatible values in which the winner takes all. Politics, in Čapek's opinion, or at least the democratic variant that he promulgated, cannot be conceived so narrowly, lest society perish. It must have a cooperative dimension, that which unites competing parties in a communal struggle. In a self-governing *polis,* political engagement is of necessity transactional, a negotiation among different positions, each of which is valid in its own limited way. The programs we advance, the causes we champion are not capricious manifestations of our will to power but reactions to similar initiatives by fellow citizens. To deal with them efficiently we must approximate their system of values, anticipate their responses to our actions, agree on the rules of the interaction, and so on. Our identification with one point of view, therefore, is not a negation of all others but rather an implicit legitimization, an affirmation of their right to exist. From this perspective, then, social activism need not be at variance with the principles of pluralism. In a democratic society Čapek saw their direct extension into the political sphere.

Such a program looks good in theory, to be sure. But its implementation in interwar Europe, where by the mid-1930s democratically elected governments represented a distinct minority, was an altogether different matter. Amid ideological intolerance and ethnic hatred, the idea of literature as an impartial display of equipollent values sounded distinctly escapist, to say the least. Authors worried about the fate of the world, most concerned intellectuals insisted, must leave the proverbial ivory tower of art and rally behind the cause they consider just, or face the consequences of their irresponsibility. Čapek himself, it must be stressed, was quite aware of the prevailing sentiment of the day. He even made it a theme of one of his apocryphas. The hero of this text, a man of literary talent, is deeply upset by the moral decay that pervades his kingdom, and in the company of two friends he ponders what he should do: seek refuge from an unpalatable reality in the world of fiction, or mobilize his people for direct action that would change the social situation to which he objects. *Tertium non datur!*

HAMLET: Write—I shall write. I've got so many subjects already—the villain was the first. The second will be about the toadying, mean-spirited courtiers—

ROSENCRANTZ: Top hole, prince!

HAMLET: The third, a comedy about a stupid old chamberlain—

GUILDENSTERN: A first-rate subject!

HAMLET: The fourth will be a play about a girl.

ROSENCRANTZ: What sort of a play?

HAMLET: Oh, just a play.

GUILDENSTERN: A most promising subject!

ROSENCRANTZ: Quite poetic.

HAMLET: And Hamlet will write. On the throne a scoundrel will grind the faces of the defenseless people, courtiers will bend their backs, and Hamlet will write. And there will be wars, things will grow worse for the weak and better for the strong, and Hamlet will write. So as not to rise and do something—

GUILDENSTERN: What, prince?

HAMLET: How should I know? What does one do against a bad government?

ROSENCRANTZ: Nothing, prince.

HAMLET: Nothing at all?

GUILDENSTERN: Well, in history you sometimes find men who place themselves at the head of the people and urge them by their eloquence or their example to rise against bad government and smash it.

ROSENCRANTZ: But that, prince, is only done in history.

HAMLET: Well, well. Only in history. And you say that eloquence can rouse people up? Grief is dumb. Someone must come who will call a spade a spade and say: Look here, this is oppression, this is injustice, an infamous crime has been perpetrated against you and the man who calls himself your king is a criminal, a cheat, a murderer, and an adulterer—that's fact, isn't it? If you are men at all, why do you put up with this infamy, why don't you snatch up swords and clubs? Or are you already gelded by your shame? Are you slaves who can bear to live without honor—

GUILDENSTERN: You are eloquent, prince.

HAMLET: Eloquent, you say? What if I came forward and as if in history made my eloquence the voice of the people?

ROSENCRANTZ: The people are certainly devoted to their prince.

HAMLET: And then at their head overthrew the rotten throne?

GUILDENSTERN: Your pardon, prince, but that's politics.[8]

According to this passage, a marriage of politics and poetics, it seems, would be an impossible proposition. Hamlet cannot be both playwright and public tribune. He must either give up his artistic ambitions to fulfill his civic duties or, for art's sake, become oblivious to the injustice that surrounds him. Yet, curiously enough, as a whole, Čapek's apocrypha hardly seems dogmatic about this issue. It is a text, we must not forget, with a subtext: a discourse comprising several semantic layers. In general, it engages all of Shakespeare's *Tragedy of Hamlet*. But on a more limited scale it draws on Hamlet's own play, *The Mousetrap*, staged in the tragedy itself. And it is precisely this play within a play that suggests one possible method for literature's social involvement.

Čapek's apocrypha alludes to Hamlet's play metonymically, through its opening lines. It starts with Hamlet questioning Rosencrantz and Guildenstern about the reception of *The Mousetrap*, which has just been performed at court. The reader familiar with Shakespeare's work knows very well that this is not an inquiry by a vain author insecure about his dramatic skills. In its original setting Hamlet's play means to be more than "just a play." It is designed as a tool of justice, a strategic textual "trap" to help the wronged author catch the culprit. Hamlet's monologue at the end of Act II divulges his plan:

> That guilty creatures sitting at a play
> Have by the very cunning of the scene

8 Čapek, *Kniha apokryfů*, pp. 204–8; *Apocryphal Stories*, trans. D. Round (London, 1949), pp. 129–31. Quotations are taken, with some slight alterations, from Round's translation. Further references will be given in the text; the first number in parentheses refers to the Czech original and the second to the English translation.

> Been struck so to the soul that presently
> They have proclaimed their malefactions;
> For murder, though it have no tongue, will speak
> With most miraculous organ. I'll have these players
> Play something like the murder of my father
> Before mine uncle. I'll observe his looks,
> I'll tent him to the quick. If he but blench,
> I know my course. The spirit that I have seen
> May be the Devil, and the Devil hath power
> To assume a pleasing shape. Yea, and perhaps
> Out of my weakness and my melancholy,
> As he is very potent with such spirits,
> Abuses me to damn me. I'll have grounds
> More relative than this. The play's the thing
> Wherein I'll catch the conscience of the King.[9]

Thus, Hamlet writes his play not to depict fictitious characters in an aesthetically self-contained manner but to reflect living counterparts in the audience. It is the staging of a murder that draws a parallel with the actual murder of Hamlet's father by his uncle in order to "catch the conscience" of the villain. At this moment perhaps the cautionary words of Čapek's Guildenstern might come to mind: "Your pardon, prince, but that's politics." Would he be right? Yes and no. True, Hamlet's play is intended to have social consequences. Yet, unlike political rhetoric, it does not "call a spade a spade," or the king "a criminal, a cheat, a murderer, and an adulterer." It makes its case "tropically," through analogy, within a neutral artistic frame. Sensitive viewers might indeed catch the intended political message (as Hamlet's uncle does), but only if they contextualize the text according to the author's concealed wish. For though not "just a play," Hamlet's play still remains a play, a semantically open piece of fiction that can always be contextualized in a nonpolitical manner as well. This is, after all, the point that Hamlet makes to deflect his uncle's ire.

But how do Čapek's apocryphas emulate the oblique mode of reference that makes The Mousetrap an effective tool of Hamlet's extraartistic design? For this technique to work, an author must make his audience aware that he is talking about something other than what he is actually portraying, without at the same time providing any explicit clues as to the true subject of his discourse. The irony of this position is that it is distinctly

[9] William Shakespeare, The Tragedy of Hamlet, Prince of Denmark, in The Complete Works (New York, 1948), p. 905.

unironic. If an ironicist, as the old saying goes, is someone who does not wish to be understood, Hamlet's objective is quite the opposite. He wants very much for his uncle to know that he knows. And he may be confident that his royal relatives will recognize themselves in his play because he shares with them the secret of their criminal act. But Čapek, with no paternal ghost to prompt him as to the secret thoughts of his audience, could never be sure that his implied message would be received. This might sound like an insurmountable problem until we realize that virtually all the apocryphas appeared initially in the daily *Lidové noviny*. And while leafing through the crumbling sheets of this newspaper we might begin to appreciate how context-sensitive most of Čapek's narratives are. The story of Christ's birth, "The Holy Night," for example, was published on December 25, and the one about his death, "Crucifixion" (originally titled "An Apocrypha"), on Easter Sunday.

It was not only the Christian calendar that prompted Čapek to write his stories. His "Hamlet" was published on October 28, 1934—Czechoslovak Independence Day—celebrating the founding of the Republic sixteen years before. The context of *Lidové noviny* furnishes one of the links between this Shakespearean play and the national holiday. On that day Čapek received the coveted state literary prize awarded yearly to commemorate writers' contributions to the Czechoslovak quest for self-determination. Written for this festive occasion, the apocrypha provided Čapek with an opportunity to reflect upon his role as literary author in the current political setting. Hamlet appears in the story as a man of letters endowed with some of Čapek's personal traits. In addition, the generating conflict in Shakespeare's play—the illegitimate transfer of power through regicide—had uncanny relevance to the concerns of 1934. In July of that year the Austrian Nazis, aided by Germany, staged an unsuccessful putsch in Vienna, killing Chancellor Engelbert Dollfuss. And in Marseilles on October 9, less than three weeks before "Hamlet" was published, Croatian terrorists trained in Hungary and Germany assassinated King Alexander of Yugoslavia, a close ally of Czechoslovakia. Čapek was deeply disturbed by the moral consequences of these actions, as he wrote in *Lidové noviny*: "Political gangsters commit something worse than political murders. They kill respect for the human being, trust in reason, and the sense that justice is to rule the world."[10] His apocrypha projected such worries into literary material. The moral decay that confronted Hamlet, Čapek warned his readers, was no longer solely a matter of a fictive Den-

---

[10] Karel Čapek, "Skoro modlitba," in *Od člověka k člověku*, vol. 3 (*Spisy*, vol. 16) (Prague, 1991), pp. 235–36.

mark but rather the political reality of Europe. Something had to be done lest the play leave the stage and the tragedy become life.

The example of "Hamlet" yields an important insight into Čapek's strategy for folding politics into his art. The apparent simplicity of the *Apocryphal Stories* is quite deceptive: there is a discrepancy between what these narratives evidently speak about and what they are actually saying. Explicitly they are amusing renditions of great tales from the history of Western civilization. If perceived only at this level, they can be read as light literary parodies. But in writing them Čapek also pursued a political agenda that is "apocryphal" in the etymological sense of the word—"hidden away." He used time-honored texts as pre-texts to comment on the pressing problems of his day. At this level his apocryphas carry a clear-cut political message and serve the author as a medium of persuasion. They are *cryptograms* insofar as they require an external key if they are to be understood in accordance with authorial intent. Their message, therefore, is not the sole property of the texts themselves but a function of the immediate context to which they are responding. Through *Apocryphal Stories* Čapek pleaded his case and engaged the enemies of his *polis*—whether internal or external. But, unlike in his nonartistic, polemically blunt pieces, here he did so indirectly, in a figurative fashion, through analogy.

Two stories from Čapek's collection are particularly telling examples of this dependence on context, for I myself was oblivious to their political purport before investigating the historical background that generated them. The first, "As in the Good Old Days," from August 3, 1926, like many other apocryphas, addresses the issue of justice. It is a dialogue between Eupator and Philagoros, two citizens of Thebes, about the scandal involving a local military leader. "Do you know what's happening?" Philagoros asks Eupator, who is fully occupied with his daily business. "They want to have our General Nikomachos up for trial! Some people say he's guilty of some sort of intrigue with the Thessalonians, and other people say he's guilty of some mix-up with the Malcontents' Party. . . . I myself believe that Nikomachos was trying to betray us to the Thessalonians; someone there said so, and he said that someone he knew had seen some letter. But one man said it was a plot against Nikomachos and that he knew a thing or two about it. They say our government's involved in it" (25–27; 20–21). Eupator, however, is unperturbed by the news and goes on with his chores. All the information Philagoros is bringing, he replies, is mere rumor. It is clearly premature to speak of Nikomachos' guilt or innocence until the matter is thoroughly investigated. And all the innuendo spread by the outraged Thebans is detrimental to the fairness of the investigation. "Confound you all," Eupator sums up his position. "I don't know if Nikomachos is guilty, but you are all damnably guilty of trying to interfere with the course of justice" (28–29; 22).

So much for the *Dichtung;* now the *Wahrheit.* On July 9, 1926, *Lidové noviny* printed a brief notice concerning a military officer, General Radola Gajda. "A few days ago," the paper announced, "General Gajda, the Vice Chief of the General Staff, received an extraordinary furlough whose length is uncertain. Conjecture about the reasons for this furlough are circulating but are yet to be confirmed."[11] The mystery deepened when the public learned through various leaks that Gajda was suspected of engaging in espionage against France for the Soviet Union. Because of the sensitivity of the issue, a special military commission was established to look into these allegations. The secrecy surrounding the Gajda affair was a welcome opportunity for opposition parties to launch a concentrated campaign against the coalition government which had dominated the news for several weeks. Hinting darkly at documents to which they were privy, they accused the government of framing the general because of his political views, and proclaimed his total innocence. The extreme right, well aware of Gajda's pro-Mussolini sentiments, jumped into the fray. Public meetings against the liberal conspiracy were convened, and the floor of Parliament was the scene of shouting matches. In this heated atmosphere Čapek's *Lidové noviny* steadfastly refused to comment on the Gajda affair despite the derision aimed at it from various quarters. It would be prejudicial, the paper maintained sensibly, to jump to any conclusion while the facts were still largely unknown. The scandal reached a climax on July 29, when the government failed to meet its own deadline for concluding the investigation.

The connection between Čapek's "apocrypha" and the Gajda affair is quite clear. The very title of the story invites the comparison. To make the parallel fully evident, I quote a few relevant passages from the editorial "What Is Going On?" printed in *Lidové noviny* just three days before the apocrypha:

> Yesterday evening the Defense Minister, General Syrový, asked journalists not to write about the Gajda case for military reasons. . . . *Národní listy* did not honor the Minister's request. On the contrary, in its edition of yesterday evening it increased the hysteria around Gajda in such a way that the committee of the coalition parties . . . [felt compelled to issue] a statement urging that the newspaper debate about this matter be conducted critically with regard for the facts. *Národní listy*, patently inspired by Gajda, attacked [Foreign] Minister Beneš and spun horror stories about an alleged conspir-

11   "Generál Gajda na dovolenou," *Lidové noviny*, July 9, 1926, p. 3.

acy against Gajda. The Milan paper *Secolo* yesterday printed an interview with Gajda that contained his direct admission of his Fascism.[12]

Within this context, no reader of "As in the Good Old Days" could miss the real identity of Nikomachos or the actual referents of these thinly veiled allusions to the Malcontents' Party and the government's plot. Čapek's intention in writing this story was equally clear. His quasi-historical simile defended the position of *Lidové noviny* on the Gajda case against all the modern Philagoroses who for narrow political motives attempted to meddle with due process. A self-governed, democratic *polis*, Čapek / Eupator argued, must respect justice. The question of guilt or innocence ought to be decided according to the rule of law, not the emotion of the streets.

This was a reasonable proposition, albeit not an entirely practical one, because none of the serious charges against Gajda—that is, planning a military takeover and spying for the Soviet Union—would pass critical legal scrutiny. And an in-house commission of the Defense Ministry secretly meted out his eventual punishment—dishonorable discharge from the army and forfeiture of 25 percent of his pension. It must be also pointed out that, at least as of August 1925, Čapek and *Lidové noviny* joined the choir of Gajda detractors and aided Beneš and Masaryk in orchestrating a newspaper campaign to discredit the general.[13] The rule of law had to be bent a bit to oust from the sensitive office he occupied the man whom many feared as a potential threat to the fledgling democracy. In this respect the Gajda affair is an excellent example of how quixotic lofty ideals are when it comes to nitty-gritty politics. Let me explain.

Gajda, to begin with, was a highly flamboyant figure who, according to the assessment of the French General Charles Mittelhauser (Gajda's commanding officer until 1925), exhibited "all the advantages and disadvantages of a condottiere."[14] With the departure of the French military mission that had helped to create the new Czechoslovak army, native officers had to be promoted to the highest posts. The charismatic Gajda—hero of the Czechoslovak Legions, which during World War I had fought on the Russian side against the armies of the Central Powers—was destined to become chief of the General Staff. But he was considered a rather unpredictable character with robust pro-Fascist sympathies. So after Marshal

[12] "Co se děje," ibid., July 30, 1926, p. 1.
[13] See Antonín Klimek et al., *Vítěz, který prohrál: Generál Radola Gajda* (Prague, 1995), pp. 123–26.
[14] Quoted from Jonathan Zorach, "The Enigma of the Gajda Affair in Czechoslovak Politics in 1926," *Slavic Review* (December 1976), 684.

Józef Piłsudski's coup in neighboring Poland in May 1925, rumors began to circulate that Gajda might use his popularity to pull off a similar caper in Czechoslovakia. Such speculations were fanned by widespread political instability. The general elections of 1925 polarized Parliament to such an extent that no bloc represented there could muster a lasting government. The only way out of this stalemate was to include moderate parties representing the German-speaking electorate into a ruling coalition—a step vehemently opposed by the Czech nationalist right with which Gajda was associated. As if this were not enough, the Soviet intelligence service sensed an opportunity to settle an old score (during the Russian civil war Gajda had joined Aleksandr Kolchak's army against the Reds) and began to feed President T. G. Masaryk fabricated stories about Gajda's being their secret agent. Masaryk, eager to get rid of the vexatious general, was more than willing to take such accusations at face value. So he did not hesitate to use all means at his disposal (some of them not entirely fair) to rid the military of a man he deemed unreliable.

Stripped of his rank and retired from the military, Gajda could finally come out of the closet, and he promptly became the leader of the Czech Fascists. In the political arena which he entered his path soon crossed that of Charles Pergler, another figure of the local far right to whom Čapek devoted one of his apocryphas. In addition to their ideological orientations, the two men shared a similar past. While Gajda had fought against the Austrian monarchy in Russia during World War I, Pergler (who settled in Chicago in 1903) had become one of the leaders of the anti-Habsburg movement among American Czechs.[15] In this capacity he not only raised substantial sums of money for the patriotic cause and recruited over two thousand volunteers for the Czechoslovak Legions that engaged the Central Powers in France, but also lobbied successfully in Washington, D.C. and arranged Masaryk's contact with many American decision makers during his support-seeking mission in the spring of 1918. So it was quite logical that he should become the first diplomatic representative of the newly formed Republic in the United States. But then something went wrong between Pergler and the captain of Czechoslovak foreign policy, Edvard Beneš, and Pergler was not included in the delegation to the Paris Peace Conference which reshaped Europe after the war. Eventually he ended up as ambassador to Japan. And even this appointment lasted only until the summer of 1922, when Pergler was rather insultingly retired from diplomatic service. Embittered, he returned to the United States, where he embarked on an academic career. But, bitten by the bug of

---

15 For biographical information about Charles Pergler, see Světlana Rysková, "K případu Karla Perglera," *Český časopis historický*, no. 4 (1992), 571–87.

power, Pergler could not stay away from politics, and in the late 1920s he reentered public life. Together with Gajda and another sworn enemy of Masaryk and Beneš, Jiří Stříbrný, he reemerged in Prague as leader of a rightist party established to give the liberal establishment a run for its money in the 1929 general elections. He even won a seat in Parliament, only to lose it some two years later under curious circumstances when the electoral court refused to affirm his mandate because, lo and behold, Pergler was not a Czechoslovak citizen. The rancorous debate that followed filled the pages of Prague newspapers for most of the spring of 1931. But eventually a financially strapped Pergler was paid off from a secret fund of the Foreign Ministry and in the summer left for the shores of the New World, never again to return.[16]

In the United States, Pergler launched a vituperative campaign against those who had injured him among the Czech minority there. In the fall of 1931 his barrage, published by the Chicago ethnic paper *Svornost* (Concord), against Masaryk's mismanagement of the donations he received during the war for the struggle against the Habsburgs became grist for the Prague journalistic mill. On November 22 *Lidové noviny* commented in some detail on Pergler's allegations. This individual, the paper stated, had a single purpose in mind for releasing his story: "to incite American Czechs and Slovaks against Masaryk. He strove to do so by charging that American collections for revolutionary activities were never accounted for, and by claiming that the President's daughter Olga lived on that money in America in a luxurious hotel and [his son] Jan Masaryk received $3,000 of it for his private use."[17] On the very same day, Čapek's apocrypha named after the scurrilous Thersites, the detractor of Achaian heroes in *The Iliad*, appeared in *Lidové noviny*. In this amusing story the Greek character is presented as a compulsive complainer and a chronic negativist whose startling revelations about the "true" state of Greek affairs are so patently far-fetched that they have no credence among his compatriots. The entire Trojan war, Thersites tells his incredulous listeners around the campfire, is being fought "firstly, so that the old fox, Agamemnon, can get a sack full of booty; secondly, so that the coxcomb Achilles can satisfy his inordinate ambition; thirdly, so that the trickster Odysseus can cheat us over war supplies; and finally, so that a country-fair songster, Homer or whatever the hum's name is, can be bribed to glorify the greatest traitors to the Greek nation for a few dirty nickels and vilify or ignore the true, modest, self-sacrificing Achaean heroes, who are yourselves" (35; 26). But Thersites' rabble-rousing has a soporific effect on

[16]   See Klimek et al., *Vítěz, který prohrál*, p. 219.
[17]   "Perglerovy žaloby," *Lidové noviny*, November 22, 1931, p. 2.

his listeners. Instead of rising up against infamy, the Achaeans think about going to bed. " 'Some day'," Thersites releases his last and heaviest salvo, " 'they will write of our time as of a period of the deepest national disgrace and subjection, infamy, pettiness and treachery, bondage and subversion, cowardice, corruption and moral rottenness—' 'We shall muddle through,' yawned Eupator. 'And I'm going to sleep. Good-night, folks' " (39; 28).

Čapek felt compelled to react to Pergler's mud-slinging, for not only did it dishonor the man who, in his eyes, represented the very idea of Czechoslovak statehood but also it denigrated the entire struggle for national liberation, which he considered the brightest moment in the modern history of his people. Since Čapek was a friend of Masaryk's, moreover, he took vilification of the president personally. At the same time, however, Masaryk's selfless devotion to the national cause before and during the war and his moral integrity were such well-established facts that Pergler's petty calumnies did not merit serious reply. Irony was called for. Thus Čapek's answer was a historical analogy, clear to anyone, which caricatured the offender as a pitiful present-day Thersites. Through this apocrypha, I would add, the author also aimed a sarcastic jab at those who impugned his own reputation. We should not overlook the fact that Thersites' slander against Homer echoed the gist of accusations leveled at Čapek, the president's official biographer. More than once Čapek's enemies alleged that his international literary fame had been purchased with government money in exchange for services to the state as its chief apologist and glorifier.

Examples of apocryphas closely intertwined with political events of the day could easily be multiplied. Evidence gathered by Karel Kapoun, for instance, convincingly documents that the story "Crucifixion" (1927) is Čapek's comment on the so-called "New Year's Eve affair"—the public auto-da-fé to which Čapek was subjected by the hostile press for a political skit he staged in his home on December 31, 1926.[18] Similarly, "Master Hynek Ráb of Kufštejn" (1933) lampoons the deputies who, during the parliamentary discussion in November 1932, criticized on nationalistic grounds the League of Nations and Beneš's disarmament initiatives. In the same manner, Alexander the Great's account of his global expansionism as a series of purely defensive measures (in the 1937 apocrypha named for him) mirrors Hitler's territorial demands made in the name of German security, and the Roman conquest of Syracuse in "The Death of Archimedes" (1938) comments on the *Anschluss* of Austria.

---

[18] In *Silvestrovská aféra* (*Zpravodaj SBČ: Informace pro členy společnosti bratří Čapků*, no. 26, [1988]).

To reduce the *Apocryphal Stories* to mere commentaries on political events, however, would narrow their ideological scope excessively. Čapek knew only too well that all practical decisions stem from a *Weltanschauung*, a general system of beliefs shared by those who hold them. In order to act properly, he maintained, citizens must first think properly. The apocryphas were also meant to promote the kind of thinking that the author considered right. There is thus another context to which these texts relate: intellectual history, the clash of ideas in which Čapek engaged. As I observed earlier, the overall design of *Apocryphal Stories* reflects a particular theoretical problem: the lack of unity in the ego. Individual apocryphas, too, are concerned with intellectual issues. The portrayal of characters and actions from the past served Čapek as a convenient vehicle to inject into his art the ideological arguments that he advanced directly in his nonfiction writings. This aspect of the book has not escaped the attention of some critics. Josef Branžovský, among others, has pointed out the parallel between the relativist notion of truth propagated by Pontius Pilate in the 1920 story "Pilate's Creed" and the epistemological postulates of Čapek's book on Pragmatism published two years earlier.[19] Likewise, Alexander Matuška has noted that the apocrypha "The Ten Righteous" (1931) reiterates the motif of the Lord's judgment on Sodom, which Čapek first used for polemical purposes in his 1924 essay "Why I Am Not a Communist" and a year later in the "Addenda" to his *Pragmatism*.[20] Since I have already acknowledged the connection between *Apocryphal Stories* and Čapek's philosophical and moral thought, I will limit my discussion to a single text, the biblical story "Martha and Mary" (1932).

This apocrypha is an extension of a tale about Christ from the Gospel of Luke (10:38–42), which forms its preface:

> Now it came to pass, as they went, that he entered into a certain village: and a certain woman named Martha received him into her house.
>
> And she had a sister called Mary, which also sat at Jesus' feet and heard his word. But Martha was cumbered about much serving, and came to him, and said, Lord, dost thou not care that my sister hath left me to serve alone? Bid her therefore that she help me.
>
> And Jesus answered and said unto her, Martha, Martha, thou art careful and troubled about many things:
>
> But one thing is needful: and Mary hath chosen that good part, which shall not be taken away from her. (92; 61)

---

[19]   Josef Branžovský, *Karel Čapek, světový názor a umění* (Prague, 1963), pp. 122–23; see also William E. Harkins, *Karel Čapek* (New York, 1962), p. 160.

[20]   Alexander Matuška, *Člověk proti zkáze: Pokus o Karla Čapka* (Prague, 1963), pp. 112–13.

Čapek, for reasons I will explain, renders the quarrel between the two sisters through the eyes of the slighted Martha. It would be wonderful, she complains to her pregnant neighbor, Mrs. Grünfeld, as she assists her with domestic chores, if she could act like Mary. Indeed, she would like nothing more than to sit at Christ's feet and listen to His words. But who then would do all the dirty work? she asks. Instead of indulging herself, she takes care of a dozen small duties: removing dirty linen, cleaning the room, fetching Christ some cold milk and bread with honey, looking after the neighbor's kids, chasing the chickens out of the yard so that they will not disturb him, and so on. "And then when everything was done," Martha continues,

> I was filled with such a beautiful certainty that now I was all ready to hear the Word of God. So I slipped quietly into the room where He sat talking. . . . And, Mrs. Grünfeld, He looked at me with such clear and kindly eyes, as if He were going to say something. And all of sudden it came over me—oh God, how thin he is! You know, He never has a square meal, He hardly even touched the bread and honey—And then I thought: Pigeons! I'll roast Him a brace of pigeons! I'll send Mary to the market for them while He rests a little—"Mary," I said, "come to the kitchen for a minute." But Mary took no notice, she might have been blind and deaf. (99–100; 64–65)

The rest of the story is known from Luke. Martha appeals to Jesus to make Mary help her and is rebuffed.

On the surface this apocrypha attempts to redress what might be perceived as a case of scriptural injustice: Christ's rebuke of Martha. It does so by reinterpreting the conflict between the two sisters as a clash between two kinds of Christian love: the love of Jesus and the love of "thy neighbor." Mary embodies the first. In accordance with her faith, she prefers staying with the savior to helping her sister. The Bible applauds her for doing so: she "hath chosen the good part." But is Martha's part worse? Čapek's story suggests that it is not. True, she is so consumed by her petty worries that she has no time to listen to Jesus. Yet her choice, the apocrypha argues, is as noble as Mary's, at least according to Christian doctrine. Martha cannot be with the messenger of universal love because she is too busy implementing his message, constantly serving everybody around her. Martha's good deeds deserve recognition, and she yearns for it. Sometimes, she confesses to Mrs. Grünfeld, you feel "that someone will say something to you or look at you somehow . . . as if they were saying: Daughter, you clothe us with your love, you give us the whole of your self, you sweep with your body and keep everything clean with the

cleanliness of your soul; we come into your house as if it were you yourself. Martha, you too have in your own way loved much—" (98; 64). But
the New Testament, Čapek's tale concludes, in glaring contradiction to
the morality it preaches, denies Martha her satisfaction.

But this apocrypha is not concerned solely with an injustice described
in the Gospel of Luke. On a more general level, it is also a critique of social
utopianism and axiological absolutism. By defending Martha, Čapek was
in fact defending himself and his own pragmatist outlook. In spirit the
story of Martha and Mary is most closely related to Čapek's essay "Save
Yourself, Whoever Can!" (1922), which analyzes the peculiar human desire for salvation. It ends with an imaginary conversation with Christ,
who rings the author's doorbell to announce that once more he has come
into the world to save humankind. Čapek's reaction to this news reveals
his reasons for defending Martha:

> Surely, I would cry, crushed by the lack of faith and nobility on my part,
> but surely I would say (or at least think): "For Christ's sake, don't do it, it's
> good for nothing. Even if it were utterly splendid and wonderful—hu-
> mankind cannot be saved. Perhaps because there is no humankind, only
> many people. Humankind cannot be saved but a human being can be
> helped. Perhaps it is a low ideal, just helping instead of saving; only help-
> ing someone, in this very place, at this miserable moment, instead of saving
> once and for good the entire world. Perhaps it is a minuscule ideal, a nickel-
> and-dime venture in saving. But how can one save the world if not every-
> thing is in order here, at the reach of my hand?"[21]

Although Martha is not mentioned by name in this passage, it is clear that
Čapek identifies with her position. Furthermore, within the context of this
essay it is equally obvious that his argument reaches beyond the bounds
of Christianity. The most famous of all the Messiahs stands as a symbol
for all doctrines that promise a universal panacea for social ills. Čapek
viewed every utopianism, regardless of its ideological origin, with great
suspicion. The world, he maintained steadfastly, can be improved not in a
grand manner, by sweeping changes carried out in the name of the highest ideals, but only in a limited, Martha-like fashion, by concrete personal
endeavor aimed at a particular social deficiency. And Čapek felt that
Pragmatism, the philosophy of practical life, provided an epistemological
basis for a realistic social policy. "Modern life," he wrote,

---

[21] Karel Čapek, "Spas se, kdo můžeš!" in *Od člověka k člověku*, vol. 1 (*Spisy*, vol. 14)
(Prague, 1988), p. 228.

is not an ideal to anyone. It is bad enough to dream up a completely different ideal of life, or bad enough to realize that it urgently requires active involvement and persistent improvement. Which of these two should one choose? Pragmatism . . . consciously opts for the latter, Martha's part. "Better it is for philosophy," says, for instance, John Dewey, "to err in active participation in the living struggles and issues of its own age and times than to maintain an immune monastic impeccability, without relevancy and bearing in the generating ideas of its contemporary present.

"These words," Čapek adds, "speak for the entire Pragmatist stance."[22]

Thus, the two protagonists of Čapek's apocrypha, Mary and Martha, are literary personifications of two attitudes toward the world: of singular devotion to an absolute ideal and of pluralist engagement with the relativity of human existence. And Čapek obviously identified fully with the latter. Single-minded adherence to absolute ideals paralyzes when we come to dealing with the problems of daily life. To tackle them one must recognize that human values do not reflect a priori universals but reveal only the factual contingencies of a given situation. Since values so conceived correspond to the vacillating needs of individuals, they are doomed to appear imperfect, insignificant, or outright ridiculous if measured against the yardstick of eternity. Yet it is precisely this "flaw" that makes them what they are: real human values. The light of the Absolute, Čapek the relativist maintained, blinds those who see it to the heterogeneity and the polymorphousness of the real world. "The only way to avoid being a relativist is to be a monomaniac. Of these two, select the better part. Either the part of Mary who listens to a single truth or the part of Martha who 'is careful and troubled about many things.' Of course, the part 'of many things' includes much that is petty and strange, unknown and even useless, for in that part lies all of reality."[23]

Čapek's political philosophy, one might say, is quite reasonable and displays many appealing points. But it contains one cardinal weakness that, with the passage of time, proved to be fateful. It takes two to tango! That is, while the proponents of competitive axiology have it easy, in a manner of speaking, for they rely solely on themselves, those who sub-

---

[22] Karel Čapek, *Pragmatismus čili filozofie praktického života*, in *Univerzitní studie* (Prague, 1987), pp. 321–22; John Dewey, "Does Reality Possess Practical Character?" in *Essays Philosophical and Psychological in Honor of William James*, ed. G. S. Fullerton et al. (New York, 1908), p. 80.

[23] Karel Čapek, "O relativismu," in *O věcech veřejných čili Zoon politikon* (Prague, 1932), p. 63.

scribe to a cooperative system of values inevitably depend on the good-will of others. And this is a factor that, as Czechoslovakia learned the hard way, can never be taken for granted. For a number of reasons (some of which I will discuss shortly) centrifugal forces prevailed, and the project of creating a lasting democratic state, with which Čapek fully identified, proved to be a failure.

It is not my intention, however, to try to sell Čapek cheap here. Though perhaps too optimistic, he was definitely not a naive idealist oblivious to the formidable political obstacles that the creators of the new Republic would encounter. One need only read the transcripts of his numerous conversations with President Masaryk, which he recorded, to realize that Čapek was cognizant of the difficulties that lay ahead. The lack of local civic traditions was definitely one of them. "We need fifty years of uninterrupted development," Masaryk observes in one conversation, "to be where we wish we were today."[24] The symbolic half century for which he asked would have been enough, he believed, to change the mentality of his fellow Czechoslovaks, to make them ready, if the need should arise, to subordinate their narrow partial interests to that of the common good of the state to which they belonged. With the benefit of hindsight one can only wonder whether such an estimate was not altogether too confident. Czechoslovakia, we must recall, was a multinational and multiethnic entity created in a part of the world not exactly known for its tolerance in such matters. Even the dominant Slavs (Czechs, Slovaks, and Ruthenians), though unquestionably consanguine, were quite unlike one another in their social and religious attitudes, and their discords, often displayed in public, did not foster national unity. The sense of belonging was also clearly lacking among the numerous groups of Germans and Hungarians who had been living for centuries in the territory of the newly formed Czechoslovakia. Masaryk was quite aware of this difficulty when he told Čapek: "We are in a situation in which the nation and the state do not coincide; we have considerable ethnic minorities, whence the pressing task for sagacious politicians: to correct the minority problem as soon as possible in such a way that all citizens of our state may be at one in their conscious citizenship."[25]

Yet it was not entirely the fault of local politicians that Czechoslovakia did not become a Central European melting pot for all the peoples living within its borders. Surrounded on all sides by states with territorial claims against this "darling of the Versailles Treaty," the leadership had to cope with ethnic minorities who sometimes openly endorsed the expansionist schemes of those neighboring states. In particular, some 3 million Sudeten

---

[24]   Karel Čapek, *Hovory s T. G. Masarykem*, 7th ed. (Prague, 1969), p. 270.
[25]   Karel Čapek, *Čtení o T. G. Masarykovi* (Prague, 1969), p. 111.

Germans living primarily along the Austrian and German borders became more than willing instruments of Hitler's aggressive *Drang nach Osten* plans in the 1930s. Neither did the future look altogether cloudless even before the Nazis' rise to power. In an article written in his last years but not published until 1969, Čapek recollected an exchange he had had with an unusually pensive Masaryk around 1928. In the middle of a silent walk the president stopped. "I only hope," he said, "that we'll be able to hold on to this republic for twenty, thirty years more. After that I'm not afraid of anything."

Čapek was somewhat taken aback. "Only to hold on?" he objected. "Isn't that too little?"

"It's not," the elderly statesman stuck to his guns. "There are a lot of difficulties ahead of us, *o'ye.*"

"Why do you think so?" the writer probed further.

"It comes from our location and other things. We must show Europe that we can govern ourselves . . . and defend ourselves."[26]

Given the fact that Czechoslovakia, with its 15 million inhabitants, was only a medium-sized European country, Edvard Beneš—the country's perennial foreign minister and Masaryk's heir apparent—based his defensive strategy on the principle of collective security. The inviolability of the Republic's borders was to be guaranteed by a number of mutual defense treaties with other countries, of which the most important was the alliance with France ratified in 1924. But the drive toward cooperation was not very strong in Europe between the wars, even among the democratic governments most threatened by the rapid growth of totalitarianism. Hitler knew only too well how to exploit the fears of a new continental war when he orchestrated the Sudeten crisis. And he succeeded in persuading England and France that peace would be best served if all Czech border districts with German populations were ceded to the Third Reich. The ultimatum signed in Munich on September 29, 1938, led to Beneš's resignation and the wholesale destruction of Czechoslovakia. Besides Sudetenland, which went to Germany, Hungary received large portions of southern Slovakia and Ruthenia, while Poland annexed a chunk of northern Moravia. The truncated Slovakia and Ruthenia each obtained autonomy from the new Prague government only to declare full independence in March of the following year, after the Nazi army had invaded the rest of the defenseless Czech lands, thus creating the Protektorat Böhmen und Mähren. War would break out in less than six months.

The debacle of 1938—blatant betrayal by the Republic's Western allies and the government's helpless assent to Hitler's demands—dealt a pro-

[26] Ibid., p. 19.

found blow to the idea of democracy in Czechoslovakia and influenced the course of its history for decades to come. As one of the most visible symbols of the previous regime, Čapek became the lightning rod for his homeland's misfortunes. All his cherished beliefs informing the *Apocryphal Stories*—political pluralism, axiological relativism, ideological tolerance—looked effete, if not blatantly counterproductive, in the face of the inevitable triumph of fanaticism. The unheroic, Martha-like concern with "many things" was no match for the single-minded effectiveness of military action. The gentle voice pleading its case indirectly, through textual analogy, stood no chance of being heard above the roar of propaganda that filled the air. Čapek's funeral, in January 1939, attended by thousands of his countrymen, became something more than just homage to a popular author. Along with Čapek they were burying an era that would never return.

A Communist journalist, Julius Fučík, junior to the deceased writer by thirteen years, was among the mourners. His obituary, "Čapek Alive and Dead," deserves to be mentioned because, curiously enough, it recapitulates once again the Hamletian dilemma discussed at the beginning of this chapter. "Perhaps none of the Czech writers," Fučík noted, "avoided political confrontations as Karel Čapek did. He worked on grand projects, but he preferred to leave things half unsaid or even unsolved rather than to say something politically too concrete, too quotidian, too 'ordinary,' as he saw it. He was attracted by the most topical themes. He rushed to them and belabored them, but whenever you thought, 'Now he will say the right word,' when all was set for it to be uttered—Čapek escaped into generalities, just to avoid saying it. He was terrified by the din of the world in literature." Hesitant, ambivalent shy: these are not exactly *epitheta ornans* in the Marxist-Leninist lexicon. But Čapek redeemed himself in his last days, Fučík concluded in his short piece. When attacked from all sides, he openly entered the political arena and fought back. "Only now, perhaps for the first time in his life, did he clearly realize the magnitude of the stakes in this everyday political struggle which always horrified him and which he avoided."[27]

We should recognize this passage for what it is: an appropriation of the past, the recasting of a dead author's image according to that of his self-assertive successor—a device cogently described by T. S. Eliot. In his last moments, the obituary suggests, Čapek finally recognized that his political evasiveness was no longer sustainable and became a Fučík-like social activist. The magnitude of this misprision boggles the mind. There are

[27]   Julius Fučík, "Čapek živý a mrtvý," in *Milujeme svůj národ: Poslední články a úvahy* (*Dílo Julia Fučíka*, vol. 3), 4th ed. (Prague, 1951), pp. 92, 94.

few Czech literati who embody all of Čapek's political phobias as perfectly as Fučík: a committed utopianist blindly loyal to his militant party, fully devoted to revolutionary change. Yet the fundamental disagreement between the two involved their respective literary tastes as well. Whereas for Fučík "reportage" was the backbone of his creative method, Čapek's attitude toward this genre was more than skeptical. "The reportage novel, which was presented to us as the novelistic type of the future, has no future whatsoever," he put it bluntly in 1934; "in the best case it might have its immediate presence."[28] He was obviously dead wrong about this, and time was just as merciless to his political views. Not only did the trauma of the Munich agreement fully disgrace in the eyes of his compatriots the liberal discourse that Čapek championed so ardently, but also it was Fučík's hard-shelled, doctrinaire *Reportage: Written from the Gallows* that would emerge from the cataclysm of World War II as the most significant Czech fiction of the era yet to come. Move over, Čapek. It's Party time!

[28] Karel Čapek, "Má reportážní román budoucnost?" in *O umění a kultuře*, 3:611. This seems to have been Čapek's belated reaction to the polemics about the necessary displacement of the traditional novel by the journalistic novel, initiated in 1929 by the leftist journalist Egon Erwin Kisch. For more details, see the discussion in Chapter 3.

3

The Past Perfect Hero

Julius Fučík and *Reportage: Written from the Gallows*

ANDREA: "Unhappy is the land that breeds no hero."
GALILEO: No Andrea: "Unhappy is the land that needs a hero."

—Bertolt Brecht, *Galileo*

Brecht's play from which my epigraph was chosen has a curious relevance for the topic of this chapter. Written by an exiled leftist author in 1938 / 39, it pondered the economy of heroism—which, given the precarious political situation in Europe at the time, was not just idle thought. Is a hero someone willing to sacrifice his or her life to affirm a noble ideal? What about somebody like Galileo, who, by ostensibly submitting to those in power, preserved his life to be able to further promulgate an ideal? By publicly renouncing the heliocentric theory of the universe, he was able to escape the wrath of the Inquisition and to return to his scientific research.[1]

Where might one place Julius Fučík in such a dilemma? Would he have sided with Andrea or with Galileo? The answer to this question is not as simple as I might wish: the signals he emits are quite contradictory. One position is suggested in his 1934 essay "On Heroes and Heroism," which asks the reader what is the heroic response to a situation in which one finds a person drowning in a treacherous stream.[2] Is it to dive in thoughtlessly and, because of the difficult conditions, not to be able to extend the intended help, even to drown in the process? Or, instead, is it

---

[1] For a comprehensive discussion of Brecht's views of Galileo and his use of the actual historical material, see Gerhard Szczesny, *The Case against Bertolt Brecht with Arguments Drawn from His "Life of Galileo,"* trans. A. Gode (New York, 1969).

[2] Julius Fučík, "O hrdinech a hrdinství," in *V zemi milované: Reportáže ze Sovětského svazu* (*Dílo Julia Fučíka*, vol. 5), 3rd ed. (Prague, 1951), pp. 19–25.

to make a calculated attempt to get a boat and without great risk to one-self save the endangered life? This is obviously a leading question. Cost-benefit analysis, separating means from ends, clearly champions effi-ciency over foolhardiness and puts Fučík squarely in Galileo's camp. Yet by his deeds, by his martyr's death at the Nazis' hands, Julius responded, so to speak, to Andrea's call for heroic self-sacrifice. Viewed from this per-spective, Fučík cuts a rather paradoxical figure, as if he simultaneously were and were not willing to risk his life. What kind of a hero, one might wonder, is such a split personality, and by which facet of his charater should he be judged? Even in his homeland, Fučík's image is far from uni-form. Was he a self-promoting narcissist whose cowardly behavior devas-tated one branch of the anti-Nazi underground in 1942, as some insist? Or was he a brave man killed in the line of patriotic duty, the author of the immortal *Reportage: Written from the Gallows*—a faithful record of his or-deal in a Gestapo prison and the most widely translated book ever written in Czech?[3]

Before jumping into this controversy, let me introduce some biographi-cal data.[4] Born in Prague in 1903 into an artistic family (his father was a part-time actor and singer), he was named after his famous uncle Julius, the Czech John Philip Sousa. Theater, it seems, was a most important in-fluence during his formative years. From the tender age of three until he was about twelve, Julius performed a number of children's roles includ-ing Little Lord Fauntleroy. In 1912 his family moved to the industrial town of Pilsen, where he finished high school. After graduation he en-tered Charles University in Prague and for about seven years studied there intermittently, without, however, receiving his final degree. He at-tended lectures and seminars by some of the most prominent literary scholars of the era, including the leading critic F. X. Šalda. During his student years he regularly contributed to various literary journals, co-translated from Russian Isaac Babel's *Red Cavalry*, and became associated with the leading Czech avant-garde group Devětsil.

In 1921 Fučík not only entered the university but, more important for his life and death, also joined the Communist Party of Czechoslovakia (founded that year as a Comintern-inspired splinter group of the local So-cial Democratic Party). In the most fateful moment in the CPCS's history, during its Fifth Congress in 1929, when the Moscow-backed group

---

[3] According to Gusta Fučíková, by the end of 1975, *Reportage* had been published in eighty-eight languages. She lists them in "Život a boj Julia Fučíka," in *Julius Fučík ve fotografii* (Prague, 1977), p. 20.

[4] I draw most of my biographical information from the memoirs of Fučík's widow, Gusta, *Život s Juliem Fučíkem* (Prague, 1971), and *Vzpomínky na Julia Fučíka*, 2d ed. (Prague, 1973).

headed by Klement Gottwald ousted the "reformist" leadership and re-cast the Party according to a ready-made Stalinist model, Fučík sided with the radical wing. He followed the Party's general line unswervingly until his untimely death in 1943. During those years he served the Party in many capacities. In 1928, for example, when the Czechoslovak authorities erected administrative obstacles to publishing and distributing Commu-nist periodicals, Julius and a few friends managed to persuade Šalda to turn over to them his literary journal *Tvorba*. Fučík promptly transformed it into a militantly leftist periodical devoted to politics and culture. A year later he joined the editorial board of the Communist daily *Rudé právo*, for which he wrote articles and reportage from various sites of labor unrest (such as the coal miners' strike in northern Bohemia in 1929). He visited the Soviet Union for the first time in 1930, and his two-month sojourn re-sulted in a book of reportage with the catchy title *In the Land Where Tomor-row Already Means Yesterday*, published the following year. He returned to the USSR some four years later as the Moscow correspondent of *Rudé právo*. Back in Prague in 1936, he continued to work for various Party pe-riodicals, including *Tvorba*.

The Munich agreement of 1938 which ceded to Hitler parts of Czecho-slovakia, and the subsequent Nazi occupation of the entire country in March 1939, dealt Fučík a profound blow. He kept an emotionally charged diary of the hectic weeks prior to Beneš's humiliating surrender to the British and the French ultimatum insisting that Hitler's territorial demands be accepted without qualification. The day after the German troops marched into Prague, he began to write an autobiographical novel conceived of as a dialogue with his imaginary unborn son Peter. The three initial chapters that were finished teem with existential anxiety and a sense of doom. Now married to Gusta (née Kodeřičová), our hero decided to move to a family retreat in southern Bohemia, where for more than a year he devoted himself fully to the study of nineteenth-century Czech lit-erary history. His essay about the leading Czech woman writer of this pe-riod—Božena Němcová—is, curiously enough, the first sustained effort at feminist criticism in Czech letters. Warned of his impending arrest in the summer of 1940, he fled to Prague, where he lived in various "safe" apart-ments and continued his literary-historical research.

The arrest of the first clandestine Central Committee (CC) of the CPCS in February 1941 apparently compelled Fučík to seek contact with the Communist underground (the Party was officially dissolved in December 1938). From July 1941 until his apprehension by the Gestapo in April 1942, he went under the nom de guerre of Professor Jaroslav Horák and was one of the three members of the newly reconstituted clandestine CC in charge of resistance publishing. In this capacity he managed to bring out about ten issues of *Rudé právo*, which, under difficult conditions, became a monthly, as well as several other journals published irregularly. Whether it was a breach of conspiratorial silence or simply an accident that led the Gestapo to the apartment where Julius and several of his fellow resistance fighters were meeting on the fateful night of April 24 is a matter of discussion—as is Fučík's refusal to use a gun to resist his captors. Equally debated is who caved in first to the Gestapo's cruel torture and triggered the avalanche of arrests that almost entirely wiped out the Party's underground. The fact remains that for over a year Julius remained at the Gestapo prison in the Pankrác district of Prague, where during the spring and summer of 1943 he secretly recorded his experience on some 167 odd sheets of scrap paper (distributed among the inmates for an altogether different purpose) which he contrived to have smuggled out. His interrogation completed, Fučík was taken to Germany in July of the same year, sentenced to death in Berlin, and with Nazi exactitude duly beheaded on September 8, 1943.

"Turning their backs to life, everyone here dies daily," Fučík reminisced about his experience in the "in-house prison" at the Gestapo's Prague headquarters in the preface to his *Reportage*. "But not everyone is reborn."[5] Fučík, I am happy to report, was among the lucky ones capable of transcending death. And what a postmortem life he has had! It all started somewhat inconspicuously. Shortly after the war Adolf Kolínský, one of the Pankrác guards during whose shift Julius was able to write in his cell and who also smuggled parts of *Reportage* out of the prison, contacted Fučík's widow and informed her of the existence of the manuscript. Additional scouting around was necessary to assemble all the separate pieces (some were discovered only after the book appeared in print), and the first edition was published in the latter half of 1945.

To judge from its reprint history, *Reportage* was received slowly. The first edition appeared in 1945 and the second in 1946. But then three editions appeared in 1947. This burst can be attributed to the ideological drive of the CPCS, which, for self-serving reasons, launched a compre-

---

[5] For reasons I will discuss later, not until very recently was Fučík's manuscript published in its entirety. My quotations, therefore, come from the first critical edition of this text, *Reportáž, psaná na oprátce: První úplné a komentované vydání*, ed. František Janáček et al. (Prague, 1995), p. 11. The English translation is taken with some modifications from *Notes from the Gallows* (New York, 1948), p. xiii. Further references will be given in the text; the first number in parentheses refers to the Czech original and the second to the English translation. The numeral zero will be used whenever the corresponding passages are missing in the latter. In general, the English edition is not very accurate. Its system of transliterating Czech names and some characteristic mistakes indicate that it was based on the Russian translation of Fučík's book rather than the Czech original. It seems certain that the Moscow-led Cominform was involved in boosting the international success of *Reportage*.

hensive campaign after the war to present itself as the only domestic political force that actively fought the German occupation of Czechoslovakia. Fučík's well-documented martyrdom fit this design perfectly. In his speech at the Eighth Congress of the CPCS in March 1946, its general secretary, the ill-fated Rudolf Slánský, declared the acceptance of the Munich dictate the heinous betrayal of the working people by the Czechoslovak bourgeoisie, and the Communist underground the beacon of anti-Nazi resistance. "Just read Julius Fučík's book," he urged the sympathetic audience. "Fučík describes how inhumanly they tormented him, how they wanted him to speak. He was beaten again and again, he was tortured, his life hung by a thread. And at this moment, recalling the May First [celebrations] in Moscow, he realized that he was not alone, that together with him millions of people waged the ultimate battle for human freedom. . . . And this awareness endowed him with strength not to submit, to persist."[6] Thus the heroic image of Julius Fučík was launched by the Communist Party, an image that, essentially without alteration, hovered high above the horizon for more than forty years.

But it was during the 1950s when the full-blown cult of Fučík was truly developed. Party propagandists appointed him as role model for Socialist youth. "No other personality of the Communist movement," ventured Václav Černý, one of the most vociferous detractors of the Fučík cult, "equaled Fučík's seduction of youth. Not by the nature, content, or significance of his resistance activity did Fučík seduce, but rather by the way in which . . . he rushed with zealous joy to face death."[7] For him to be a role model, however, Fučík's image had to be better packaged. So his prosopopoeic presence in the text was augmented by a real face: an idealized portrait drawn from a profile by the Art Nouveau–style painter Max Švabinský: "almost girlish, effervescent, pure, and so beautiful," as Milan Kundera put it mockingly, "that perhaps those who knew Fučík personally preferred this noble drawing to their memory of a real face."[8] And an appropriate slogan was selected from *Reportage* as a condensed substitute for the entire book, a shorthand verbal accompaniment to the visual icon. The merger of the concluding two sentences—"People, [I liked you.] watch!" (91; 112)—dovetailed perfectly with the image of the book as a

6   Rudolf Slánský, "Komunistická strana v boji za svobodu národa," in *Za vítězství socialismu: Stati a projevy 1945–1951*, vol. 2 (Prague, 1951), p. 92.
7   Václav Černý, *Pláč koruny české* (Toronto, 1977), p. 325. Further references will be given in the text.
8   Milan Kundera, *Žert* (Prague, 1967), p. 188. Quoted from *The Joke: Definitive Version Fully Revised by the Author* (New York, 1992), p. 190. Further references will be given in the text; the first number in parentheses refers to the Czech original and the second to the English translation.

monument to heroic self-sacrifice proffered so that there would be no more imperialist wars.

It is not possible to enumerate here all the accolades bestowed on the martyr. Since 1946 the honorific "National Hero" has been used regularly in front of his name, and in 1948 he was posthumously decorated with the highest Czechoslovak military medal, the Order of the White Lion. At the 1950 Congress of the Moscow-backed Conseil Mondial de la Paix in Warsaw, a "watchful" jury headed by the Italian Socialist Pietro Nenni awarded Fučík its Peace Prize for his immortal book. The Chilean poet Pablo Neruda (who by chance borrowed his pen name from the nineteenth-century Czech poet Jan Neruda, Fučík's favorite) declared in his address to this distinguished international gathering that "we live in the literary epoch which tomorrow will be called the epoch of Fučík, the epoch of simple heroism."[9] And to make sure that this prophecy would not go unfulfilled, the Czechoslovak Youth Union (the local version of the Soviet Komsomol) instituted in the early 1950s a new tool of indoctrination aptly called the "Fučík Badge." A candidate for this honor had to undergo a thorough examination of his or her knowledge of the books selected from a prescribed list, including *Reportage* as one of the obligatory texts. The coveted prize for passing this rite was a pin bearing Fučík's authorized profile which the fortunate ones could sport on their blue shirts—the Union's official gear.[10] And there was no better place to show it off than Fučík's Park of Culture and Relaxation (as the old Prague fairgrounds were renamed in the 1950s).

Needless to say, Fučík also become an object of literary adulation, and not only by run-of-the-mill propaganda hacks. Poets of Pablo Neruda's and Milan Kundera's stature felt an urge to pay homage to the dead martyr.[11] To boost his image as the premier man of Czech letters, comprehensive publication of Fučík's oeuvre was carried out from 1947 to 1963. This undertaking was actually suggested by the hero himself in his "last will," embedded in *Reportage,* which also appointed a friend, Ladislav Štoll, as editor. But whereas Fučík had envisioned his collected works as a "modest" five-volume project, Štoll, aided in his valiant efforts by the hero's

---

[9]   Pablo Neruda, "Bor'ba i pesni," trans. F. Kel'ina, *Literaturnaya gazeta,* December 28, 1950, p. 1.

[10]   By 1953 about eighty thousand young Czechoslovaks had been awarded the Fučík Badge and, according to a resolution of the Central Committee of the Czechoslovak Youth Union, their number was to be doubled within a year. See "Za masové rozšíření Fučíkova odznaku: Usnesení předsednictva Ústředního výboru ČSM," in *Za masové rozšíření Fučíkova odznaku,* ed. E. Hrych (Prague, 1953), pp. 12–13.

[11]   Pablo Neruda, "Conversación de Praga: A Julius Fučík," in *Obras completas* (Buenos Aires, 1956), pp. 682–88; Milan Kundera, *Poslední máj: Báseň* (Prague, 1955).

widow, managed to extend it to twelve volumes. And it surely could not have hurt the sales of Fučík's collected works to have been edited by the man who was not only a member of the CPCS Central Committee, one-time minister of education, perennial director of the Literary Institute of the Czechoslovak Academy of Sciences, but also and above all the top Party Cerberus in literary matters.

What has been so far left out of my account, however, is the special status of Fučík's *Reportage* in post–World War II Czechoslovak society. It was more than just fabulous, a hagiographic account of what happened to a man who personified essential Communist virtues; it was scriptural, a Holy Writ animated by the last breath of the dying hero. The metaphor of Saint Veronica's handkerchief—the direct imprint of Christ's face on a piece of fabric—employed by the avant-garde Czech poet Konstantin Biebl in his "Fučík in Prison" conveyed the special status of *Reportage* as a textual *vera ikona* signifying the immediate presence of the author.[12] So when quoted at pregnant moments it was perceived not as just another prosaic instance of reported speech but as if Julius's authoritative voice itself had just resounded (the first-person form of his narrative was quite helpful in this respect).

Given the nature of a totalitarian regime, it is not surprising that the Party-sponsored cult of Fučík lasted untarnished for so long. True, a few troublemakers claimed to remember some facts quite differently from how they were presented in *Reportage*. But they were quickly hushed up, and their heterodox views did not become known to the general public until much later. The only dissenting voices came from abroad, from those émigrés who had known Fučík before the war and whose recollections of him were very unlike the official legend. The most sustained text of this kind, successfully kept away from Czech readers by the Iron Curtain, was a long essay by Fučík's erstwhile friend, the writer Egon Hostovský, published as a pamphlet in April 1953 by the National Committee for a Free Europe. Hostovský's attempt to puncture as many holes as possible in the Communist hero's nimbus is quite unflattering in every conceivable respect. Yet, despite its rancorous tone, some of its observations appear remarkably insightful as far as the origins of *Reportage* are concerned. "Fučík," Hostovský volunteers, "nurtured immense admiration for vaudeville magicians, and he himself had learned many tricks that remained unbeknown to his friends for a long time. . . . It amused him to play a double role and the problem of treason fascinated him to an extent

---

12   Konstantin Biebl, "Julius Fučík ve vězení" in *Dílo: Bez obav 1940–1950*, vol. 4 (Prague, 1953), p. 28.

almost pathological. . . . If Fučík really was great," Hostovský concludes his exposé, adding insult to injury, "then his era was desperately petty."[13]

With the passage of time and gradual erosion of the Communist ideology for which the image of Fučík was an important prop, the 1960s marked a significant decline in the hero's popularity, although his official status remained the same. The Czechoslovaks grew tired of being watchful all the time and instead they started to ask some pretty embarrassing questions about the book. What questions? Well, how, for example, could such an extensive text have been written in a closely guarded prison? And why was the facsimile of the manuscript never released in its entirety but only as a few isolated sheets? Or, how could this sworn archenemy of the Nazis roam at leisure through the streets of Prague with the Gestapo interrogator Böhm at his side, as described in *Reportage*? And what was the ultimate meaning of Julius's heroic gesture anyway? This last question was addressed head-on by Milan Kundera—one of the lionizers of Fučík during the previous decade—in his 1967 novel *The Joke*, which derided the hero's superhuman bravery as sheer histrionics. And a year later, during the hot summer of 1968, the young journalist Miroslava Filípková, in the popular weekly *The Young World*, suggested for the first time in public that Fučík's text contained certain discrepancies that not only ought to be closely scrutinized but also cast a shadow of doubt on his alleged supreme heroism.[14]

The "fraternal aid" of the Red Army in August 1968 that suppressed the short-lived experiment with "democratic" Socialism brought an end to all such blasphemies. The larger-than-life statue of Fučík—a war hero and above all a true friend of the Soviet Union—was ceremoniously dusted off and put back on its pedestal. But it was more and more difficult to get young people (for whom World War II was but a few boring pages in school textbooks) excited about this didactic figure so closely identified with the Stalinist era. True, as penance for his political sins committed in the heady atmosphere of Prague Spring, the respected writer Ladislav Fuks published in 1978 a novel focusing on Fučík's childhood; a full-length feature movie about Julius was released at about the same time; and in 1987 the one-and-only Fučík Museum opened in downtown Prague next to Café Slavie, the favorite hangout of Czech dissidents. But despite all this worthy toil, the enthusiasm of yore for the resistance martyr was never again to be fully resuscitated.

---

13   Egon Hostovský, *The Communist Idol Julius Fučík and His Generation* (New York, 1953), pp. 5–6, 16.
14   Miroslava Filípková, "Fučík," *Mladý svět*, no. 28 (1968), 9–12.

One of the denizens of Café Slavie, the literary historian Václav Černý, in his 1977 memoirs published abroad but with a sizable underground circulation at home, subjected Fučík's *Reportage* to the closest critical examination up to that point. Černý's comments were perceived as especially incisive because of his firsthand experience of the Pankrác prison during the war. For, like Fučík, he too was a member of the Czech anti-Nazi resistance and a captive of the Gestapo. Some of his questions reiterated the same doubts: the mystery of Fučík's manuscript, his unusual socializing with a Gestapo interrogator. But Černý's inquiry probed still further. If Fučík was such an important underground operator, why was he not kept in solitary confinement? And how could he have become a prison trusty before his interrogation was finished? The purpose of Fučík's text, Černý declared, was to finger a scapegoat for the author's own failings. More than anything else it was a rhetorical exercise in persuading readers that it was not he who had caved into the Gestapo's torture but his second in command, Jaromír Klecan. So far we had only Fučík's word to this effect—absolute and all too shrill, Černý asserted. But if he were telling the truth, why, Černý asked slyly, were the 1945 protocols of Böhm's interrogations by the Czechoslovak authorities never released, especially if they would substantiate Fučík's version of what transpired the first night at Gestapo headquarters?[15] But Černý could only pose troublesome questions, for the relevant documents were safely beyond his reach.

And they remained inaccessible to virtually everyone until the Velvet Revolution of 1989. This sudden historical turnabout finally abolished all the taboos of the ancien régime and the *causa* Fučík entered its final stage. Now some of the most conspicuous passages from *Reportage* could be critically examined, above all the scene of our hero's arrest by the Gestapo on the fateful evening of April 24, 1942. Fučík, according to his own account, came to a clandestine meeting and immediately reproached other participants gathered there for not observing strict conspiratorial rules. Alas, his wise words were uttered in vain, for, just as tea was being poured to refresh the plotters, Gestapo agents began to bang on the door. Nine Nazis entered the apartment through the kitchen while Fučík, armed with two 6.35–mm pistols, observed them from behind the partially opened door to the adjacent bedroom. Clint Eastwood would have known what to do: the "Krauts" would simply have made his day. Then again, Eastwood is not particularly famous for his writing skills. Fučík, a man of letters, proved to be much less trigger-happy. "If I shoot," he soliloquized for two or

---

15 Černý, *Pláč koruny české*, pp. 321–31. Černý, it might be mentioned in passing, had an axe to grind. In 1938 Fučík had rather savagely attacked Černý's new journal *Critical Monthly*, launched that year. See Julius Fučík, " 'Sklep ze slonoviny,' " in *Stati o literatuře: Literární kritiky, polemiky a studie (Dílo Julia Fučíka*, vol. 6), 1st ed. (Prague, 1951), pp. 269–71.

three seconds, "I wouldn't save anything except myself from torture. But in vain would I sacrifice the lives of four comrades. Is that so? Yes! It's decided. I leave my hideout" (13; 2).

Riva Friedová-Krieglová, the only participant in this meeting who survived the war, remembered what happened on April 24 somewhat differently. After her return from a Nazi concentration camp in 1945, she even gave a written deposition (sounding more like an indictment) about that touchy event; it promptly disappeared, however, in the bottomless Party archives. Not until after 1989 could her voice be heard, crisp and clear. According to Krieglová, Fučík's lack of resolve during the Gestapo bust was something she clearly did not expect:

> We ran to the [other] room from the kitchen. We pulled up the blinds and opened the window. . . . Outside [as if] glued to the wall stood a Gestapo man. I was quite disappointed by Comrade Fučík's behavior. Instead of fulfilling his duty and using the weapon against the Gestapo man, he hid it under a quilt. Had Comrade Fučík killed the Gestapo man under the window he and other comrades would perhaps have been able to escape. Meanwhile, Gestapo men broke down the door. How many of them I do not remember. And still Comrade Fučík did not use his weapon. [16]

It would be utterly futile to try to adjudicate after so many years which version of the event is more accurate (though, apparently, the detail about how the guns were concealed so unheroically in a bed was corroborated independently by a member of the arresting team, Kommissar Josef Böhm, during his postwar interrogation by the Czechoslovak authorities). What would have happened if Fučík actually had offered armed resistance we can only conjecture. Most commentators agree, however, that his refusal to use his weapon and his irenic surrender to the Nazis was very much out of character with the cruel ethos of the Communist resistance, whose deliberate unwillingness to distinguish POWs from traitors was notorious.

But Friedová-Krieglová's testimony—regardless of its informational value—was not the greatest surprise of the season. With archive doors wide open, answers to most inquiries about Fučík could finally be provided on the basis of evidence, not hearsay. A team of historians led by the late František Janáček sieved through all relevant sources and came up with a bundle of surprises. The manuscript of *Reportage*, the forensic laboratory of the Czechoslovak police attested, is genuine and has not been altered mechanically or chemically. Also, a comparative graphological analysis carried out by the same lab established that the handwriting is Fučík's and his authorship of the text is indisputable. Furthermore, from what could be culled from existing Gestapo archives and from the testimony of Gestapo personnel after the war, Fučík—Janáček and the members of his team are absolutely insistent on this point—did not provide any incriminating evidence against his fellow resistance fighters, and Klecan was indeed the first one to talk. Whether this investigation dispelled all doubts about Fučík's behavior in German captivity remains to be seen. But it is, surely, the best proof we have so far.[17]

Fučík, however—and here comes the kicker—did talk to the Gestapo. He even mentions this fact at the very end of *Reportage*:

> For seven weeks I did not give any evidence. I was aware that no word could save me but could endanger comrades outside. My silence was my action. . . .
>
> Seven weeks with the Gestapo taught me a lot. . . . I realized that even here I have an opportunity to fight; by different means than outside but with the same purpose and the same direction. To remain silent meant not to exploit this opportunity. More was necessary so that I could tell myself that I fulfilled my duty in every place and in every situation. It was necessary to play a high-stakes game. Not for one's own sake—I would lose immediately. But for the sake of others. They expected a sensation from me. I gave it to them. They expected a lot from my talking. So I "talked." *How*, you will find in my protocol.
>
> The results were even better than I expected. I turned their attention in a completely different direction. . . . I gained their trust and I continued. For a few months they were chasing a mirage which—like every mirage—was greater and more attractive than reality. . . .
>
> That I postponed my death in this way and that I gained time that could perhaps help me was a reward which I did not calculate.
>
> For a year I was writing a theatrical play with them, one in which I ascribed to myself the lead. It was sometimes amusing, sometimes exhausting, but always dramatic. But every play has its own ending. Climaxes, crises, denouements. The curtain falls. Applause. Spectators, go to sleep! (90–91; o)

The reason why nobody knew about this was that the passage was excised from all pre-1989 editions of *Reportage*.

---

[17]   See František Janáček, "Pochybnosti i jistoty: Stručně ke starým otázkám," in the critical edition of *Reportage* (see note 5), pp. 301–37; and Alena Hájková, "Kauza Fučík: Ediční poznámky na pokračování," *Tvar*, nos. 7–13 (1996), 17.

It is not difficult to understand why the editors of Fučík's *Nachlass* resorted to this radical measure. As if it were not enough that their man refused to shoot at the Nazis, he was even fraternizing with them! A Communist who, for whatever reasons, might ingratiate himself with the Gestapo to gain their trust would hardly have been an inspiration to Czechoslovak youth. How, after all, can you tell the dancer from the dance?[18] But within the context of the book, Fučík's admission of his covert "play" provides a plausible explanation for some of the most controversial passages in *Reportage*, such as his excursions in Böhm's company to a pub in suburban Bráník and to the Hradčany hill overlooking Prague. Unable to refer to Fučík's duplicitous scheme, official propaganda had to employ some pretty tenuous construals to justify them, such as depicting these odd perambulations as the Gestapo's desperate attempts to break Fučík psychologically, to soften his resolute stance by exposing him to the spring beauty of his native Prague. Milan Kundera's lengthy poem *The Last May* (1955), for example, presents an extended argument why Fučík had to emerge victorious from this existential duel. Obviously, the editors found it more palatable to publish such dark passages than to expose the hero's motives to potentially embarrassing second-guessing. Furthermore, they may have also preferred to see this segment deleted because it imbued the hallowed phrase "People, watch!" with undesirable connotations. In the conclusion of his text Fučík was juxtaposing a somnolent theatrical audience with alert participants in real life, where "there are no spectators." The spin doctors, however, used Fučík's words in a way that had nothing to do with dozing versus being awake. They wanted people to "Be on guard!" against all the nefarious imperialist schemes threatening the welfare of humankind.[19]

With all this information at hand, we can now return to the issue of heroism with which this chapter began. Was Fučík a hero? Well, he participated actively in the anti-Nazi resistance—a deed of which very few of his countrymen may boast. He held his own under torture by the Gestapo

---

[18] According to the moral canon of Socialist Realism, Abram Tertz (Andrey Sinyavsky) argues convincingly, the very act of talking to the Germans during World War II, even with strategic objectives in mind, was perceived as tantamount to treason. He illustrates this point in a scene from Leonid Leonov's novel *Russian Forest*, the winner of the Lenin Prize for Literature in 1957: "The brave girl Polya, entrusted with a dangerous mission, makes her way to the rear of the enemy—the action takes place during the Patriotic War. As camouflage she is supposed to collaborate with the Germans. She plays this part for a while in talking to a Nazi officer, but with great difficulty: it is morally painful to her to talk the enemy's language. Finally she cannot stand it any more and reveals her true self and her superiority to the German officer. . . . The fact that by this pompous tirade Polya betrays herself and moreover harms the mission with which she has been entrusted does not disturb the author in the least" (*On Socialist Realism* [New York, 1960], pp. 54–55).

[19] This is how the last sentence of *Reportage* was rendered in the English edition (see note 5).

and was not, it seems, the primary cause for the wholesale destruction of his underground group. And if we take into account his "functionalist" understanding of heroic behavior, according to which the ends justify the means, we can understand the telos of the "high-stakes game" he played with his captors, despite the bad aftertaste it may have left in the mouths of some. Yet there still remains to be considered one of Fučík's actions that does not neatly coincide with this straightforward heroic interpretation: Why did he not resist arrest while armed against such an event? There was no conceivable gain to be derived from this decision other than saving his own life. He could not have known in advance that he would withstand brutal interrogation or that he might successfully mislead the Gestapo under the pretense of providing them with valuable information about the Communist underground. Moreover, to continue in my role of Monday-morning quarterback, had Fučík turned that Prague apartment into the O.K. Corral, the ensuing shoot-out would have diminished considerably the number of potential "weak links" able to lead the Gestapo to the rest of the Communist underground. True, this is all just a chain of probabilities, but the odds do seem stacked against Fučík.

So why did he not shoot? In the realm of speculation which this question usually elicits, the answer offered by Fučík's friend and fellow member of the Communist resistance, Vladimír Vrána, is most intriguing: "I believe that the real reason why Julek [a nickname for Julius] gave up the fight was his reporter's passion, his curiosity about what would follow. Julek simply could not leave life like that, like blowing out a candle. He could not leave without writing his big reportage about the CPCS's resistance against the invaders, about which—I noticed—he was thinking at each step" (92). Whether Vrána's insight into Fučík's psyche is correct ultimately depends on one's personal opinion. But his observation introduces a refreshingly new twist into my discussion of Fučík. The reason why this man, who was not exactly a household name in prewar Czechoslovakia, provoked so much ado after his death is not just a function of his courageous achievements. Without detracting from Fučík's actual merits, one can concede that Černý's assessment of his role in the Communist underground—"his significant resistance activity was of limited duration [and] it consisted of fulfilling directives coming from the agencies or personalities truly in command" (324)—does not seem altogether off the mark. What really matters about Fučík, and this should be obvious by now, is not his heroism per se but its representation—or self-representation, to be more precise.

Fučík, hero or not, was a child of his own epoch, and his writings carry an indelible imprint of the time. This said, I must emphasize that the 1920s and 1930s were a turbulent period in Czech culture, the age of modernist experimentation and of political radicalism, which, moreover, often went hand in hand. Given this confusing context, a short discussion of the avant-garde theories with which Fučík was familiar is necessary if we are to ascribe him to an appropriate place.

In his 1934 essay "What Is Poetry?" the vice chairman of the Prague Linguistic Circle, Roman Jakobson, pointed out what he perceived to be the fundamental dichotomy inherent in every act of representation: "Besides the direct awareness of the identity between sign and object (A is A_1)," he ventured, "there is a necessity for the direct awareness of the inadequacy of that identity (A is not A_1)." It is the latter tendency toward non-sameness (*différance*, in more recent parlance) which characterized artistic signification for Jakobson. Such a semiotic bifurcation might appear, at first glance, quite convincing. We have, on the one hand, opaque, nonreferential texts of avant-garde writers (whether Khlebnikov or Joyce) and, on the other hand, Fučík's forthright reportage—clear-cut examples of a utilitarian, journalistic mode of writing. And Fučík never tired of swearing again and again to the documentary veracity of his texts. But is the matter really so simple? And was it not, to be sure, Jakobson himself who in the same essay warned us to be cautious, to watch out for literati speaking with forked tongues: "Do not believe the critic who rakes a poet over the coals in the name of the True and Natural. All he has in fact done is to reject one poetic school, that is, one set of devices deforming material in the name of another poetic school, another set of deformational devices. The artist is playing no less [of a] game when he announces that this time he is dealing with naked *Wahrheit* rather than *Dichtung*."[20]

What is the source of this anxiety, one might ask? Why would creative writers repeatedly repudiate the very premises of their art? The reason, I suspect, has something to do with the spirit of the time. In scrutinizing the modernist paradigm for an answer, I could not help but notice that one of its most salient features is the idea of transgression (the frustration of expectations, the power of the extraordinary, and various modifications thereof). A brief look at writings stemming from the very different fields of knowledge and / or from authors of very dissimilar political orientations of interwar Europe supports this hypothesis. "*It must be possible for an empirical scientific system to be refuted by experience,*" wrote Karl Popper emphatically in 1934, making the principle of "falsifiability" the mother of all scientific methods.[21] And though the probability of an errant slice of bread flying up instead of landing on the floor (with its buttered side

20   Roman Jakobson, "What Is Poetry?" trans. M. Heim, in *Language in Literature*, ed. K. Pomorska and S. Rudy (Cambridge, Mass., 1987), pp. 378, 370.
21   Karl Popper, *The Logic of Scientific Discovery* (New York, 1968), p. 41.

down) is pretty slim, it must exist for the law of gravity to have scientific status. In a similar vein, the political theorist Carl Schmitt argued that the ultimate criterion of legality is not the adherence to law but, on the contrary, its breach: "The exception is more interesting than the rule," he affirmed in 1922. "The rule proves nothing; the exception proves everything: It confirms not only the rule but also its existence, which derives only from exception. In the exception the power of real life breaks through the crust of a mechanism that has become torpid by repetition."[22] And to revitalize a dormant legal system, Schmitt proposed the institution of a Godlike sovereign with absolute decision-making power who at any moment could transcend the existing order, destroying its reduplicative self-sameness.

It is uncanny how close the rhetoric of Schmitt's decisionalism comes to that of Slavic modernist aesthetics (with which my argument started) and its dialectics of defamiliarization / automatization. Art, in Viktor Shklovsky's 1914 dictum, was precisely the creative impulse capable of "bringing back to a human being its experience of the world, resurrecting things and killing pessimism"; the antinomy of *byt*—"an immutable present, overlaid," as Jakobson put it eloquently in 1930, "by a stagnating slime, which stifles life in its tight, hard mold."[23] This theory, I believe, accounts well for the strange behavior of artists that earlier puzzled me so much. What motivated their negative attitude toward the past was the premium that modernism placed on novelty. The keen urge to reject a particular mode of representation has nothing to do with its inherent significatory characteristics, but everything to do with its historical status. A replacement is used not necessarily because it is semiotically more appropriate than that which is discarded but simply because it is more exciting. And within this simple developmental scheme one could perhaps argue that if at a certain moment the artistic canon mandates a high degree of identity between signifier and signified, it will be succeeded by a system appreciating their maximal non-sameness. Or vice versa. The heuristic value of this model lies in its appealing simplicity. The actual historical material at hand, however, muddles things somehow. Making the process of artistic representation as complex as possible did not by any means fully exhaust modernist radicalism. Its ultimate gesture was transgressive to the point of self-annihilation. What true modernist iconoclasts desired

<hr/>

[22] Carl Schmitt, *Political Theology: Four Chapters on the Concept of Sovereignty*, trans. G. Schwab (Cambridge, Mass., 1985), p. 14.

[23] Viktor Shklovsky, *Voskreshenie slova*, reprinted in *Texte der russischen Formalisten*, vol. 2, ed. W.-D. Stempel (Munich, 1972), p. 12; Roman Jakobson, "On a Generation That Squandered Its Poets," trans. E. J. Brown, in K. Pomorska and S. Rudy, *Language and Literature*, p. 277.

was not just to displace the works of their venerable predecessors with their own creations but to smash the vicious circle of denial and affirmation that hitherto had characterized the history of art, to end this "strange" activity once and for all.

I do not wish to comment here on the feasibility of such a project, but some of its formulations, as I will illustrate shortly, had considerable impact on Fučík's writings. Let me, therefore, introduce just one example relevant to my argument: Marcel Duchamp's ready-made sculpture *Fountain*, which rendered an ordinary urinal a work of art. And before getting to the thorny issue of what this artifact may or may not stand for, I want to mention only a single aspect, its shocking sign-vehicle—the fact that it recycled as artistic material an "undignified" object connected with the lowest bodily functions. Fučík's *Reportage*, too, I would remind those who have meanwhile grown impatient with my digression, has a peculiar material substratum: it was written on scraps of toilet paper. The Duchamp-Fučík analogy—and I am prepared to take the fire—might look quite strained, to say the least. The French sculptor, an objection might go, had full liberty to employ any material he wished, and his use of a urinal was a well-calculated choice made with a specific purpose in mind: to *épater le bourgeois*. The Czech writer, by contrast, imprisoned by the Nazis as a resistance fighter and writing his *Reportage* in an environment more than hostile to such a pursuit, was forced to use the only paper he could get hold of. Moreover, the result of this illegal toil is a fairly straightforward account of his ordeal at the hands of the Gestapo, a readily digestible reading produced to enlighten the masses, to steer them in a particular ideological direction. So is it legitimate to compare his *Reportage* to Duchamp's *Fountain*? Some further discussion is obviously needed.

Anyone who inspects the manuscript of Fučík's *Reportage* cannot help but notice that its physical appearance was not dictated entirely by harsh prison conditions.[24] The author cared what it looked like. Thus, in a situation in which those who smuggled the individual pages of his manuscript out of prison were literally risking their own lives, Julius did not hesitate to expand the contraband by an additional sheet of paper—a front page to the book—that contained nothing but the title, the date, and its place of origin, and the author's customary pen name, "-jef-". Furthermore, it should be observed that Fučík's experimentation with a genre of illicit prison writing (*motáky* in Czech) that employs unorthodox media predates his encounter with the Gestapo by more than a decade. In February

---

[24] The manuscript is kept at the Museum of the Labor Movement which has found its uneasy domicile on the campus of Charles University's School of Physical Education in Prague—Vokovice.

1930, for example, while incarcerated for ten days at the Prague police headquarters, he managed to get out a missive (to the lady he was to marry some nine years later) inscribed on an unfolded cigarette box, his text artfully woven around the commercial graphics on the wrapper.[25]

As if emboldened by the results of that endeavor, he decided to go public with such epistolary efforts at the next available opportunity. And he did not have to wait very long. Arrested in August 1931 for crossing the Czech-German border with someone else's passport and held for about two weeks in investigative detention at the Pankrác prison (of all places), he wrote another contraband letter, this time to Kurt Konrád, Fučík's temporary replacement as editor in chief of the weekly *Tvorba*. Well aware that his epistle would be reformatted for print, the author was more than eager to call attention to the unusual physical appearance of his note, written "on scraps of paper with a match found in the courtyard and dipped into a stinky solution from a cigarette butt."[26] Yes, Fučík conceded, his legal status entitled him to write regular letters, but then, going through official channels would take much too long. Was this a credible argument? From the editorial commentary appended to Fučík's text in *Tvorba* of August 27 (the letter itself was dated August 18), the reader learns that Konrád received this contraband correspondence on the very same date that its author was released from detention.

The point I am trying to make is that Fučík, not unlike other modernists, was attracted in his creative praxis to strange and unusual materials. In contrast to true aesthetic experimentalists such as Duchamp, however, he did not defamiliarize his medium in a playful, detached manner but strove to ground this act in existential circumstances. Such a grounding, however, should be recognized for what it actually is: a ploy for justifying phenomena that, from a practical perspective, make very little sense. Thus, Duchamp's and Fučík's creative modi operandi may easily be seen as opposite sides of the same avant-garde gesture: signing art's death warrant. If even a urinal can be elevated to the level of art, Duchamp's sculpture suggests, then art as a privileged category of special artifacts does not exist. Fučík's use of a cigarette box or toilet paper as writing material, however, is like a label whose warning to the user might be summarized as: What you are going to read is not belles lettres or fiction. This is a factual account of what really did happen, produced under

25 "Guště do Prahy" of approximately February 2 or 3, 1930, in Julius Fučík, *Korespondence* (*Dílo Julia Fučíka*, vol. 12), 1st ed. (Prague, 1963), p. 67. For a photographic reproduction of this "letter," see *Reportáže z buržoasní republiky: Z let 1929–1934* (*Dílo Julia Fučíka*, vol. 7), 3d ed. (Prague, 1955), insert between pp. 88 and 89.

26 Julius Fučík, "Moták," August 18, 1931, in *Politické články a polemiky: I. část z let 1925–1934* (*Dílo Julia Fučíka*, vol. 8), 1st ed. (Prague, 1953), p. 185.

the described circumstances as certified by the physical appearance of this document.

But wait a minute, a sensible reader might exclaim at this point. Duchamp's attitude toward artistic material truly revolutionized our understanding of what representation is all about. He was among the first to shock the public with one of the greatest truisms of our age: the medium is the message! From this perspective, Fučík, for whom the material had only a secondary, authenticating function, appears to be a premodernist retrograde naively striving to depict the outside world "as it is."This charge can be countered in a number of ways. In historical terms, modernism is not a synchronous, homogenized structure but a period comprising antithetical trends and competing generations. In the latter respect, one might observe that Duchamp was Fučík's senior by some fifteen years, which in those turbulent times was not a negligible gap. And it follows very much from the anti-normative spirit of modernism that a mode of representation affirmed by one generation would have been spontaneously challenged by the next. Within the dialectical scheme of change discussed earlier, the automatized semiotic formula $A \neq A_1$ so dear to the likes of Duchamp would be replaced by its opposite, $A = A_1$ championed by Fučík and his cohorts.

This negation of the status quo, however, does not imply a return to the status quo ante: a wholesale abandonment of the modernist canon for nineteenth-century realism. What had changed in the meantime was not only the concept of reality itself but also the sense of how literature should relate to it. The world around us, Marxist-Leninist doctrine (whose impact on modernist thought can hardly be overestimated) proclaimed, is the product of economic relations invisible to the naked eye. Furthermore, these relations exist in real time and develop according to their own logic: from capitalism to Communism, if only to speak about the final sequel of this historical series. Although the direction of history is clear, the timetable of the transition from an exploitative to a classless society is not. It all depends on how quickly the proletariat mobilizes for its "last battle."And this is where the literature championing progress can find its new role: to educate the masses, to steer them in the right direction, to mourn martyrs and celebrate heroes.

The reason why some modernist artists found Marxist-Leninist ideology so attractive is quite obvious. Earlier I drew a parallel between Schmitt's decisionalism and avant-garde aesthetics based on the proclivity toward transgression that they both shared. This similarity, however, should not obfuscate the significant difference between the two normative spheres these theories treat: politics and art. An unprecedented decision of the Schmittian sovereign would impact significantly on the lives of all his subjects, whereas even the boldest artistic experiment always concerns only very few and carries virtually no existential consequences. Or, to put it differently, of all the norms governing human actions, the aesthetic ones seem the least obligatory and socially relevant. So what is the point in transgressing them if nobody really cares? Subscribing to the theory of history as class struggle and the progressive function that literature can effectuate within it promised to release artists from their proverbial ivory tower, to boost their bruised egos, to put them where the real action was. By accepting this new social engagement, however, writers eager to play ball had to adjust their discursive strategies accordingly.

What marginalized modernist literature above all was the hypertrophy of exclusive, esoteric, and experimental texts that it generated. If this trap is to be avoided, the message of art cannot be its medium, they recognized clearly, but must be political action. Trotsky's polemics with the avant-garde theorists who conceived of verbal art as the art of language neatly encapsulates this point. "They believe," he charged from the Marxist position, "that 'In the beginning was the Word.' But we believe that in the beginning was the deed. The word followed as its phonetic shadow."[27] One need not be an Einstein to figure out what "deed" meant to Bronshteyn, the architect of the October Revolution. If art is just a function of politics—and this is, I believe, what he was actually saying, albeit more elegantly—then literature as an autonomous field of human creativity is dead indeed. For, as an instrument of social engineering, or, more apropos, a weapon of class struggle, there is only one yardstick to measure its value: its utility for the revolutionary cause.

It was the Russian writers and critics around the group called the Left Front of Art (Lef, or the New Lef after 1928) who, in my opinion, elaborated the modernist program of *littérature engagé* in the most systematic way. The fallacy of traditional literary mimesis, these challengers of the status quo maintained, was not its intention but its implementation. Texts written by the esteemed members of various realist and / or naturalist schools might indeed have been intended to depict the world as it is, but as works of fiction they succeeded merely in producing a pale semblance, verisimilitude. Drawing an unflattering analogy with another form of deceptive inauthenticity—religion—the modernists declared belletristic prose to be "an opium for the masses" and "the shamanism of literary priests."[28] To retain its right to exist, literary praxis had to be fundamentally transformed from fiction-making into factography (*literatura fakta*), or, even more radically, replaced by certain forms of expository writing.

[27] Leon Trotsky, *Literature and Revolution*, (New York, 1925), p. 183.
[28] Nikolay Chuzhak, "Pisatel'skaya pamyatka," in *Literatura fakta*, ed. Nikolay Chuzhak (Moscow, 1929), p. 28.

Because of its social function, it was printed journalism that attracted the young iconoclasts' attention. What gives this medium its punch, they correctly assessed, is its referential mode of signification. In reading a newspaper we do not have to suspend our disbelief about the actual existence of the events and personalities reported. On the contrary, we pick up a paper every morning firmly convinced that the knowledge derived from this source is about the world not *as if* but *as is*. And in comparing its form to that of the "realistic" novel, the theoreticians of Lef were quick to point out why the latter failed in its mimetic project. The novel, first of all, developed as a concatenation of several short stories. The law of the genre, however, required the author to obfuscate this fact, to provide some "credible" motivation for the fusion. The psyche of its hero, for example, provided a convenient unifying frame for the typical nineteenth-century novel. It is precisely the patch work quilt structure of a newspaper that exposes the make-believe nature of this convention. It presents individual articles for what they are, without false pretense of interconnectedness. Second, a newspaper piece is capable of rendering reality more faithfully, the theoreticians of Lef believed, because its narrative need not fit the procrustean bed of literary emplotment. It tells a story as it actually unfolds, without scrambling the order of events for the sake of composition. And finally, unlike the traditional novel, to get its message across journalism utilizes some completely nonnarrative devices, such as photographs, statistics, and graphs. These iconic / indexical signs no doubt further enhance the potential of the print medium for presenting what has happened in a way that seems authentic and verifiable.

Lef's quest for the new prose I have briefly described had its definitive merits. By drawing attention to the technology of writing per se (the "making of the work"), the champions of factography succeeded in highlighting those aspects of the literary process that traditional critics had hitherto neglected. And by creatively appropriating formal principles and devices from the non-artistic realm, avant-garde writers effectively transformed the artistic praxis as well. Yet, all of these achievements necessarily had only limited repercussions—far too limited for those whose appetite for transgression knew no bounds. For them mere change of an artistic canon was too lame an affair. To jolt the audience thoroughly, the use of journalistic devices could not have been an end in itself but above all was a means for imparting a radical political message. It was intended to foreground not "an organized violence of poetic form over language"[29] but the violence of one class over the other: not to *épater le bourgeois* but to annihilate it. This sounds pretty heady and might have remained just an-

---

[29]   Roman Jakobson, *O cheshskom stikhe preimushchestvenno v sopostavlenii s russkim* (Berlin, 1923), p. 16.

other intellectual pipe dream if not for the unique historical situation in which the Russian avant-garde found itself in the 1920s. The Bolshevik Revolution of 1917 and the subsequent civil war violently rent Russian society, and the champions of change (whether artistic or political) joined the strife as comrades in arms. The vacuum created by the destruction of the existing social fabric had to be filled, and the young modernists eagerly stepped into the void: for a while they became the official representatives of the new Soviet culture. To justify this identification with victorious political power, a theory of "social command" (*zakaz*) was advanced, according to which the best art of every epoch expresses the interest of the most progressive social class of the moment. So the appropriation by the avant-garde of Bolshevik ideology—the language of Marxism-Leninism—was explained as an instantiation of this general historical law.

As far as Lef's project of *literatura fakta* is concerned, it was scientific Communism that provided the factographers with the cognitive lens through which to observe and report the "objective reality" surrounding them. But as the Soviet system became firmly entrenched and its backbone, the Party apparatus, grew stronger and stronger, the range of creative possibility for serving the proletarian cause remaining to leftist writers grew proportionately narrower and narrower. It was no longer up to them to decide how their works could contribute to the welfare of the new Communist state. The Party became the ultimate arbiter of "literary" taste, and, with all the coercive power at its disposal, the innovative quest for the most direct and truthful rendition of social reality backslid quickly into a ritualistic exercise in preapproved political propaganda.

A narrative about Beauty marrying the Beast and then becoming just like it would not in itself be particularly new or interesting. History is full of examples of rebellious writers turned state's apologists. But the Russian avant-garde added another twist: the Beast changing into Beauty. The poets who forged their pens into arms for class war declared politics to be the continuation of poetics by other means. The never-ending game of rendering the artistic form strange lost its purpose, members of Lef were happy to announce, because the proletarian revolution itself had totally defamiliarized the world. Literature was dead because life had finally become artistic! In 1926 the "poet of Revolution," Vladimir Mayakovsky, told the visiting Prague writer (and a close friend of Fučík) F. C. Weiskopf as much when the topic was broached:

"Literature . . . literature is already passé."

"?"

"Yes, because it's more boring than Soviet life. More boring, for example, than a meeting of citizens suffering a housing shortage. . . . I attended such a meeting recently and I tell you that what the simple speakers 'from the crowd' related about their family lives, small adventures, and about their plans was much more interesting than the best-constructed novel. . . . And a Komsomol demonstration in Red Square is better than any one of my poems . . . with the exception, of course, of advertisements, like the one for Mosselprom [a Moscow food store]."[30]

And to keep Soviet life that way, a Schmittian sovereign was needed: a demiurge with the power and will to prevent it from relapsing into normalcy, into an automatized, "torpid-by-repetition," non-artistic state. Many might have been pretenders to the title of the "Grand Defamiliarizer," but nobody was better suited for the job than the man whose truly breathtaking campaigns—collectivization, industrialization, purges, political trials, and wars—for decades prevented Soviet citizens from ever having to endure a single dull moment: the *coryphaeus* of arts and *poeta laureatus*, Iosif Vissarionovich Stalin.[31]

This detour has been necessary, I believe, to place Fučík's writings into the context in which they rightly belong. For within the tradition of Czech letters alone, Fučík's factographic reportage is usually miscatalogued. His calculated rejection of the norms of belletristic fiction for the rendition of documentary truth has all too often been taken at face value, as Fučík's turning his back on literature and applying his talents solely to partisan journalism. And there are good reasons why Fučík's anti-poetic gesture was taken seriously. The Czech literary avant-garde, first of all, never generated a full-fledged theory similar to Lef's. This is not to say that the leftist Czech writers did not discuss the possibility of journalism's taking over the role of traditional prose genres. But such pronouncements never reached the scope or intensity witnessed in Russia, and, moreover, they came at a moment when the political fortunes of Lef began to decline dramatically.[32] Thus in 1929, for example, the legendary "furious" (*rasend*) reporter Egon Erwin Kisch provoked some Czech literati with his short,

---

[30] F. C. Weiskopf, "Kapitola . . . také o literatuře," in *Literární nájezdy* (Prague, 1976), p. 39.
[31] This conclusion reflects, to some degree, Boris Groys's sustained critique of modernist aesthetics formulated quite provocatively in *The Total Art of Stalinism: Avant-Garde, Aesthetic Dictatorship, and Beyond*, trans. C. Rougle (Princeton, 1992).
[32] Fučík's postscript to the Czech edition of Isaac Babel's *Red Cavalry* of 1928 which he co-translated indicates his familiarity with contemporary Russian criticism including that of Lef. He even quotes from Shklovsky's essay "Isaak Babel" published in *Lef*, no. 2 (1924); see Julius Fučík, "I. Babel," in I. Babel, *Rudá jízda*, trans. A. Feldman and Julius Fučík (Prague, 1928), pp. 140–46. This piece, however, was never included in Fučík's collected writings. After the Communist coup in Czechoslovakia, the book itself ended up among other *libri prohibiti;* from Babel's arrest in 1937 until the mid-1950s, the name of this "enemy of the people" vanished completely from Soviet literature.

provocative, and Lef-like manifesto: "The Novel? No, Reportage." "What do I think of reportage?" Kisch asked bluntly. "I believe that it is the literary victuals of the future. Of course," he continued his staccato barrage, "a high-quality reportage. The novel has no future. There will be no novels, books with fictitious plots. The novel is the literature of the previous century."[33] The lively discussion that Kisch incited proved, however, to be short-lived. With the ideological streamlining of Soviet arts in the late 1920s, the death sentence meted out to traditional literature by Lef was suddenly perceived by Party pundits as alien to the spirit of "Proletarian Realism" (Socialist Realism after 1934). So, just a year later, the not-so-furious Kisch in an "Open Letter to Revolutionary Writers in Czechoslovakia" from the International Congress of Revolutionary Literature held in Kharkiv, Ukraine, in November 1930 repudiated his thesis about the supremacy of reportage over the novel as a "leftist deviation" and a "sectarian, formalistic stance."[34]

Furthermore, the situation in post–World War I Czechoslovakia was very unlike that in the USSR. The relative political stability of the new Republic guaranteed that a Soviet-like revolution would not take place while at the same time the boring bourgeois system allowed modernist artists to play their amusing role of enfant terrible. So with great fervor they embraced the most extreme cause at hand: the violent transformation of society according to the doctrine of Marxism-Leninism. It also should not come as a total surprise that for a long period of time, aesthetic and political radicalism worked in tandem. "New, new, new is the star of Communism," the members of Devětsil declared jointly in 1921. "Its collective work creates a new style and there is no modernity without it."[35] Within a couple of years young avant-gardists had an excellent chance to put their money where their mouth was.

The Czech leftist literary scene was far from uniform. Among the writers actively supporting the CPCS one may distinguish two groups separated by a generation gap of some twenty years and by correspondingly

[33] E. E. Kisch, "Román? Ne reportáž," *Čin*, December 5, 1929, p. 121. For more information about the discussion generated by Kisch's article, see Mojmír Grygar, "Fučíkovy umělecké reportáže," *Česká literatura*, no. 6 (1958), 373.

[34] E. E. Kisch et al., "Otevřený dopis revolučním spisovatelům v Československu," *Tvorba*, December 24, 1930, p. 794.

[35] Quoted from Jaroslav Seifert, *Město v slzách*, 3d ed. (Prague, 1929), n.p. The authorship of this catchy phrase is usually attributed to the Czech avant-garde writer whom Fučík, according to *Reportage*, met by chance at Gestapo headquarters just hours before his execution on June 1, 1942—Vladislav Vančura; see, e.g., Milan Kundera, *Umění románu: Cesta Vladislava Vančury za velikou epikou* (Prague, 1960), p. 64. In his letter to Ladislav Štoll of September 9, 1950, however, F. C. Weiskopf claims it to be his own brainchild; see Ladislav Štoll, *Z kulturních zápasů: Vzpomínky—rozhovory—portréty—stati—korespondence* (Prague, 1986), pp. 279–80.

different aesthetic sensibilities. In the first group were authors born around 1880, such as S. K. Neumann, Marie Majerová, and Ivan Olbracht. Associated initially with the anarchist movement, they entered the literary scene before World War I as representatives of fin-de-siècle poetics. The other circle consisted of avatars of postwar avant-gardism—writers born around 1900 and organized in Devětsil. The political conflict of the two generations reached its apogee in 1929 during the Fifth Congress of the CPCS, when the Moscow-backed Klement Gottwald took over the Party's helm and molded it into a Bolshevik-like instrument of revolution. Neumann and his cohorts reacted to this change by demonstratively leaving the CPCS, whereas their younger colleagues threw their unqualified support behind Gottwald and his hard line. In an open proclamation published by Fučík's *Tvorba* on March 30, the twelve signatories stated unambiguously: "We are convinced that the genuine development of modern culture depends upon the revolutionary labor movement and its victory is determined by the victory of the working class. We are convinced that it is the Communist Party that should and of itself could be the leader of revolution and the vehicle of our cultural efforts. . . . We voice our opinion," they informed the elders who had quit the Party, "not to correct [your] mistake—but to emphasize that from now on our paths have diverged."[36]

Yet, despite this strong rhetoric, in its artistic praxis the Czech avant-garde tended to be distinctly aesthetic rather than political. The predominant mode of its writing was poetry, which, after a short-lived "proletarian" phase in the early 1920s, gravitated toward experimental, self-centered texts. Both poetism—the only genuinely autochthonous Czech "-ism"—and the *fabriqué en France* surrealism, which became fashionable in the 1930s, always reflected more interest in the linguistic and / or psychoanalytic dimensions of the literary process than in a correct depiction of social reality. This was in stark contrast to the "didactic verse" of the older leftist writers such as Neumann, accused in 1925 in a Devětsil journal "of making poetry into a contraband smuggled [into print] under the pretense of communicating needed truths to the proletariat," [37] or the novels of Majerová and Olbracht from the 1920s and 1930s which thinly dressed the radical political message in a traditional "realist" garment.

It is apparent that Fučík's output does not fit into either of these categories. His texts are clearly aimed not toward the message itself but toward the social context that they strive to influence. Nevertheless, even a

---

[36] "Zásadní stanovisko k projevu 'sedmi,' " *Tvorba*, March 30, 1929, p. 177. Among the signatories of this declaration were, besides Fučík, Vítězslav Nezval, Konstantin Biebl, František Halas, Vladimír Clementis, and others.

[37] Roman Jakobson, "Konec básnického umprumáctví a živnostnictví," in *Pásmo: Revue Internationale moderne. Éd.: Devětsil*, nos. 13 / 14 (1925), 2.

cursory look at Fučík's first book of reportage from 1931 suffices to illustrate how much it differs stylistically from similar travelogues sympathetic to the Soviet Union, such as Olbracht's *Pictures from Contemporary Russia* (1920) or Majerová's *A Day after the Revolution* (1925). Plenty of statistics, graphs, photographs, and quotes from journalistic and historical sources (these last often set for authenticity's sake in a typewriter-like font) augment the fragmentary, newspaper-like narratives in Julius's text with imaginative headings. Repeated rhetorical questions, the frequent use of verbal leitmotifs and of nominal sentences, sometimes set one per line: these and other devices fit the aesthetic sensibility associated with the program of Lef, including the unabashed glorification of the Soviet Union as the first proletarian state in the world and the tomorrow of all humankind.

The syncretism of Fučík's style, deliberately straddling politics and poetics, makes the question of whether he was just a partisan journalist or a creative writer impossible to answer. Such a traditional distinction, however, makes little sense when one is dealing with an author for whom literature was a weapon of class struggle and class politics the continuation of art by other means. But what can be said for sure is that the Marxist-Leninist lens provided Fučík with a most peculiar vision of the world. If his was a factographic program, it was a very strange one indeed. Contemporary Czechoslovakia in his rendition was such a monstrous abomination and the USSR such a wonderful never-never land that I am tempted to speak of Fučík's "mythopoetic universe" rather than of a documentary prose. This claim, however, requires closer scrutiny, and I will return to it immediately. But as far as the reception of Fučík's blatantly utopianist discourse is concerned, within the Czechoslovak context it wielded robust defamiliarizing potential. And as a credible threat to the existing political system, it exhibited considerable transgressive appeal. Local authorities, it must be stressed, collaborated with Fučík in this respect (albeit unwittingly) by frequently censoring those segments of his manuscripts they judged seditious. The published texts, perforated liberally by blank spaces (the author intentionally refrained from substituting anything for the expurgated material), endowed Fučík's writings with an aura of the forbidden, the uncanny.

So how factual was Fučík's factography? The answer to this question depends on whether or not one shares his set of beliefs about reality: words are mere arbitrary signs that turn into facts only if interpreted that way. Galileo's trouble with the church was precisely the clash of two understandings of the universe, of two cosmologies. But if it was the heliocentric view that eventually carried the day, better corresponding to the cosmic state of affairs, this did not happen as a matter of facts. On the contrary, an abstract scientific explanation was needed to shatter humankind's down-to-earth experience that it is the sun doing all that revolving. And passing from palpable phenomena to intangible social reality only increases our dependence on interpretive frameworks of various kinds. Whether we see profit as a necessary stimulus of economic growth, beneficial for everybody, or as the fruit of exploitation, the root of all social misery, depends entirely on which *Weltanschauung* we subscribe to. Fučík, as should be clear by now, made his choice relatively early in life, and his writings refracted the world according to the achromatic prism of Marxism-Leninism.

I do not wish to engage here in an involved argument about the merits and shortcomings of this once-popular ideology. What interests me at the moment is its formal structure, which inherently exhibits a specific generic predisposition. In *The Secular Scripture*, Northrop Frye called attention to certain parallels between the structure of the romantic narrative and Marx's theory of history. Romance, according to Frye's broadest definition, is a tale concerned with "man's vision of his own life as a quest," fueled by his keen desire to transcend the unsatisfactory situation to which he is confined.[38] Such stories are constructed around disrupted harmonies, to be subsequently realigned, and the mental landscape that these tales project reflects this fact. They are made up of clear-cut polar oppositions in which the good guys are very, very good and the villains, bad beyond the pale. A romance begins with its hero's fall from a happy and secure setting into a world of suffering and horror. In this process his identity is questioned—the hero is confused, bewitched, metamorphosed—only to be reasserted as genuine at the end of the story. Through this happy return to the beginning, however, the narrative potential of romance is exhausted. Truth, justice, or beauty has triumphed over lies, injustice, or ugliness, and there is nothing more to speak about. The romance ends.

History, according to Marx, follows this romantic plot quite closely, though its hero is not one but many: the entire working class. Once upon a time, the story goes, there was a society that produced only as much as it could consume, so its members lived in peace with one another. But alas, increased productivity created a surplus, and its unequal distribution spoiled everything. A division of labor resulted, together with a host of other undesirable phenomena: alienation, exploitation, and so on and so forth. Good men and women became slaves, serfs, or proletarians, depending on the socioeconomic formation into which they were born. As

---

[38] Northrop Frye, *The Secular Scripture: A Study of the Structure of Romance* (Cambridge, Mass., 1976), p. 15. Further references will be given in the text.

bad as it looks, however, Marx's story has its happy ending. The inescapable proletarian revolution will eventually come to wrest away the means of production from those who usurped them and abolish all private property. And since the division of humankind into antagonistic classes was begun by a skewed distribution of surplus, in a classless society people will be rewarded solely on the basis of their natural needs. Only then will initial harmony return, albeit on a dialectically higher level.

Lenin's embellishment of Marx's basic design, made in his *What Is to Be Done?* (1902), piles additional romantic overlays onto the scheme. First of all, he conceived of the revolution in terms of a quest for identity. The Achilles' heel of the labor movement, his argument went, is the proletariat's unawareness of its signal historical role. And its spontaneous striving for immediate economic gains (shorter work hours, higher salaries) by ameliorating social inequities in fact prolongs the existence of retral capitalism instead of overthrowing it. The only way to bring about the desired revolutionary change, Lenin argued, is to impregnate the minds of the masses with socialist ideology, the Marxian romance of their own ascension, to raise them from their self-oblivion, to make them conscious of what they really are: not passive objects of history but its ultimate makers.

The split of the Russian Social Democratic Party into reformist Mensheviks and revolutionary Bolsheviks which Lenin's book had heralded was a powerful reaffirmation of the Manichaean view of the world so proper to the genre of romance. Those striving toward gradual improvement in the situation of the working class were diverting the proletariat from its destined revolutionary path, and so they were nothing but traitors, unwitting assistants of the oppressors. Bolshevik logic, their leader declared, is disjunctive: "The *only* choice is—either bourgeois or socialist ideology. There is no middle course."[39] Such a black and white picture of the world, I am ready to admit, might appear quite shallow in every conceivable respect, yet it is not entirely devoid of appeal. By freeing the decision-making process from all embarrassing doubts or incomprehensible dilemmas, it corresponds to the fundamental human yearning for pure and simple justice from which, Frye reminds us, the genre of romance draws its inspiration.

With this in mind, I now return to Fučík to illustrate how his writings (and here I concentrate primarily on his pre–World War II texts) reflect

---

[39]   V. I. Lenin, *What Is to Be Done? Burning Questions of Our Movement*, trans. G. Hanna et al. (New York, 1969), pp. 40–41.

the romantic predisposition of Marxism-Leninism which I have just out-lined. To this effect let me call attention to Julius's description of a specific creative project of his in a letter to Gusta dispatched from Moscow in Feb-ruary 1935. It concerns the material he collected on his trip to Soviet Asia about Interhelpo—an industrial cooperative in Kirghizia—established there in 1925 by Czechoslovak immigrants eager to contribute their skills to the fledgling Soviet state. "I was there for a second time," an elated Fučík confides to his girlfriend, "and only now have I grasped what 'In-terhelpo' means for understanding the difference between the Soviet Union and capitalist countries. How, through it directly, through its living history and living people one can show this difference without having to commit any compositional violence." He goes on to provide a general plan for the book he would like to write. It was to unfold along three major thematic lines: how the building of Interhelpo transformed the for-mer citizens of a capitalist country into new people of Socialist Kirghizia; how this poor and backward Russian colony grew into a rich and modern Soviet republic; and, finally, how those Czechoslovaks who, frightened by initial hardship, had unwisely returned to their capitalist homeland, pined there jobless wishing they could go back to Interhelpo.[40]

Fučík's plan sounds fascinating, and one can only regret that he never executed it. But what does the quoted passage say about his creative method? Let me, first of all, attempt to explain what he meant by the "compositional violence" he wished to avoid. Julius, it seems, had in mind traditional literary emplotment, a device particularly abhorred by the Lef group. The engine of his book, the letter suggests, would be not the tension stemming from a sequential dislocation of events within the narrative, but the conflict generated by a juxtaposition of facts. The same he would render as different or the different as same by presenting it in two unlike contexts. And the quoted passage also suggests two basic ways of doing this: temporalization and spatialization. The theme of re-turning somewhere after a prolonged absence is, on the one hand, one of Fučík's favorite methods of temporal juxtaposition. The same location can look surprisingly strange during a second visit. Or it might, equally sur-prisingly, remain as it was before. The oscillation between Czechoslova-kia and the Soviet Union, on the other hand, provides Fučík with a conve-nient vehicle for the spatial interplay of sameness and difference. The two pairs of appurtenant oppositions, "now / before" and "here / there," however, appear in Fučík's narrative not as disparate categories but as a united chronotope.

What is important about the difference detected through iterative visits

---

[40] "Gustě do Prahy," February 9, 1935, in Fučík, *Korespondence*, pp. 212–15.

to the same place is not change per se but its directionality. Julius uses repetition to present facts as historical phenomena evolving along the progressive trajectory sketched clairvoyantly by Karl Marx. The spatialization of time in Fučík's universe entails the temporalization of its space. Distant localities might look unexpectedly similar because of their isochrony (measured by the Marxian timetable of historical change), or their geographic proximity might be totally overshadowed by their belonging to quite different historical time zones. Thus, movement in space implies in Fučík's travelogues a simultaneous movement in time. Going from Czechoslovakia to the Soviet Union is not just a mundane matter of traversing some thousand miles or so but, more important, a journey into the future: from retrograde capitalism to "the land where tomorrow already means yesterday." But what happened to today, a curious reader might ask? Significantly, it is absent from Fučík's chronology. For he sees historical time not as a continuum where what-has-been passes smoothly into what-will-be via some indefinitely long what-is. To return to Lenin, a capitalist society does not gradually evolve into a Communist one; the latter is established only through violent destruction of the previous socioeconomic order. The past, in Fučík's writings, is totally separated from the future by the imposing caesura of the Great October Revolution, which makes any mediation between the two simply impossible.

Earlier I argued that the major defamiliarizing device of Fučík's reporting is the juxtaposition of the same fact in two different contexts. The effectiveness of this device, needless to say, is directly proportional to the degree of contrast between the two contexts that provide the comparative backdrop. Whether they are truly disparate or not, they must be made so if only to prevent readers from yawning. And Fučík is not at all subtle in this respect. Although the past and the future are mutually disconnected, they relate to each other in a particular way. Historical repetition, Fučík learned, most likely from Marx's *Eighteenth Brumaire*, is the ironic subversion of the old by the new. If in capitalism, as an old anecdote has it, a man exploits his fellow men, in Socialism it can only be the other way around. And so what was initially tragic turns comic the second time, negative becomes positive, sour, sweet, and so on. Viewed through this lens, Soviet Russia is not merely a more just society, an incomparably better economic system, but capitalism's absolute antipode. A festive carnival, it is the world turned upside down, or, more precisely, the world turned as it should be, and in whose mirror the truly perverted nature of capitalism stands stark naked.

The absolute antinomy between the past and the future is manifested tropologically in Fučík's reportage. Let me return once more to the passage from the letter to Gusta to point out what I see as Julius's most basic metaphor. "Living people" and "living history" are just two tokens of the image "life" which he uses consistently to characterize the Soviet Union. And, not surprisingly, its polar opposite—the image of death—is equally consistently applied in reference to capitalist society. Fučík lays bare his usage of this essential human antinomy in the concluding part of the "Introduction" to his 1931 book of reportage *In the Land Where Tomorrow Is Already Yesterday* (dedicated to "comrades of the Interhelpo commune"). Pondering, as every other author does, how his travelogue will measure up with other books of this kind, he writes: "I wish to do nothing more than to bring a picture of your creation before the eyes of the people with whom I live in the same subjugation. An exact, good, honest picture. And I admit that I know what it means. It means to place it at the crossroads of two worlds and to inscribe on the outstretched hands of the road sign: Way to life. Way to death. You [the Interhelpo members] are already traveling along the first path."[41] Who are the poor wayfarers along the second one, moving toward doom and extinction? The author remains eloquently silent. But we should not fail to notice that by returning to his homeland, Fučík chose this very road. A subliminal suicidal gesture on his part? More about this later.

The overarching image of life generates in Fučík's writings a veritable host of other metaphors—whether spring, youth, or vigor—with the individual reportage as their respective permutations. Portrayed in this manner, the Soviet Union appears not as a static structure but as a dynamic, self-perfecting process by which the best is constantly getting better and better. Fučík, for the sake of credibility, is willing to admit that here and there not everything is yet entirely rosy in the USSR. But his vitalistic frame of reference easily explains these shortcomings. Some are compared to infectious diseases contracted from a bygone era. Like invisible germs, the unrepentant members of the defeated class have been wrecking the Soviet economy from within, stealthily undermining its health. This is the imagery Fučík employed in his quasi-medical report about the 1928 Shakhty case against the prerevolutionary technical specialists—the first show trial of the Soviet era—with the dreaded secret police (then the OGPU) portrayed as doctor (280). Other imperfections of Soviet society are portrayed as mere dislocations stemming from too ebullient a growth: "Soviet poverty—it is not rags on the wasted, crippled body of a beggar. Soviet poverty—it is clothes on the body of a child who is growing out of them." Never mind the clothes, Fučík admonishes his reader, but look at the growing boy, "at his young, strong figure, broad chest, and legs which support him firmly" (340–41).

Such an incessant onward drive of Soviet society makes it virtually im-

---

[41] Julius Fučík, *V zemi, kde zítra již znamená včera* (*Dílo Julia Fučíka*, vol. 2), 5th ed. (Prague, 1949), p. 27. Further references will be given in the text.

possible for an outside observer, Fučík confesses to his audience, to keep abreast of the true life there. Hence the necessity for repeated visits through which the colossal positivity of changes can be fathomed almost instantaneously. Yet no sum of its discrete states can substitute fully for the fluidity of organic change. And, by extension, no written record, including Fučík's own reportage, can ever do justice to the protean dynamism of Soviet life. So, in a Mayakovsky-like gesture, a "frustrated" Fučík, in the same "Introduction" to his 1931 book of reportage, declares his text already passé, hopelessly limping behind real life: "Literature capable of capturing your contemporaneity for an hour," he intimates to an imaginary Soviet reader,

> is just a stenographic abbreviation of a telegram. . . . Thus, my book is a *historical* reportage. A conscious historical reportage, because I feel sorry for it, because I feel sorry for a weak pen that cannot keep up with you, because I want it to live at least as a segment of your ever-growing work. I wished to depict the curve of this segment's growth; you yourself will extend it further. Beyond the pages of this book it will ascend higher, and there, in its continuation, further and higher, somewhere at that elusive point, there are you—today, tomorrow, or, again, already yesterday. (25–26)

One would assume that Fučík—the "necro-romancer" portraying the demise of bourgeois society—would have a much easier time. Death is, after all, something so fixed that comparing it to a doornail is not entirely off the mark. Moreover, he had some respectable models to follow. The Czech leftists, it must be stressed, exhibited a somewhat morbid infatuation with this subject. Such a tendency can be attributed, at least in part, to the popularity of Jiří Wolker, the leading figure of proletarian literature after World War I. This sickly young author, about whom Fučík wrote a good deal, prematurely succumbed to tuberculosis at the age of twenty-four. But before that he managed in a number of his most memorable poems to thematize dying and death within the context of class struggle. And before Wolker it was the local Decadents who creatively exploited the great transgressive potential that the representation of this unpleasant topic carries in bourgeois society.

Fučík's obsession with death was not, it seems, for public consumption only. It spilled over into his private correspondence as well. As he wrote to his close Moscow friends (in whose apartment he often used to stay) soon after his return to Prague in mid-1936: "This is what initially had the greatest impact upon me here: that this street appears as before, life here has not changed. . . . And this seems absolutely improbable to the man who in your country got used to life that changes every day. . . . Only I have fewer friends now. . . . Fritz F[euerstein] jumped into the Vltava River. He was jobless for many years. Alcohol killed Longen. A landslide in his 'wild' mining pit buried Weiner. Well, this too is life."[42] Once again, the passage involves repetition, this time of coming home. Only now the same is reiterated as selfsame, affirming from the opposite vantage point the absolute difference between the buoyant Soviet Union and torpid Czechoslovakia. If change is the most obvious symptom of life, then the only vital sign Julius detected in his native land was the death of his friends.

Depicting its terminus, however, proved for Fučík almost as impossible as representing life itself, albeit for different reasons. Czechoslovak authorities were always ready to deny him the dead bodies he staked out, to snatch corpses away from him. This is what Gusta tells us in her memoir about a chance encounter with her sweetheart in October 1928. That month an unfinished building collapsed in downtown Prague, burying in its debris almost fifty construction workers. A few days after this fatal incident she was going by the construction site, from which, to her surprise, Julius emerged exhausted. "From his unshaven face, sunken, drowsy, feverish eyes stared at me. 'What are you doing here?' I looked at him surprised. 'I am watching the dead,' " he replied. Julius, she goes on, and one of his comrades "had not budged from the scene of the catastrophe for days. Literally, they watched so that not a single . . . corpse could be denied. The builder and the authorities attempted to do so because they were afraid of workers' riots."[43]

For Fučík, to be sure, death was not just a matter of simple arithmetic. The corpses were to be not merely counted but paraded publicly. The opportunity for doing so came some sixteen months later during a period of labor unrest in northern Bohemia. In a confrontation with the police, four rioting miners were shot dead, and Julius made a beeline for the place. But the problem was that the corpses were stowed away in the local morgue under police guard. Fučík's plan was to get in to take a picture of one dead man's face and publish it. He knew that the authorities would not permit this, so he cut a hole in his trousers pocket, where he hid a small camera. The bulge near his crotch, he calculated, could easily be mistaken for a slight erection. An ingenious idea, indeed, but thwarted, to the plotter's chagrin, by vigilant security personnel on account of a single flaw: the noise produced by the opening of the shutter. Fučík's female assistant in this adventure told Gusta later what had happened, and she immortalized this incident in her memoir. The experiment worked fine during its

42 Quoted in Ida Radvolina, *Rasskaz o Yuliuse Fuchike* (Moscow, 1963), p. 34.
43 Fučíková, *Život s Juliem Fučíkem*, pp. 145–46. Further references will be given in the text.

dry run, we learn, "but things took a turn for the worse in the morgue where policemen flanked Fučík on both sides. And they did not like it a bit that he was just standing there staring. So in this graveyard silence he pushed the button. Policemen searched him immediately and that was it for the picture" (238).

But Fučík refused to give up. Prevented from obtaining a graphic portrayal of death, he opted for its verbal representation. Yet, once again, those in power foiled his efforts. Death was effectively whitewashed. Fučík's "Introduction" to his 1931 book, from which I quoted earlier, contains a highly dramatic account of the horrors the author witnessed in his native Czechoslovakia (as a striking counterpoint to his positive experience in the USSR). Aside from some minor inconveniences that the local proletariat had to endure, according to Fučík—unemployment, homelessness, crime-inducing poverty—his damning list contains a few truly morbid items: "I saw a man dying of hunger," the avid death-watcher begins his litany. "I saw a woman pulled out of a river. . . . I saw female workers burned to death in an explosion of dynamite. . . . I saw four boys in the morgue of a mining town . . . " (28–30). These last, a discerning reader will undoubtedly recognize, were the bodies Fučík tried to photograph. But the fist of the law struck once more. The censor confiscated the entire register of grievances (about seventy-three lines), and the "Introduction" appeared with a gaping blank space instead, a fact mourned with glee by the "injured" author in a new introduction to the second edition of his book.

By focusing exclusively on the victims of bourgeois society, Fučík managed to draw a highly unflattering picture of contemporary Czechoslovakia—a place of human misery and existential jeopardy. But there is more to his obsession with death than this sheer negativity. By casting the binary opposition of capitalism and communism as the metaphoric antinomy of death and life, Fučík apparently departed somehow from the tenets of Marxism-Leninism. Class antagonism, according to this romantic script, has its obligatory positive outcome: the proletarians vanquishing the bourgeoisie. But can there be a happy ending to the terror of the Grim Reaper? Can the dead be resuscitated, revivified? Perhaps not in an ordinary hospital but certainly in a romance! Too weak to depict life but strong enough to defeat death, Fučík's numinous pen turned into a mighty instrument of resurrection. In the universe of fulfilled desire, good guys and girls cannot simply perish, disappear into a void. The dead must rise, if only symbolically. "Oh indeed," Fučík tells his future readers in *Reportage*, where the theme of coming back to life plays a central role, "even dead we will live somewhere in a bit of your great happiness because we have invested our lives in it" (46; 48). Judged from this angle, Fučík, it seems, was concerned not so much with the representation of death as with the possibility of rendering the dead present yet again. Once captured, recorded, portrayed, they can be always wrested away from lethal oblivion and reincorporated into a new living presence. In the just world of the romance unjust suffering cannot go unredeemed. After the final victory of the proletariat, comrades fallen prematurely on the road to a better future should be able to partake somehow of the classless Elysium, living happily ever after in the memory of all.

Which brings me obliquely to the issue of Fučík's return home: his taking the "way to death" instead of, as one would expect of this apostle of life, the opposite path. But from what we have just seen it is clear that his choice was not suicidal at all. On the contrary, according to his own understanding of the matter, it was a rescue mission. Like Jesus, who upon hearing of Lazarus' infirmity returned to Judea despite the danger he would face there, Julius abandoned the succor of the Kirghiz sun and willingly descended into the perilous underworld of shadows to deliver the Czechoslovak proletarians. And, to extend my scriptural metaphor further, the Message he was bringing had a distinctly Christological ring: "I am the resurrection, and the life: he that believeth in me, though he were dead, yet shall he live" (John 11:25). Only the kerygma he was preaching to the masses was somewhat different: *ad resurrectionem per insurrectionem*. The Soviet revolution, Fučík's chief article of faith, validates fully the Marxist-Leninist historical romance about the ascension of the downtrodden. Come forth, he loudly bade the workers of Czechoslovakia, and follow them! Complete this story on your own and bring history to its felicitous resolution!

So far I have been dealing primarily with Fučík's prewar writings. There is, however, a good reason for this self-imposed limitation. The profound political changes brought about by the fateful year 1938 significantly affected not only Julius's life but his writing as well. Despite all of its shortcomings, the Czechoslovak Republic was a liberal democracy with a broad spectrum of political parties represented in Parliament and an independent judiciary. Not exactly "an earthly paradise at first glance," as its national anthem would have it, but perhaps nearly so if compared to its neighboring countries. It was precisely this social system that allowed Fučík to play his transgressive modernist games without much personal risk (as his criminal record clearly indicates).[44] A closer look at some of his most notorious infringements of the law, like his 1930 trip to Russia

---

[44] After the war Fučík's wife, Gusta, researched court archives and established that he was "arrested twelve times, most often by the Prague police, and received short . . . sentences for a total of thirty-two days which he served partially at Pankrác and partially at Prague police HQ prison" (ibid., p. 216).

without valid travel documents, reveals a thick histrionic layer to his character. His childhood involvement with theater had taught him well the importance of props and costumes. If we are to trust his widow's memories, his "illegal" return home from "the land where tomorrow is already yesterday" had been short of spectacular: "Jula walked across [the border] dressed in a Red Army summer uniform. He only hid a white cloth cap with a five-point star on his chest during the crossing." And to make sure that everybody would know about his caper, he wore this gear around Prague for a few days after his arrival (207–8).[45] With the Nazi invasion, all such charming jests turned into a distant memory. The risk became real and death not just a figure of speech.

So how did the political situation evolve as of 1938? The blatant betrayal of Czechoslovakia to Hitler by its trusted allies England and France at the Munich conference in the fall of that year, which has given "appeasement" a bad name ever since, totally discredited all democratic parties in that country. It was also a bonanza for Communist propagandists, who never tired of presenting this tragic moment as an instance of high treason by the Czech bourgeoisie. Instead of exercising its defense treaty with the Soviet Union, so the legend goes, the class-conscious government of capitalists acquiesced to a lesser evil—Nazi occupation. This story, however, quickly became superannuated. The Molotov-Ribbentrop pact of September 1939 which followed the partition of militarily defeated Poland between the Germans and the Soviets made the Communists and the Nazis official allies. And the CPCS, always following the Kremlin's lead, suddenly seemed reconciled with foreign occupation.

Fučík, as far as I can tell, did not deviate from the Party line—at least not in public. But it had to be a bitter pill to swallow for the man who on so many occasions had insisted that the Soviets were the only true enemy Hitler would ever have. In light of this, one might wonder whether his retreat to southern Bohemia and his compulsive preoccupation with liter-

[45]   One might even wonder how illegal Fučík's first trip to the USSR was. In his account Fučík reports that the hostile Czechoslovak police refused to issue him a passport. According to Gusta, however, Fučík's confrontation with the authorities concerned an extension of his expired travel documents. In either case the question remains how Fučík managed to cross the other borders separating Czechoslovakia from the Soviet Union. We learn from Gusta that during his first trip with an expired passport in 1930, Julius had to wait in Berlin for over two weeks to receive a Soviet visa (ibid., p. 196). But to be eligible he had to have valid travel documents. For, as she tells us some forty pages later, Julius had to abort his second journey to the USSR in 1931 after twenty-two days of waiting in Germany "because the Soviet visa could not have been issued to an invalid passport" (ibid., p. 248). Unless, of course, the Soviet authorities modified their visa policy between April 1930 and July 1931, Fučík's first trip could not have been as unlawful as he would like us to believe. It was upon his return home in August 1931 that he was arrested at the border for using somebody else's travel documents.

ary-historical studies was not for Fučík a form of self-imposed exile. His letter to Ladislav Štoll of April 1940 from that locale hints at its author's disillusionment with the deceptive world of international politics ("I am finding now more and more, diplomacy has absolutely nothing in common with clarity").[46] And he sounds quite rueful about the years 1939–41 in his short history of the Communist resistance sketched in *Reportage*; he characterizes this as the period "when the Party was deep underground not only vis-à-vis the German police but the people as well" (87; 108).

Closer scrutiny of his literary-historical output from these troubled times reveals a curious fact. Fučík's essays entertain certain themes—treason, duplicity, illicit writing in captivity—that would subsequently occupy the central position in his *Reportage*. The piece that, in this respect, has traditionally attracted most attention is his essay "On Sabina's Betrayal," written in 1940 as a chapter of a larger study devoted to the Czech Romantic writer Karel Sabina (author, among other things, of the libretto to Smetana's *Bartered Bride)* and a radical political figure. After serving a long prison term for his role in the uprising of 1848, the destitute Sabina accepted the role of paid police informer, a move that, curiously enough, provided him with the financial means to continue his anti-Austrian political activities. His secret, however, was revealed in 1872. Ostracized by his former friends, Sabina became a pariah in Czech society. One could expect this case of quid pro quo ethics to have intrigued Fučík. But, strangely enough, his condemnation of Sabina is unequivocal. The "crown" stops here, Julius declared: accepting money for such services represents moral and psychological degradation from which there is no return.[47] And this conclusion might explain a seemingly gratuitous remark about the strictly not-for-profit nature of his "collaboration" with the Gestapo that Fučík made at the end of *Reportage*: "That by doing so I postponed my death, that I gained time that could *perhaps* help me, was a reward which I did not calculate" (91; 0).

If Fučík found Sabina's duplicity reprehensible because of its pecuniary motivation, he was clearly attracted to other deceitful characters from Czech letters with more complex behavioral patterns. I have in mind Jaroslav Hašek's protagonist the good soldier Švejk, whose deeds never fully match his words, but whose perfidy cannot be interpreted unequivocally. Fučík wrote several critical essays about this hero and, according to some, even emulated his conduct. As recalled by one of Gottwald's top lieutenants, Václav Kopecký, who knew Julius well, he "was not only ex-

---

[46] "Ladislavu Štollovi do Prahy" April 25, 1940, in Fučík, *Korespondence*, p. 256.
[47] Julius Fučík, "O Sabinově zradě," in *Tři studie: Božena Němcová, Karel Sabina, Julius Zeyer (Dílo Julia Fučíka*, vol. 6), 3rd ed. (Prague, 1951), p. 92.

tremely fond of Hašek's *Švejk*, but . . . by his nature and talent he was close to Hašek's jocularity and witty humor, and . . . during his stay in the Soviet Union Julius Fučík was often called a Švejk, this despite his handsome and knightly appearance."[48] As I illustrated in the chapter dedicated to this text, Fučík returned to Hašek's novel once again in 1939 to reinterpret its protagonist from a new and strikingly different perspective. Whereas earlier he had praised Švejk for his stolid passivity capable of corroding any oppressive system, now he conceived of him as a potential fighter. One may only speculate how much of Fučík's strategy in his game of deception with his Nazi captors was inspired by his insight into Hašek's character. But he was definitely not the only modernist, I observe in passing, who conscripted the good soldier to the anti-Hitler campaign. In a curious coincidence, Brecht's *Schweyk in the Second World War*, written almost exactly at the same time as *Reportage*, rendered Švejk an interrogatee at the very same Prague Gestapo headquarters where Fučík underwent his ordeal, but with one small difference: Brecht's protagonist manages to finagle his way out of this tight spot.[49]

Karel Havlíček-Borovský—a mid–nineteenth-century Czech journalist and satirist, is the third literary-historical figure about whom Fučík wrote in early 1939 in a way that seemed to foreshadow his own *Reportage*. Though politically less radical than Sabina, in the conservative ambiance of the years after 1848 Havlíček too was deemed subversive by Austrian authorities. Unable to indict him in a court of law, they committed Havlíček in 1852 to administrative exile in the Alpine city of Brixen (Bressanone). There, under the nose of watchful police, he managed to compose and smuggle out to Bohemia some of his most pungent antigovernment poetic satires. Returning home in 1855 only to die of tuberculosis a year later, Havlíček immediately became a national martyr. "Indeed, the time of his enforced stay in Brixen was lost neither for Havlíček, nor for Czech culture," Fučík lauded the man whom he would soon join in the national pantheon. "It was heroic work. Havlíček was under strict surveillance all the time; police officials could freely enter his room at any moment and at any moment they could also confiscate any of his writings." And "it was equally difficult to preserve what had been already written, pass it on to the Czech public."[50] True, Fučík's own experience of carrying on a clandestine prison correspondence well preceded his essay. But it is

[48]   Václav Kopecký, *ČSR a KSČ: Pamětní výpisy k historii Československé republiky a k boji KSČ za socialistické Československo* (Prague, 1960), p. 460.
[49]   Bertolt Brecht, *Schweyk in the Second World War*, trans. W. Rawlinson, in *Plays, Poetry, and Prose*, vol. 7, *The Collected Plays*, ed. John Willett et al. (London, 1976), pp. 80–85.
[50]   Julius Fučík, "Básník ve vyhnanství," in *Milujeme svůj národ: Poslední články a úvahy* (*Dílo Julia Fučíka*, vol. 3), 1st ed. (Prague, 1951), p. 138.

not difficult to see that Havlíček's situation as portrayed in the 1939 piece matched the conditions that Fučík was to encounter in the Gestapo jail a few years later more closely than the old-fashioned ambiance of Czechoslovak penal institutions.

Earlier I mentioned Fučík's unfinished novel, *The Generation before Peter*, conceived one day after the German troops annexed the rest of his homeland to the Third Reich. This text, I believe, marks a significant shift in its author's style. Suddenly the motifs of existential anxiety totally absent in earlier works become predominant. In many respects this novel can be seen as a prefiguration of *Reportage*. It is an autobiographical account, a flashback triggered by the author's sensing his imminent end, addressed to an implied future reader apostrophized in the text as an unborn son, Peter. And the two works are mirror images of each other, the novel focusing on Fučík's birth and his early childhood, *Reportage* recording his last few years. The antinomy of life and death so essential to Fučík's earlier writings is maintained in *The Generation* but redefined accordingly. Social change is seen no longer as a mere succession of classes but as a succession of generations. The author and his coevals are presented as preterit people or, more optimistically, as a provisional transition between the sordid past and the bright, as yet unborn future represented by Peter. The organic trope is modified to include not only healthy growth but also mortal decay. "We are the spring crop, Peter, sown underneath. This is our generation. . . . Not all of us will germinate, not all of us will grow when the spring comes. Each of the hobnailed boots walking above our heads can trample us down. Can crush us—whether by accident, hatred, or the joy of destruction—and we know that. And we live with that."[51]

The metaphor of a seed eventually yielding its fruit had been used by Fučík earlier and would sprout once again in *Reportage*. But in his unfinished novel he imbued it for the first time with a distinctly eucharistic spirit. Earlier I argued that in his prewar writings Fučík presented himself as a Christ-like figure capable of bringing the dead to life. This image, however, was only implied and never used explicitly. Now the scriptural analogy becomes unmistakable. But it is a different Jesus who emerges from the writings of a man facing the possibility of his own death: not the one who resurrected others but he who was himself resurrected. "But, Peter," Fučík continues the dialogue, "do not think that we are scared. Not all of us will grow but neither will all perish. We know this and live with it too. The rustling of mature ears of corn will obscure the footprints of graves, they will be forgotten, all will be forgotten—the worry and the

---

[51] Julius Fučík, *Pokolení před Petrem: Stati, články a pozůstalost z let 1938–1942* (*Dílo Julia Fučíka*, vol. 11), 1st ed. (Prague, 1958), p. 29. Further references will be given in the text.

grief. Only the crop will tell your generation on behalf of us, dead and alive: Take, eat; this is our body!" (29). *Hoc est corpus [meum]*. Not too bad for someone who quit the Catholic Church at the tender age of sixteen because he could not accept, on zoological grounds, the biblical story of a whale swallowing the poor prophet Jonah![52]

We turn now to *Reportage: Written from the Gallows*. Let me first point out its extreme heterogeneity. The text is a montage of narrative and descriptive passages which include the story of Julius's arrest and ordeal at the hands of the Nazis, but also a plethora of verbal portraits of other prisoners and their captors. These two main ingredients are interspersed liberally with, among other things, Fučík's recollections of different events and places, a record of his torture-induced delirium, a short history of the Communist resistance, his last will, and above all his ex cathedra comments about various matters, instructions to his relatives, his future audience, and humankind at large about how to read his text and understand his feelings, or equally elevated exhortations on how to behave. If one discounts such insertions and flashbacks, the text is organized chronologically. And this "natural" order of events is intended, I would argue, to underscore the nonfictional character of Fučík's *Reportage*.

There are two other important exceptions to this ordering principle. First of all, only at the very end does Fučík mention his "trafficking" with the enemy—the fact that much earlier in the game he had decided to protect his comrades at large by feeding the Gestapo false clues to throw them off their scent. This information casts new light on his chummy relationship with his interrogator Böhm, thus providing not only a surprising resolution to a problem that might have puzzled many readers throughout the book but also, and more important, an entirely new perspective on the author himself. At the same time, it could be argued that this time lapse was dictated not solely by the norms of literary plotting but by life itself. To divulge his furtive plan while it was still being executed would, if the manuscript fell into the wrong hands, compromise it, blow it to shreds. So Fučík had to hang on to his secret until the last minute when everything was over.

The other exception to the linear sequencing of the story is more complicated. It concerns a year-long lag between the beginning of the narrated events and the event of narration itself. Fučík was arrested in April 1942, but he dates the inception of his text (on its title page) to the spring of 1943, so most of it is a relatively distant recollection. The two take place not only within different spaces (one mental, the other actual) but also at

---

[52] See Mojmír Grygar, *Žil jsem pro radost: Životopisná črta o Juliu Fučíkovi* (Prague, 1958), p. 46.

different speeds (the former faster than the latter) until they merge at the end of the text when memory turns into living presence. Throughout the text Fučík highlights this discrepancy by interrupting the story with details not belonging to it but, instead, concomitant with the very act of writing. This effort seems to anchor the immaterial realm of what is being represented in the "reality" of the representational process as such, authenticating, in this way, its nonfictional origins.

There are plenty of other markers in *Reportage* indicating its factual status: exact dates and real places are rendered in detail that only an eyewitness could provide. The same can be said about the copious verbal portraits of the living people (with their proper names always mentioned) who populate the book. In the absence of a camera at the Pankrác prison, they are a close approximation to the documentary photographs that Fučík used to employ in his previous reportage. Some other strategies for achieving the intended reality effect may be subtler. The title of a subchapter, "Suspenders: An Intermezzo" (60; 67), which yokes together a somewhat comical object of everyday use and an artistic term charged with lofty operatic connotations, ironically implies how inadequate is the conventional aesthetic taxonomy for grasping the reality of a Gestapo prison.[53] And Fučík's confession to positively weird behavior—the guessing of his future predicament from the shapeliness of women's legs glimpsed on the way to his interrogation—suggests that the author is hiding absolutely nothing from the reader.

Although, obviously, *Reportage* has its documentary dimension, a careful reader of the book will notice small details whose truth-value might seem somewhat compromised. I have in mind not the reality of some of the presented events—the traditional target of Fučík's detractors—but just small textual clues (certain temporal data, for example) whose neatness seems to contradict the typical sloppiness of life. The first chapter, for example, starts on the evening of April 24 at five minutes to ten (12; 1) and ends on the twenty-fifth at 9:55 P.M. and not a single minute later (17; 8). One may be equally doubtful about the exact duration of Fučík's silence during his interrogation by the Gestapo. "For seven weeks," he insists, "I have not provided any evidence" (80; 0). While the former example is unmistakably an instance of a conventional literary device of circular fram-

---

53 To Czech readers the technique of an embedded "intermezzo" calls to mind the most famous Romantic poem of their literary tradition—Karel Hynek Mácha's *May*—which, moreover, relates to *Reportage* thematically as well. Like Fučík, its main protagonist, the robber Vilém, is in jail awaiting his impending execution. This textual parallel, as I will illustrate in Chapter 5, is fully exploited in Kundera's eulogy of Fučík, *The Last May*. Julius's allusion to *May*, however, seems rather parodistic, while such Romantic props as the "Choir of Spirits," a "Skull," and the "Moon in the Zenith" populate Mácha's "intermezzi," profane objects such as "suspenders" definitely do not occur there.

ing (the first and the last sentences of the chapter are identical save for the date), the latter, because of its magic numerological valence (seven times seven), exudes the aura of the mythical.

This brings me once again to the question of the factuality of Fučík's reporting which I faced when discussing his prewar writings. As I tried to illustrate, his texts were above all creative applications of a specific ideology whose cognitive lens refracted Julius's interpretation of the world in a very specific way. *Reportage: Written from the Gallows* adds another wrinkle to this process. This is not to say that Fučík suddenly abandoned the tenets of Marxism-Leninism, with its impetus toward a romantic narrative. On the contrary, as I will argue shortly, his last book, if generically anything, is a romance. The complication that *Reportage* introduces stems from the fact that, in contrast to his earlier texts, what is represented is not primarily segments of external reality but the author of the book himself. For, as I suggested earlier, *Reportage* is, above all, Fučík's self-presentation.

The autobiographical nature of *Reportage* is underscored in its short "Introduction" by a pun on the word *biograf* ("movie theater" in Czech)—the inmate's nickname for the "in-house" prison at the Gestapo headquarters where the detainees wait for their interrogation. The setting—rows of benches where prisoners sit facing a blank wall—evokes in Fučík's imagination the idea of captives mentally projecting "films" of their lives upon the wall they face. "I have seen my own film here a hundred times, a thousand times its details," he says about the origin of his text; "now I'll try to tell it" (11; xiii). And even though the author, following the tradition of Marxist romance with its plural heroes, praises the collectivity of prisoners and sketches the portraits of others besides himself, he is clearly the star of the book. It is his arrest, torture, dying, his secret game with the Gestapo and his testimonial to what happened, and above all his emotions and ideas that *Reportage* conveys. The charge of overpowering authorial self-indulgence was one of the shocking blasphemies Kundera's novel *The Joke* leveled at this sacred book (as I show in Chapter 5).

Kundera's reproach to Fučík can be extended, mutatis mutandis, to all literary self-portraitists and autobiographers. For any writing in which one and the same person fulfills the triple role of author, character, and reader might be seen, to a great extent, as narcissistic. To deflect this unflattering image, authors of such texts often invoke a higher authority to legitimize their blatantly self-gratifying impulse. They mold their life stories along the lines provided by the biographies of authoritative figures sanctioned by the appropriate cultural tradition. This strategy (whether applied consciously or not) might absolve them from the deadly sin of vainglory, but such pardon does not come for free. At stake is, first of all, the credibility of the narrative itself. For the reader might recognize that the alleged biographical facts are instead mere pseudo-facts, ready made *loci communes* derived from elsewhere. Equally troublesome is the issue of the narrator's identity. After all, what would you call an individual who presents somebody else's curriculum vitae as his own? An impostor? Many autobiographers engage in a secondary game of concealment, obfuscating as much as possible the affinities to the originary source.

Applying these insights to *Reportage*, I will show how the events from Fučík's life presented in the initial four chapters closely trace the trajectory of Christ's death and resurrection in the Gospels. My point is that most of the controversies about the documentary veracity of the book center precisely on passages that bear maximal scriptural similarity. As far as Fučík's "anxiety of influence" is concerned, his attitude toward the textual model that he emulated is delightfully equivocal. Although the number óf biblical allusions is far too high to allow us to assume that Fučík was unaware of his presenting himself *in figura Christi*, *Reportage* makes quite clear that he does not endorse in any way the products or opinions for which this figure stands. Not only did Julius have his own well-defined *Weltanschauung* to peddle, but also, as some of his earlier writings clearly indicate, he considered religion to be entirely counterrevolutionary. And though *Reportage* deals with the Christological topics of death and resurrection, it is quite clever in displacing a religious symbolism with a Communist one. More about this later.

Reader reception of *Reportage* reflected this ambiguity. On the one hand, poets, who by the nature of their craft are the most sensitive to the figurative use of language, detected from the very beginning the strong parallel between the Fučík of his last book and the story of Christ. It was not only Konstantin Biebl who exploited this image but also, to some degree, Pablo Neruda and many others. On the other hand, literary scholars (notoriously slow on the textual uptake) have almost completely ignored this dimension of the book. Perhaps, in officially atheistic Communist Czechoslovakia, Party ideologues were willing to condone scriptural analogy as a matter of poetic license but not as a matter of fact. As far as I was able to determine, Vladimír Macura was the first critic who, in 1985, dared (albeit quite sheepishly) to bring into the open *Reportage*'s obvious borrowing from the Gospels: the motif of the temptation of Christ on the mountain (Matthew 4:8–10; Luke 4:5–8).[54] "Sometimes after a day-long interrogation," Fučík reports about his mysterious exploits with Böhm, "he put me into a car and took me through evening Prague to the Castle above Neruda Street. 'I know that you like Prague. Look! Don't you want to re-

---

54 Vladimír Macura, *"Reportáž psaná na oprátce jako dílo literární,"* in Julius Fučík, *Reportáž psaná na oprátce*, 25th ed. (Prague, 1985), p. 102.

turn to it? How beautiful it is! And it will be beautiful even when you aren't around. . . . ' He played the role of the Tempter well." One might only wonder what this temptation was all about, because such trips to the city were organized, Fučík has us believe, only after he became—at least in the Gestapo's eyes—their willing informer. But to keep the biblical parallel intact, Fučík like Christ, had to reject the Satanic lure. Interrupting Böhm, he retorts, "and it will be even more beautiful when you aren't around" (59; 67).

This scriptural allusion, however, should not have come as a total surprise to readers, for there are small clues dispersed throughout *Reportage* hinting in that direction. Most significantly, Christ's name is explicitly mentioned twice at the beginning of the book. In the second chapter, titled "Dying," a delirious Fučík hears his fellow cellmates singing a religious song about "that eternally blazing star / Jesus himself, Jesus himself," invoking life in heaven (18; 9). The second mention of Christ's name, in the next chapter, is more opaque because it is an implicit dialogue with another text: Jan Neruda's "Christmas Lullaby."[55] In this poem the speaker comforts the infant Jesus in his Bethlehem manger, imploring him to sleep on rather than enter the treacherous and cruel world. Fučík makes a point of disagreeing with his favorite poet: "Oh, Neruda's infant Jesus, there is no end to humankind's road to salvation. But: you don't sleep any longer, don't sleep any longer!" (24; 18). What interests me here is not simply the image of Christ as a social activist in a Fučík-like mold. A careful reader will recall that it is not just the infant Jesus whom Fučík urges not to sleep in *Reportage* but, in its ultimate sentence, all of humankind. "People, I liked you. Watch!" These are the famous last words, as Fučíkian as his impish smile and his love for anything Soviet. But within the Christological context evoked by the reference to the infant Jesus, the authorship of this sound bite becomes somewhat problematic. "And what I say unto you I say unto all, Watch" (Mark 13:37). Yes, it is Jesus speaking now, wrapping up his sermon on the Mount of Olives in which he warns his followers of false prophets and other natural disasters, admonishing them, at the same time, not to be caught napping when the Lord finally cometh.

Could this be just a coincidence? Yes. But my surprise would be unbearable. For *Reportage* replicates more than just isolated words of Christ. Its affinity with the Bible is much more thorough. Let me be more specific. Entering the book we behold the conspirators' last communion—if not supper, at least tea. And Fučík's very first words are fittingly vatic: "Com-

---

[55]   Jan Neruda, "Ukolébavka vánoční," in *Zpěvy páteční*, vol. 2 of *Spisy Jana Nerdudy: Básně*, (Prague, 1956), p. 204.

rades, I'm glad to see you, but not together this way. This is the best road to jail and death. You'll either stick to the rules of conspiracy or quit working with us, because you endanger yourselves and others. Understood?" (12; 1). Yet, another participant at this gathering, Riva Friedová-Krieglová, insists vehemently that what was said that evening was something completely different. Fučík's resistance identity, she recalls, as Professor Horák—a limping older gentleman with a full beard—looked too histrionic (he was only thirty-nine years old) and was attracting unwanted attention. Thus, according to her, the words of caution about the compromised conspiracy were not made by Fučík after all but addressed to him by others.[56] Is she right? It is her word against Fučík's, so who can say? The controversy, however, can be easily defused if we realize that it might not have been concern for documentary truth that controlled Julius's pen in this instance but his adherence to the scriptural model. For the Christological parallel necessitates absolutely that it be Fučík who, in his providential wisdom, warns his followers about an impending catastrophe, not the other way around.

"And as they sat and did eat, Jesus said, Verily I say unto you, One of you which eateth with me shall betray me' " (Mark 14:18). Fučík, verily, was not so explicit in his monition as Christ, but a Judas was sitting at his table too. Which brings me to the villain of *Reportage*—Fučík's "adjutant" Klecan—the man whom Fučík personally chose as his closest collaborator and whom he trusted fully. This is also the man who gets blamed for all the subsequent misfortune. Fučík goes so far as to ground his passivity during his arrest in his belief that Klecan would not talk to the Nazis under any circumstances, and so a suicidal shoot-out was not called for: "A man who fought in Spain, a man who lived two years in a concentration camp in France, who made it illegally in the midst of war from France to Prague—no, he won't betray us" (13; 2). Is this a credible excuse? I have already spent enough time thrashing out this point from many different angles. A biblical perspective, though, might suggest why Julius included this unheroic incident in *Reportage*, despite its strong reputation-damaging potential. Jesus, too, we might recall, not only did not resist his captors in the garden of Gethsemane but even bade the pugnacious Apostle Peter to lay down his sword.

The star-crossed Klecan did, however, crack up, and from this moment his fall from Fučík's grace was absolute. The fire and brimstone that Klecan drew in *Reportage* was so strong that it startled many commentators, Černý the most vocal among them. Fučík's censure, he wrote, "is so total,

---

[56] Riva Krieglová et al., "Julius Fučík aneb pohrdání pravdou," *Listy: Nezávislý dvouměsíčník*, no. 2 (1991), 20.

so mercilessly undifferentiated, that one is tempted a hundred times to beg from Fučík mercy for his most faithful friend, a little charity shaded by the admission and the qualification that it was a slip of the tongue, that his comrade just blurted out, and that through this aperture of a little word not checked in time, the Gestapo, by force and irretrievably, penetrated the secret of the two. But Fučík is merciless: Klecan—traitor" (325). The categorical nature of Fučík's judgment, Černý suggests, might have something to do with Fučík's own feeling of culpability—an attempt to find a convenient scapegoat for the havoc which the arrest wreaked in the Communist underground. Leaving psychology aside, within the scriptural context this absolute condemnation makes perfect sense. To question it is like wondering why the four Evangelists did not find any extenuating circumstances for Judas Iscariot's behavior, a single kind word for the services he had previously rendered to the movement.

"And the men that held Jesus mocked him and smote him" (Luke 22:63). In Fučík's case, though, the beating came before the ridicule: "A tall SS-man stands over me, kicking me to get up.... [S]ome woman passes me a medication and asks where it hurts and it seems suddenly that all the pain is in my heart. 'You don't have a heart,' a tall SS says" (16; 7–8). And later, " 'Don't you understand,' " Fučík recalls the chief of the Gestapo's anti-Communist Department telling him during an interrogation, " 'it's the end, get it, you lost the game.' 'It's only I who lost'," the uncontrite captive replies. " 'You still believe in the victory of the Commune?' 'Of course.' 'He still believes,' asks the Chief in German and the tall Commissar translates, 'he still believes in the victory of Russia'?" (21; 14). And then the demise—preceded by long and painful passions culminating in terminal thirst quenched by water from a toilet bowl. In their informative commentary on *Reportage*, historians have gone to some pains to point out that at the Pankrác prison such a method of drinking was impossible and called Fučík's account "an expressive hyperbole."[57] Perhaps. But where, for Christ's blood, was the dying Fučík supposed to get a vinegar-filled sponge upon hyssop for his last drink? The death following Fučík's "hyperbolic" sip of water was, as to be expected, only clinical. Were this Julius's true and ultimate end, *Reportage* would have been not only much shorter but also much less scriptural. For like J. C., J. F. could not simply have died. The death certificate already produced in his name was torn up next day by the flabbergasted doctor who had issued it a short time previously, and Julius stepped miraculously into his second life. "Resurrection," muses the smug Fučík at the beginning of Chapter 4,

---

[57] František Janáček et al., "Na okraj motáků: Vysvětlivky a komentáře," in the critical edition of *Reportage* (see note 5). Further references will be given in the text.

"is an unusual affair. Strange beyond words" (31; 28). Christ's empirically minded apostle Thomas could only have agreed with this assertion, to be sure. But I wouldn't dare to put my fingers into Fučík's wounds, knowing perfectly well that no amount of sensory data can ever establish mythological truth. For "there are also many other things which [Julius] did, the which, if they should be written every one, I suppose that even the world itself could not contain the books that should be written" (John 21:25).

So far I have been trying to illustrate the remarkable fit between Fučík's book and the New Testament. But, as I argued earlier, despite the reiteration of the Christological narrative of sacrificial death and resurrection, the collective set of beliefs underlying *Reportage* is completely different. And in order to assert its ideological distinctness, the text had to undercut the scriptural analogy somehow. How did Fučík manage to draw the line? Each myth, so the general claim goes, manifests itself in everyday life through specific ritualistic actions. For Christianity, it is the celebration of Easter that symbolically reenacts the sequence of events centered on the crucifixion of Jesus. So, arrested on Friday, April 25, and having a way with words, Julius could easily and effectively have linked his own predicament to this holiday. But instead he deliberately drew attention to the celebration of another feast, one that, though Easter-like in its content, is, from the Marxist-Leninist perspective, far more politically correct—the international Labor Day of May 1. Commemorating the judicial murder of seven American labor leaders in connection with the Chicago Haymarket massacre of May 4, 1889, this holiday provides a suitable ritualistic backdrop for Fučík's own dying. Listening to the endless litany of cheery euphemisms about "Jesus—the eternally blazing star" from his singing cellmates, our hero bridles a bit: "O people, people, cut it out. It is, perhaps, a nice song, but today, today is the eve of the First of May, the most beautiful, the most joyful human holiday. . . . First of May!" And a few hours later Fučík, just before taking a last sip, projects his martyrdom into the politically correct rite of spring: "In these hours on the streets of Moscow the first ranks take their place for the May Day parade. And in these hours today millions of people are waging the last battle for human freedom and thousands are dying in this struggle. I am one of them. And to be one of them, one of the soldiers of the last battle, that's beautiful. But dying is not beautiful. I'm choking. I can't exhale" (22–23; 15–16).

Not surprisingly, given the author's penchant for repetition, May Day reappears in *Reportage* once again, this time pertaining to May 1, 1943. Though separated from the moment of Fučík's "death" by a year-long interval, this second May Day celebration actually comes in the text just a few pages after the first, at the beginning of Chapter 4. This proximity is motivated ostensibly by the timing of the writing itself. By chance May 1 found Fučík at this very spot in his manuscript, and the significance of the holiday absolutely necessitated that he interrupt his recollection of the past to note the present. This "coincidence," it is easy to recognize, enabled Fučík to employ his favorite device of reiteration, of juxtaposing the same as different, which I discussed earlier. In this way Fučík introduces the death-transcending nature of the May Day celebration. For a May Day parade is not just a commemoration of fallen comrades but, above all, a symbolic act affirming the continuation of their heroic quest and uniting the dead with the living. If the dying Fučík of May 1, 1942, was joining the ranks of memorable Communist martyrs joyfully sacrificing their lives for others, the resurrected Fučík of May 1, 1943, reenters the ranks of fighters for a better future. And he does so even though under harsh prison conditions the symbols of the ongoing struggle can only be furtive: a clenched fist, gestures imitating hammer and sickle during morning exercise, and so on. But they are by no means less powerful, Fučík insists, than their full-blown counterparts displayed elsewhere. "All is in such minor details," Fučík cautions his future audience, "that who knows whether you who did not live through all this will ever understand it as you read. But try to understand. Believe me, there is force in it" (32; 29–30).

The recurrence of the international Labor Day festivities in Fučík's book should not, however, be seen just as an isolated implementation of the author's favorite device. More important, this repetition is a function of the overall structure of *Reportage* as a romance. To substantiate this claim, let me retrace my steps a bit. Earlier I argued that Fučík's prewar writings display certain stylistic markers—mode of emplotment and selection of protagonists—proper to the romantic genre. And there is a common feature these markers share: the tendency toward symmetrical organization. A quest for self-identity is a process entailing its initial loss and eventual recuperation; heroes and villains are grouped into neat pairs. But there are other narrative reduplications in a romance, Frye tells us, which mirror each other. The hero's passage from self-oblivion to anamnesis usually consists of two opposite movements: a descent to the lower world of sheer negativity and an ascent to the altogether positive higher world. A closer look at Fučík's text reveals such a bipartite organization. The resurrection, I believe, is the dividing point in *Reportage* which separates downward movement from the journey up, the world of the hero's passive suffering from that of his active defiance. From this perspective, each of the two references to the May Day celebration neatly fits this scheme, capturing through a single symbolic rite the dual thrust of the hero's search for his true self: the martyrdom of descent and the pugnacity of ascent.

Approaching *Reportage* now as a romance, I quote in full its brief "Intro-

duction," which in a remarkably economical way manages to bring out
some of the most salient features of this genre:

> To sit at attention with your body rigidly erect, with your hands pressing
> against your knees, and with your eyes riveted to the point of blindness on
> the yellowing wall of an "in-house prison" at the Petschek palace—this is
> certainly not a position most appropriate for thinking. But who can force a
> thought to sit at attention?
>
> Once upon a time, someone—we will probably never find out when or
> who—called the "in-house prison" in the Petschek palace a "movie house."
> A stroke of genius. The spacious room, six long benches in a row occupied
> by the rigid bodies of interrogatees and an empty wall in front of them like
> a movie screen. All the production companies of the world could not shoot
> as many movies as the eyes of the interrogatees, waiting for new question-
> ing, for torture, for death, have projected on this wall. The movies of entire
> lives and of life's most minute segments, movies of your mother, of your
> wife, of your children, of a destroyed home, of a ruined existence, movies of
> a brave comrade and also of a betrayal, to whom you gave that illegal
> leaflet, of blood that will flow again, of a firm handshake that obligated me,
> movies full of horror and of resolve, of hatred and love, of anxiety and
> hope. Turning one's back to life, everyone dies here daily in front of his
> own eyes. But not everyone is reborn.
>
> I have seen my own film here a hundred times, a thousand times its de-
> tails, now I'll try to tell it. If the hangman's noose tightens before I finish,
> millions will remain to write its "happy ending." (11; xiii–xiv)

The structural core of a romance, to exploit Frye's insights into the regu-
larities of this genre, "is the individual loss or confusion or break in the
continuity of identity, and this has analogies to falling asleep and entering
a dream world. . . . If I dream of myself I have two identities, myself as a
dreamer and myself as character in dream" (104; 106). The beginning of
Fučík's *Reportage* offers a variation on this opening gambit. The "Introduction" starts by drawing attention to a strange transformation of a
human body. It is petrified, frozen, turned into a peculiar statue watched
closely by a special type of audience—prison guards. This passive rigid-
ity, however, is only a matter of appearance, of a corporeal façade concealing very unruly mental processes. Thoughts, we are reminded, are always restless, always free. The captors might be able to immobilize the
prisoners' bodies but not their minds.

Fučík, it seems, is utilizing a traditional romantic motif of "sleepwatching" which, according to Wendy Steiner, fascinated modernists such as

Piccasso and Joyce. It stands, among other things, as a symbol of unwelcome artistic exile, the viewer's inability to get beyond an opaque, static object into the concealed realm of dream and fantasy.[58] The situation presented by Julius at the beginning of his book is, obviously, somewhat different. Here it is a dreaming artist who certainly does not wish the sleep-watchers' gaze to penetrate his mind. The cinematic metaphor, in my opinion, functions as an empowering stratagem, a device enabling the narrator to escape his psychic trauma. The *Ichspaltung* (ego split) thus created reverses completely the mechanism of power and authority ruling the world outside. It is no longer the guards who watch and control Fučík but the other way around: internalized, they became mere performers in his "home movie." As the sole maker of this film, he is in charge of determining who will play what. And given his unenviable situation, it is only human that in this show Julius reserve the best role for himself. At the same time, the "Introduction" exhibits the opposite impulse on the part of its author. While Fučík surely wished to shield his fantasy from the Gestapo, he desperately wanted to share it with others. Why else would he record it? Which fact adds yet another level of complication to the previously mentioned identity deficiency (or excess): Fučík the writer imagining himself watching a third Fučík muddling through his own life!

As to the "film" itself, its dramatic tension derives, quite expectedly, from the clash of two diametrically opposed settings: the serene world of before and the demonic world of now. Naturally the action is in the oppressive present, an idyllic past providing merely a contrastive background against which the depravities of the day loom large. And, as always in romances, the moral system of the "film" is fearfully symmetrical: it comprises two pairs of feuding sins and virtues identified by Frye as violence and fraud against force and cunning (65). Even a perfunctory look at the "Introduction" reveals that at least three of these categories are present. The brutality of Gestapo interrogations and betrayal (by a yet unnamed comrade) figure prominently among the sins listed. The list of virtues includes such manifestations of force as bravery, obligation, and resolve. But the craft of cunning so instrumental for the very existence of *Reportage* is curiously omitted. It is not until the fifth chapter that Fučík unites, quite unexpectedly, force and cunning: "For thirteen months now have I been fighting here for my life and that of others. By bravery and ruse" (49; 52). This remark is obviously too cryptic to be understood by readers until the very end of the book, when Fučík reveals the "high-stakes game" that he played with the Gestapo.

[58]   Wendy Steiner, *Pictures of Romance: Form against Context in Painting and Literature* (Chicago, 1988), p. 76.

Yet, upon closer scrutiny, one may detect a clear parallel between the opening of *Reportage* and its closure. The "Introduction" lumps together somewhat hastily two fundamentally different activities: a mental representation of the past (the "home movie") and its secondary verbal recording. It is obvious that in the inner sanctum of our souls we are ultimately free to imagine whatever we wish, and Fučík exploits this liberty to the hilt. When ushering our daydreams into the external world, though, we must deal with many practical obstacles—especially in a Gestapo prison with a death sentence lurking around the corner! To be able to write his book, Fučík had to resort to a literary device allegedly invented by another famous romancer, Scheherazade, for the purpose of saving her life from King Shahriyar's misogyny: death-defying narrative suspense, but with one important difference. *The Thousand and One Nights* was both the means to keep Scheherazade alive and her actual literary output. In Fučík's case, the tales he fed to the Gestapo were a mere pretext to prolong his own life so that the real text of his *Reportage* could be written on the sly.

The role of double agent that Fučík assumed for this purpose clearly continues the theme of split identity already developed in the "Introduction." We have a docile Fučík obeying the Gestapo's orders, a wily Fučík thwarting the Gestapo's plans, and his shadowy alter ego busily composing *Reportage*. Once again this multiple personality syndrome is couched in a histrionic metaphor, albeit not a cinematic but a dramatic one: "For a year I was writing with [my interrogators] a theatrical play in which I ascribed to myself the lead role" (91; 0). This play, Fučík writes, is now coming to its denouement. But what could this mean for his co-authors? Its only dramatic resolution could have been the Nazis' realizing that Fučík, for quite a while, had been leading them around by their noses—which, I believe, was not the case. Instead, the denouement of the drama coincides with the end of the film, or, to be more precise, with the end of *Reportage*. Only via the conclusion do surprised readers learn the piquant secret that Fučík has withheld from them throughout the text: of the misalliance that has begotten this unusual book.

Unlike his readers, Fučík knew about his sub rosa game with the Nazis when he started to write his book. And he was aware how delicate the role of a double agent is, how indistinguishable in its outer manifestations from actual perfidy. So it is perhaps no accident that the "Introduction" touches the topic of treason twice. Besides being mentioned directly, "betrayal" is also couched in the proto-Fučíkian opposition of life and death. This antinomy, it might be useful to recall, is linked in Fučík's mythopoetic universe to his overall understanding of the logic of history: of helping or hindering progress toward a Communist future. The cinematic metaphor employed in the "Introduction" surprisingly renders the two existential categories as an asymmetrical pair. Dying is presented as an iterative process ("everybody dies here daily in front of his own eyes"); not so resurrection ("not everyone is reborn"). This curious discrepancy suggests that Fučík's "home movie" is not just another instance of a work of art in the age of mechanical reproduction. Such an identity split provides the basis for moral rather than aesthetic judgment. Betraying secrets of the Communist underground to the Gestapo even under torture clearly trifles with the emplotment of the Marxist-Leninist historical romance, which offense, in the bailiwick of poetic justice, is punishable by death. "The sight of someone whose conscience was damaged," Julius amplifies this idea subsequently, "is worse than the sight of one whose body was crippled. . . . What kind of a life could it be if paid for by the life of a friend! This perhaps was not the first thought that passed through my mind when I was sitting in the "movie house" for the first time. But it often came to me there" (34; 33). And pointing his finger at Klecan—the bête noire of the book—Fučík declares a few pages later: "A coward loses more than his own life. He has lost. . . . And even though still alive he is already dead" (39; 39).

If romantic villains die before their actual demise, heroes, for the sake of symmetry, must be able to transcend their own deaths. It is the last sentence of the "Introduction" which broaches the issue of Julius's own mortality: an author on death row pondering the appropriate poetic closure to his autobiographical project. A romance cannot end badly, and Fučík seems well aware of this generic requirement. At the same time, however, it was quite clear to him that getting out of his present mess unscathed and living happily ever after was highly improbable. Marrying the formulaic with the realistic, Fučík ingeniuously employed the device of an implied happy ending, written, in case of his badly timed hanging, by the millions who remain. The Nazis might execute him, Julius seems to be saying, but they cannot spoil the positive outcome of his book. Wishful thinking? Perhaps. But one firmly rooted in the historical script of Marxism-Leninism that fully guarantees the victory of progress or your money back. What *Reportage* depicts, if viewed this way, is perhaps the last battle of the long war for the better future of humankind. Many, Fučík included, might perish fighting. But this is no reason for grief, the author comforts his audience. Sooner or later the selfless sacrifice of fallen comrades will be redeemed by the ultimate triumph of the cause in which they joyfully invested their own lives. And *Reportage* makes sure that they will not be forgotten.

Besides affirming the book's happy ending, the last sentence of the "Introduction" exhibits yet another salient feature of the romantic genre: the fusion of the author with the audience. "The artificial creation story in genesis," Frye reminds us, "culminates in the Sabbath vision, in which God contemplates what he has made. In human life creation and contemplation need two people, a poet and a reader, creative action that produces and a creative response that possesses" (185). The appeal of a romance, one might paraphrase Frye's argument, rests in its ability to entice its audience, to compel it to identify with the quest put forth by the text. Fučík—and there is no doubt about it in my mind—was well aware of the propagandistic potential of this genre when he began to write his *Reportage*. The book, one might argue, is an excellent example of what Frye calls a "kidnapped" romance, used for promoting or proselytizing a particular social mythology. The closure of the "Introduction" is a calculated gesture in this direction. The bridging of the gap between the author and his audience, or, more precisely, the empowerment of the reader to conclude the text properly, is a rhetorical device invoking the sense of an ideological bond and a historical obligation. It is a hand extended by the man to be executed to those who come after him, an appeal to continue the mission for which Fučík offered his own life.

Earlier I commented on the bipartite structure of *Reportage* with the scene of resurrection serving as narrative pivot. Fučík's descent into a world of horror and suffering displays many motifs that Frye mentions as typical of this portion of the romantic quest: the nocturnal setting with which the journey opens, Fučík's altered appearance and name, the clock meticulously marking every hour of his torture, the dog Julius sees in his death struggle, a symbolic sepulcher (prison cell 267) where his incapacitated body is subsequently deposited, his desperate wish yet once more to see the sunrise—the list could go on. But these are mere details which in themselves do not carry much significance. What matters, I believe, is how diametrically our hero's characteristics change during the ascent that follows his miraculous rebirth: passivity gives way to activity, isolation to comradeship, endurance to cunning.

One example of this metamorphosis already mentioned earlier is the two modes of celebrating May Day. Let me amplify. The opening scene brings us to the room that serves as an in-house prison within Gestapo headquarters where traumatized detainees await their turn for interrogation. Motionless, they stare at the yellowish wall ahead, and in mental solitude their life stories unfold in front of their eyes. Only later does the reader learn that there is yet another in-house prison in the building, on the fourth floor, reserved for Communist captives. This is where Fučík is taken almost daily in the second part of *Reportage*. And what a difference: "Downstairs in the 'movie-house' the SS guards were pacing in high boots and they shouted at every blink of your eye. Here in Room 400 Czech inspectors and agents from Police HQ ... did their duty as either the Gestapo's servants or—as Czechs. Or, also, as something in between. Here it was no longer necessary to sit at attention with your hands on your knees and with your eyes riveted ahead; here you could sit more relaxed, look around, wave your hand and could do even more depending on which of your three friends was on duty" (40–41; 41). But it is not just the more humane ambiance that Julius finds praiseworthy. In contrast to the first-floor waiting room where detainees absorbed in their own thoughts submissively await what the future will bring them, in Room 400 they forge at once an esprit de corps and carry on, even while imprisoned, their anti-Nazi struggle. This is not a "movie house," Fučík shifts his metaphor to describe it, but "a very advanced trench completely surrounded by the enemy, under a concentrated fusillade from all sides but not including a single sigh of surrender. The red flag flies above it" (41; 41).

Fučík's characterization of Room 400 in terms of a battlefield is an exaggeration made to fit the upbeat spirit proper to the theme of ascent. According to the commentary appended to the critical edition of *Reportage,* this place served the prisoners primarily as a channel for clandestine communication through which, in addition to messages, food was smuggled in. But the Gestapo was soon able to detect this leak, and the facility was closed even before Fučík started to write his book—in early December 1942 (169–71). Given the enormous power in the hands of the jailers, it is clear that cunning was the only virtue truly available to the detainees to counter Nazi violence. So, in this respect, it is not the metaphor of open warfare but of a theater used by Fučík in the conclusion of *Reportage* that seems better suited to grasp the nature of his resistance activity in prison. But even this figure of speech, I would stress, signals a departure from the mode of existence suggested by the cinematic trope that unfolds in the first-floor "movie house." While the "home movie," very much in accord with the overall passivity of the theme of descent, is just an instant replay of a story only too familiar to Fučík and fully confined to his solitary imagination, the "play" co-authored with the Gestapo is a step out of this mental isolation into the social sphere, an interactive manipulation of the enemy through the histrionic skills that Julius was lucky enough to acquire early in life.

There is yet another important parallel to be drawn between the beginning and the end of *Reportage.* As Frye points out, the loss of a hero's true identity with which a romance begins, and its eventual recouping with which it ends, are sometimes informed as a difference between sleeping and waking (53). Fučík's book, I would argue, unfolds along these very lines. The cinematic opening has an ambiance that can be seen, I argued earlier, as a variation on the theme of sleepwatching. In contrast to this, the theatrical ending—the scene in which we recognize the hero for what he truly is—suggests an alert state of mind. Technical terminology from the vocabulary of literary criticism (climaxes, crises, denouements) underscores a detached, almost a analytical attitude toward the "play" on the part of its author. But this revelation is not the true conclusion of Fučík's book. *Reportage*'s happy ending, the "Introduction" forewarns us, will be written not by the doomed Fučík but by the millions who remain. Like any other spectacle, Julius's comedy had only a limited duration. Through it he was able to fool the Nazis for a while, achieving his strategic objectives. Its finale, however, marks a relapse into the somnolent state characteristic, in the romantic universe, of an alienated existence: "The curtain falls. Applause. Spectators, go to sleep!" (91; 0).

But no romance true to its generic definition can end on such a note. A final wake-up call is necessary to establish lost harmony. So a special coda is appended which signals a return to the prelapsarian state of affairs preceding the sharp descent with which *Reportage* begins. The close of Fučík's play is portrayed not merely as the usual termination of a single spectacle but as something more radical—the transcendence of the very process of theatrical representation, the exit into the world of unpremeditated spontaneity, of a singular, undivided identity: "Well, my play too is coming to its end. But that I haven't written. That I don't know. It's no longer a play. It's life. And there are no spectators in life." It is the affectionate appeal to the millions who are to furnish Julius's book with its proper epilogue— never to succumb to sleep—that marks the ultimate awakening from the nightmare of *Reportage* and, hence, the end of this romance: "The curtain rises. People, I liked you. Watch!" (91; 112).

The romantic structure of *Reportage*, I have illustrated, clashes in places with the factographic claims of the book. But as I argued earlier, the correspondence between words and facts is always a matter of interpretation. And Fučík's writings, produced above all to exemplify an ideology committed to radical social change, deliberately strove to reflect the world not as it is but *as it should be*. The genre of romance, it seems, was ideally suited for this task. Its narrative, fueled by desire (whether erotic or revolutionary), is not about reality but about wish fulfillment. But what is truly amazing about this genre—"the structural core of all fiction" (15) according to Frye's assessment—is the enormous range of its application: from fairy tales, to both lowbrow and highbrow literary works, to some of the most holy myths of humankind. All these disparate types of texts, Frye argues convincingly, are formally very much the same. What distinguishes fabulous from infantile or sacred from trashy is the authority ascribed to particular romances by the collectivity for which they are written.

The unusual aspect of Julius's romance is the relatively wide variation in its social reception. Its timely publication just a few months after the end of the war made it a sought-after source of firsthand information about the German repressive mechanism which was hitherto well hidden from public view. The intriguing history of its origin together with the fate of its author accounted for the initial mass appeal of *Reportage*. Yet, from the way in which the editors handled the manuscript, it was obvious that they, from the very beginning, did not view this book either as just a piece of literature or as an authentic record of its author's exploits. By censoring the plot's resolution, they, on the one hand, ruined the intended aesthetic effect of the work and, on the other hand, imbued the story of its chief protagonist with an eerie suggestion of mystery. This decision, sanctioned by the highest Party officials, indicates that from early on *Reportage* may have been earmarked for a very special destiny: to become one of the founding myths of Czechoslovak Communism. This task, I might add, was facilitated by the very genre of *Reportage*, which easily accommodated such social utility. Moreover, given all the Christological parallels, one might even suspect that the author himself conceived of his own image along these very lines. The solemn tone of his speeches addressed to posterity has a decidedly otherworldly ring. But decisive for these efforts was the Communist takeover of 1948 which gave the Party spin doctors a virtually unlimited range of possibilities for rendering Julius's book a new form of Holy Writ. Aided in these efforts by their Soviet colleagues with more resources at their disposal, they spread the word around the globe.

But there is a cloud to every silver lining. Becoming one of the most important symbols of Communist ideology had its drawbacks, too. As such, the book could be judged solely on the basis of the beholder's political convictions, and Fučík-bashing provided a suitable rallying point for opponents of the regime. Given all the imponderables surrounding this text, as well as its sacrosanct status, *Reportage* clearly seemed to them a perfect target for settling their scores with the government. So, not surprisingly, whenever the Party's iron grip over society loosened somewhat, vexing questions about the Fučík case came to the fore. Prague Spring of 1968 was one such period. But the same holds for the very end of Czechoslovak Communism in 1989. On October 27 of that year—just three weeks prior to the Velvet Revolution's kick-off—the Party daily *Rudé právo* considered it necessary to publish a special article refuting the persistent rumor that Bolivia had offered to return the remains of the recently deceased Fučík to his homeland.[59] An omniscient vox populi had it that Julius, the Gestapo informer, had made it to South America after the war when a secret deal was struck with the leadership of the CPCS. He would be officially declared executed by the Germans if his name could be used to authorize the book concocted by the Party's propagandists for the sole purpose of glorifying the Communist anti-Nazi resistance.

59   Jiří Kohout, "Pravda o smrti Julia Fučíka," *Rudé právo*, October 27, 1989, p. 2.

With the popular imagination running wild, the long-awaited 1995 publication of the full edition of *Reportage*, with appropriate critical apparatus and copious commentaries, added the final twist to this already convoluted history. Yes, it introduced some previously unknown facts, solved certain textual riddles, and cast Fučík's image in a somewhat different light. But it affirmed, to the great astonishment of many, what Communist propaganda had been claiming for all those long years: that Julius Fučík was a hero!

My word . . . This script sounds all too familiar: a quest for identity with a happy ending, a fifty-year-long journey through a cloud of confusion to the ultimate recognition of the protagonist for what he truly is. Am I following Fučík's lead and emplotting his story as a romance? Rather than answer this question directly, let me return to the epigraph from Brecht's play with which I began this chapter. A second look at the dialogue reveals another difference between Andrea's and Galileo's respective positions. Whereas the former, it seems, comprehends heroism as a quasi-natural process of breeding, for the latter it is clearly a social phenomenon, a behavioral pattern corresponding to a specific social demand. So, which need did Fučík's text satisfy? In my introductory chapter to this book I pointed out that his *Reportage* managed to bring together almost seamlessly the Czech nationalist myth of sacrificing one's life to defend the motherland against the ever-present German menace with the Marxist-Leninist romance of the proletariat's ultimate ascent.[60] To legitimize the Party's claim for absolute political power, its propagandists insisted again and again that the CPCS had earned this privilege deservedly through its principled anti-Hitlerite stance. Where others had washed out, the Communists had measured up to their patriotic duty, fighting Nazi invaders not only from abroad but on the domestic front as well. Because of its track record, the Party, together with the USSR—the only ally socialist Czechoslovakia would ever need—represented an unmatchable barrier against any future German revanchism.

The truth about the Czech anti-Nazi underground of the period when Fučík joined it, however, was far less glorious, one academic historian informs us: "Whether waged by the Communists or by Beneš's followers . . . the actual extent of resistance activities remained insignificant." And a

---

[60] To achieve this seamless fit, however, the manuscript of *Reportage* had to be sanitized, purged of all passages that could be interpreted as pro-German. Eliminated was Fučík's memory of the May Day celebration in Berlin (32; 0) and his attempt to persuade Böhm that only Communism could save Germany's future (59; 0), not to mention his "shocking" revelation, bordering on treason, that he was prosecuted in the former Czechoslovakia because of his "defending too urgently the right of Sudeten Germans to self-determination" and "seeing too clearly the consequences of the Czech bourgeoisie's national policy for the Czech nation" (24; 0).

factual comparison further deflates any grandiloquent claims: "Even at the height of the terror in the fall of 1941, when the Gestapo was especially busy, the incidence of arrests for political offenses in major cities in the Protectorate did not exceed that in Germany itself."[61] Fučík's testimony, so rhapsodic in its tone and vivid in its depiction, was acutely needed by the Party to dispel any doubts some might justifiably have harbored about the seriousness and intensity of the Communist resistance. Well written and entirely persuasive, Fučík's *Reportage* was an effective ploy in the power game that unfolded in Czechoslovakia after the war, if only because none of the political competitors could boast of even a near-comparable document.

It was the Velvet Revolution in 1989 that provided the Fučík story with its curiously ironic closure, radically altering its generic label. A romance suddenly became a satire. By removing all injunctions with which the previous regime had surrounded its cherished myth, it stimulated extensive inquiry into the authenticity and veracity of *Reportage*, as well as the conduct of its author while in Gestapo captivity. With most of the facts revealed, the darkest suspicions about Julius appeared groundless, and his exemplary status, despite all the well-entrenched skepticism, might finally have been verified. Yet this was not to be, for very few really cared! With the Soviet Union gone, along with Communist dictatorships in its former satellite states, the social demand for Fučík's heroism diminished considerably. The new political elite wasted no time filling up the national pantheon with anti-Nazi martyrs of their own ideological bent, such as the Czech and Slovak commandos Beneš had dispatched to assassinate Reinhard Heydrich, who, after accomplishing their mission on May 27, 1942, perished some six weeks later in a shoot-out with Nazi pursuers. Too visible a symbol of the Stalinist era, too closely identified with the unpopular ideology of Marxism-Leninism, Fučík may have been a hero, but alas, one who was no longer needed. *Havel havelim*, saith the Preacher, the son of David, king in Jerusalem. Amen.

---

[61] Vojtěch Mastný, *The Czechs under Nazi Rule: The Failure of National Resistance, 1939–1942* (New York, 1971), p. 205. Internal German documents published after World War II indicate how little the Nazis were concerned about the activities of the Czech underground. See, e.g., the entry in Joseph Goebbels's private diary of February 15, 1942, summing up a lengthy conversation with Reinhard Heydrich about the situation in the Protectorate of Bohemia-Moravia: "Sentiment there is now much more favorable to us. Heydrich's measures are producing good results. It is true that the intelligentsia is still hostile to us. But we must rally the rank and file of the people to our side against them. The danger to German security from Czech elements in the Protectorate has been completely overcome." *The Goebbels Diaries: 1942–1943*, ed. and trans. L. P. Lochner (New York, 1948), p. 88. It was this "unseemly" lack of domestic resistance that, according to some sources, prompted Beneš to order the killing of Heydrich, carried out by Jozef Gabčík and Jan Kubiš, two Czechoslovak exiles who were parachuted into the Protectorate from England in late December 1941.

4

The Poetics of a Political Trial

Working People vs. Rudolf Slánský and His Fellow Conspirators

We are the party of the Czechoslovak proletariat and our highest revolutionary headquarters is indeed Moscow. And we go to Moscow to learn. You know what? We go to Moscow to learn from the Russian Bolsheviks how to wring your necks. (*Shouting*) And you know that the Russian Bolsheviks are masters in this! (*Noise. Shouting.*)

> —Klement Gottwald, "We Are Fighting and Are Going to Fight for a Proletarian State, for a State of Workers, for a State of Peasants: The First Parliamentary Speech of December 21, 1929"

The logic of Klement Gottwald's famous address seems, at first glance, quite clear. The new general secretary of the Communist Party of Czechoslovakia revealed publicly the two main pillars of his political program: homicidal hatred of the bourgeoisie and self-abnegating devotion to his Soviet comrades—the masters of revolutionary terror. But, cutting through the surface of this utterance, the avid reader of personal ads in the tabloids will glimpse a rhetoric that he or she knows well: the dual thrust of S/M which speaks in the same breath of torment and joy, of mastering and submitting. Within the duplex structure of such a desire, experts tell us, the pleasures of inflicting and/or receiving pain are inseparably interconnected—violence folding in upon itself. Does this explain why, after finishing with the bourgeoisie, the Czechoslovak Communists unleashed their pent-up orgasmic energy with equal zeal upon themselves, torturing and killing one another?

But is it fair to read into somebody else's words one's own peccadilloes? Let me, therefore, change my hermeneutic optics somewhat and tackle the text, instead, from a more detached, linguistic perspective.

Pronominal shifters constitute a notoriously slippery verbal category: as syncategoremata they are semantically empty, deriving meaning solely from the context of the speech situation. Once this changes, they often acquire curious and unexpected referents. And Gottwald's opposition between first- and second-person pronouns is a good example of this point. The "we," which presumably refers to the CPCS (whose head Gottwald became at its Fifth Congress in February that year), enabled him to gloss over the important fact that his party had just changed considerably. After protracted infighting, a Comintern-supported group headed by Gottwald (which also included Rudolf Slánský) gained the upper hand and transformed the CPCS into a branch of international Bolshevism fully dedicated to the revolutionary overthrow of capitalism according to the tried-and-true Soviet recipe. Those members not in favor of this ideological program left the Party either voluntarily or otherwise. That Gottwald's ideological stewardship diminished the CPCS's popular appeal is quite obvious if we compare the results of the 1925 and 1929 parliamentary elections. In the crass language of a petit bourgeois merchant, the antireformist, radical program registered a net loss of about 30 percent of the Communist seats in the National Assembly: a decline from forty-one seats to thirty.[1]

Within the context of this book it is important to note that Gottwald's "we" excluded, among others, a number of prominent intellectuals whose adherence to the proletarian cause had been quite apparent less than a year previously. Among them were seven leading Communist writers (including the future Nobel Prize winner Jaroslav Seifert) who in March 1929 had published an open letter to Communist workers warning them of the perils of the sectarianism then pervading the Party.[2] And, as if to prove them right, the signatories were promptly expelled from the CPCS. In explaining his position to the doyen of Czech criticism, F. X. Šalda, one of the seven who had impeccable revolutionary credentials, Ivan Olbracht, wrote:

> I do not criticize [the new leadership] because it wants to foment world revolution, to support the USSR's world policy, to permanently unsettle the capitalist economy, to disturb the rationalization of production, and to struggle against fascism and reformist illusions. [I criticize it] instead because it only knows how to regurgitate the theses read in last week's *Inprekor* [the Comintern's bulletin *Internationale Presse-Korrespondenz*] into dis-

---

[1]   Eva Broklová, *Československá demokracie: Politický systém ČSR 1918–1938* (Prague, 1992), p. 42.
[2]   "Komunističtí spisovatelé o rozvratu KSČ," *Právo lidu*, March 26, 1929, p. 1.

tasteful phrases; because it publishes an indigestible newspaper read by nobody; because it has lost all influence among the working masses; because
it deceives workers and the Comintern (the latter to obtain further moral
and financial support); because it is organizationally incapable even of preventing the police from knowing of its most secret directives before the factories do; because for maximal benefit of its own group it consciously
causes maximal harm to the workers; because it has destroyed a strong
mass-supported party and continues to do so. I would not follow such leadership to the nearest tram stop, not to mention in serious fights.[3]

Olbracht's scathing remarks about the usefulness of the reconstituted
Party for the proletarian cause poses an interesting problem vis-à-vis the
pronominal dichotomy informing Gottwald's broadside. On which side
of the barricade was Olbracht actually standing? Was he "we" or "you" ?
Although it is obvious that the general secretary's threat of bodily harm
was directed above all at exploiters of Czechoslovak workers and peasants—capitalists, bankers, and similar parasites—in the National Assembly it was addressed to some 270 non-Communist deputies (or whatever
the actual number in attendance). True, as lackeys of the bourgeoisie they
deserved to share the fate of their masters. Yet, in casting before the public his disparaging words about the Party's new leaders, did not Olbracht
de facto join the ranks of the enemy, and should not his neck have been
wrung as well? Is this a purely academic question? I wish it were.

"In February 1948," Milan Kundera immortalized the scene, "Communist leader Klement Gottwald stepped on the balcony of a Baroque palace
in Prague to address the hundreds of thousands of his fellow citizens
packed into Old Town Square. It was a crucial moment in Czech history—
a fateful moment of the kind that occurs only once or twice in a millen-
nium."[4] Gottwald had just arrived from Prague Castle, where, as the
country's prime minister, he had been bullying President Beneš into accepting the resignation of twelve non-Communist cabinet ministers who
had abdicated in protest of the flagrant contempt for the government's decisions demonstrated by the Communist minister of the interior. The
champion of the proletarian cause had prevailed in this confrontation
with the aged and ailing Beneš, and he came to Old Town Square to announce to his compatriots that he had obtained presidential permission to
fill the vacated seats with candidates of his choice. The victory of Com-

---

3   "Dopis Olbrachtův," *Šaldův zápisník*, no. 2 (1929–30), p. 191–92.
4   Milan Kundera, *Kniha smíchu a zapomnění* (Toronto, 1981), p. 9; *The Book of Laughter and Forgetting*, trans. M. Heim (New York, 1981), p. 3. Quotations are taken from Heim's translation. Further references will be given in the text; the first number in parentheses refers to
the Czech original and the second to the English translation.

munism in Czechoslovakia promised by Gottwald in 1929 was finally at hand and the wringing of necks could begin in earnest.

This time, however, Gottwald did not have to travel to Moscow to learn from the Bolsheviks how to seize the oppressors' necks; now he could be tutored at home. Thus, just twenty years after his first parliamentary appearance, Gottwald sent a cable (drafted by the number two man in the CPCS, Rudolf Slánský) to the highest revolutionary headquarters requesting that they dispatch somebody who could help him with his task. Just a month later, two of Lavrenty Beria's trusted men, Generals Likhachev and Makarov, arrived in Prague to lend an experienced hand. The mission of these advisers, whom the Czechoslovak security men aptly dubbed "our teachers,"[5] was succinctly described by Likhachev himself in a rebuff to an insubordinate Slovak colleague: "Stalin sent me here to organize trials and I cannot waste my time. I did not come to Czechoslovakia to argue but to wring necks [svorotit' golovy]. I prefer wringing 150 other necks to having my own wrung."[6]

Kundera, however, concealed from his readers an important fact: the baroque palace from whose balcony Gottwald delivered his epoch-making speech had at one time housed Hermann Kafka's store, and Franz himself had attended high school in that very edifice. It was the genius loci of the building that, without doubt, gave proletarian justice its Kafkaesque spin. As in an odd old novel, the line between guilt and innocence became less and less clear. Pronominal confusion descended upon Prague. Strange things were happening. Party cadres were arrested without having done anything wrong, some even turning overnight from meritorious comrades into "rats whose world is mud and stinking, putrefied cesspools."[7] Letters from outraged readers demanding, in the words of the poet Ivan Skála, "a dog's death for [such] dogs" bombarded newspapers.[8]

---

[5] See, e.g., chap. 4 of Eugen Loebel's Stalinism in Prague: The Loebel Story (New York, 1969), pp. 45–50, titled "Our 'Teachers.' "

[6] Vilém Hejl and Karel Kaplan, Zpráva o organizovaném násilí (Toronto, 1986), p. 63. Providence granted General Likhachev his wish. His neck remained intact. According to Pravda of December 24, 1954, he was sentenced to death with Abakumov and other associates of Beria and promptly shot. Fortuna was less kind to his successor in Prague, Colonel Boyarsky, who replaced Likhachev as chief Soviet security adviser in July 1950. After he was recalled from Czechoslovakia a year later, in part because of embezzlement and in part because of incorrect suspicions of his being Jewish, Boyarsky beat the legal rap. But then, au bout de son latin, he succumbed to the lure of an academic career in the fields of history and geology. Until 1989, when his sordid past surfaced, he was a senior researcher at the Soviet Academy of Sciences and a professor at the Moscow Mining Institute. For a detailed biography of this colorful figure, see Yevgenia Albats, The State within a State: The KGB and Its Hold on Russia—Past, Present, and Future, trans. C. Fitzpatrick (New York, 1994), pp. 120–67.

[7] St. Oborský, "Zrůda," Rudé právo, November 27, 1952, p. 7.

[8] Ivan Skála, "Tři lavice," ibid., November 28, 1952, p. 2.

Thanks to the relentless toil of the Soviet "teachers" (whose ranks quickly swelled to about fifty), a monstrous plot was soon discovered within the CPCS with tentacles reaching into the highest corridors of power. In his report to the Central Committee three years after that victorious February, Gottwald exposed a most perfidious scheme of the now vanquished capitalists. Two types of agents were employed by the bourgeoisie to subvert the labor movement: petty canaries who provided the police with bits of information gathered at party meetings and " 'grand'-style agents in policy-making positions of workers' parties, who were bought and controlled by the bourgeoisie and sometimes the police." Bohumil Jílek and Václav Bolen—two leaders of CPCS ousted in the 1929 shakeup—had been of the latter type, Gottwald insisted. But unfortunately they were definitely not the last. And it was precisely now, at the very moment of its demise, that the defeated bourgeoisie in a desperate all-or-nothing move had decided to pull from its sleeve "its last but highest card . . . the mobilization of its agents within the Communist Party."[9]

And what agents there were to be mobilized! According to Karel Kaplan's table of "political trials of leading communists," in the years 1950–54 seventy-three such persons were publicly tried and sentenced for nefarious activities.[10] Divided by the prosecution into small, manageable groups according to their professions or the charges against them, they included prominent members of the security and military establishments, the Party apparatus, and virtually every facet of Czechoslovak political and economic life. None of these trials, however, achieved more notoriety than that of fourteen members of the "anti-state conspiracy center headed by Rudolf Slánský," which took place in Prague from November 20 to November 27, 1952. An indictment charging high treason and related capital offenses brought together the following VIPs:

- Rudolf Slánský, former secretary general of the CPCS Central Committee (CC)
- Bedřich Geminder, former head of the International Section of the Secretariat of the CPCS CC
- Ludvík Frejka, former head of the Economic Department of the Chancellery of the President of the Republic
- Josef Frank, former deputy secretary general of the CPCS CC
- Vladimír Clementis, former minister of foreign affairs
- Bedřich Reicin, former deputy minister of national defense

---

[9] *Zpráva soudruha Klementa Gottwalda na zasedání Ústředního výboru Komunistické strany Československa dne 22. února 1951* (Prague, 1951), pp. 26, 25.
[10] Karel Kaplan, *Report on the Murder of the General Secretary*, trans. K. Kovanda (Columbus, 1990), pp. 289–91. Further references will be given in the text.

- Karel Šváb, former deputy minister of national security
- Artur London, former deputy minister of foreign affairs
- Vavro Hajdů, former deputy minister of foreign affairs
- Evžen Löbl, former deputy minister of foreign trade
- Rudolf Margolius, former deputy minister of foreign trade
- Otto Fischl, former deputy minister of finance
- Otto Šling, former secretary of the CPCS Regional Committee in Brno
- André Simone, former member of the editorial staff of *Rudé právo*[11]

After confessing at a public trial to all crimes, the felons got what they deserved. With the exception of three who merely received life sentences (London, Hajdů, and Löbl), they were condemned to death and hanged on December 3, 1952. Their bodies were cremated and the ashes, according to some accounts, scattered over an icy field near Prague.[12]

The same day that the sentences were meted out, the CPCS daily *Rudé právo* (its title means something like "Red Justice") carried a column titled "The End of a Traitor" by the now National Artist Ivan Olbracht. Reminiscing about his youth, as septuagenarians often do, he wrote: "All of us had worked with Slánský for long decades; we older comrades had worked with him since his boyhood. And yet, since the 1920s Slánský had been an informer of the Prague police! And none of us knew or recognized it."[13] But surely Olbracht had had a hunch about it in 1929, when he complained to Šalda that under Gottwald's leadership (Slánský was an important member of his team) Party secrets were routinely leaked to the police. How could he forget that letter? Was it senility or a strategic oversight intended to save his own neck? For Olbracht was well aware that his old tergiversation could easily come up at the next political trial, about which, as a defendant, he would not be writing for *Rudé právo*. Fortunately for him, he passed on just three weeks after Slánský to that "eternal CC high up in the skies" where no questions need be answered any longer. And so they sit there, forever, the two old revolutionaries, side by side in their rockers, savoring expertly chilled vodka, better even than what they used to get at the buffet at the Hotel Lux in Moscow, rocking

[11] *Proces s vedením protistátního spikleneckého centra v čele s Rudolfem Slánským* (Prague, 1953), pp. 7–8; *Trial of the Leadership of the Anti-state Conspiracy Center Headed by Rudolf Slánský* (Prague, 1953), pp. 7–8. Quotations are taken, with some alterations, from this translation. Further references will be given in the text; the first number in parentheses refers to the Czech original and the second to the English translation.

[12] See, e.g., Karel Kaplan, "Poslední dopisy," *150 000 slov: Texty odjinud*, no. 25 (1990), 145. All last letters from prisoners are from this source; page numbers are given parenthetically in the text.

[13] Ivan Olbracht, "Konec zrádcův," *Rudé právo*, November 28, 1952, p. 2.

slowly to the rhythm of Winston Smith's sweet tune which blissfully suspends all pronominal dichotomies:

> Under the spreading chestnut tree
> I sold you and you sold me:
> There lie they and here lie we
> Under the spreading chestnut tree.

But there is yet another reason why the line between friends and foes of Communism remained somewhat fuzzy, a reason connected, I believe, to the explicitly stated purpose of Gottwald's pilgrimages to Moscow—"to learn from the Bolsheviks." At a quick glance, it may seem strange to cast revolutionary praxis in terms of pedagogy—but only at a quick glance. Harking back to Hegel, the *Urquell* of Marxian dialectics, we realize that it was that great *Denker* who first conceived of the historical process as the interplay of knowledge and the lack thereof. The trajectory of evolution, he insisted again and again, is the Absolute Spirit's journey toward self-comprehension—its tortuous passage from unconscious to conscious (if this sounds like German idealist philosophy, it should). Yet, was it not Marx who energetically assailed the Hegelian idea of "history marching on its head" and instead located the engine of progress in the sphere of material production, in uninspired economic bases? In his parliamentary speech Gottwald (and this is no laughing matter) may have been intellectually too close to Hegel's idealist mode of thinking, so unbecoming to a true historical materialist. But if so, he was not the only one guilty of such a *lapsus*.

It was Lenin, one should not forget, whose conception of a revolutionary party effectively turned Marx on his head. *What Is to Be Done?* (it is no accident that Lenin borrowed his title from a nineteenth-century Russian novel) performed this carnivalesque stunt with remarkable dexterity. Written in 1902, just before the Russian Social-Democratic Party split into Bolshevik and Menshevik factions, the pamphlet is an essential manual for rabble-rousing. It is not objective economic antagonisms that hinder the development of the means of production but, above all, the proletariat's awareness of its historical devoir which is the necessary precondition of revolution, Lenin argued. The working masses, he recognized clearly, couldn't care less about the Marxist philosophy of history, despite the fact that they were the stars of its scenario. It was only the radical intelligentsia (people like Lenin himself) who took Marx's script seriously, though, paradoxically, because of their bourgeois origins they have been cast as the villains of his show. But Lenin found a better role for them. Like a Socratic midwife or a Freudian analyst, the intellectuals were to render conscious what proletarians felt spontaneously: by matching their immediate, unreflected social experience to Marx's master story about the history of humankind, the *penseurs* were to convert the workers from passive objects to active subjects of the historical process, from a class *an sich* to a class *für sich* or, put differently, from exploited wage laborers to future owners of it all. Without this mental revolution, and this is the gist of Lenin's message, there can be no social revolution.

Teacher-pupil relations, however, are much less harmonious than this picture might suggest. Stormy undercurrents of rivalry and resentment lurk behind the enlightened façade of those associations. As every educator knows only too well, it is precisely the best disciples who pose the greatest threat to one's authority and, obversely, an authoritarian teacher who stunts most effectively the academic growth of his or her students. In the Leninist scheme of revolutionary edification, though, the instructor is on the bottom. The knowledge, which the intelligentsia has to offer to the workers, is in and of itself somewhat cerebral, effete; and the exploited masses are cognizant of it anyway, though merely empirically, in a visceral, unreflected manner. Furthermore, as if by an invisible umbilical cord, these pedagogues are forever connected to the capitalist class and therefore incapable of fully engendering genuine proletarian consciousness. In other words, through learning the workers will become intelligentsia-like but not vice versa. Thus, lacking an innate proletarian instinct, brainy revolutionaries will forever be consumed by an inferiority complex, by fears of fallibility and inadequacy; and these traumata will only be reinforced by the suspicions with which the *true* workers will treat them. (It is not out of place to mention here that the very first political show trial in the USSR, and the model for all to follow, was the 1928 Shakhty case against veteran engineers accused of "wrecking" and sabotage).[14]

Such mental duress, one might safely assume, could not have been entirely alien to Lenin—a petit bourgeois intellectual himself. But he knew how to handle his phobia. The masses need a master, he had declared, more assertive than a bunch of self-effacing wimps. This was a task for professionals, for the managers of revolution. And within an organization or a political party made up of such professional revolutionaries, "*all distinctions as between workers and intellectuals*" (Lenin italicized his thought)

[14] See, e.g., Robert Conquest, *The Great Terror: Stalin's Purge of the Thirties* (New York, 1973), pp. 730–33. According to an assessment of Karol Bacílek, then the minister of national security, it was "as if the trial of Slánský and his gang brought together not only the Soviet experience from the period of the Shakhty trial but also from the trial against the Trotskyite gang of 1937" (*Poučenie z procesu s vedením protištátneho špionážneho a sprisahaneckého centra na čele s Rudolfom Slánským* [Bratislava, 1953], p. 18).

"[would have to] be effaced."[15] Perhaps. But the hierarchical structure of such a corporate body would inevitably impose a new type of knowledge deficiency on its constituency. There would be those who, because of their elevated positions, would have greater access to information than their comrades lower down. As if to exacerbate this problem further, Lenin had postulated that his revolutionary party would have to be conspiratorial, with all its secret functions centralized in the hands of a few. And though he had maintained that the discreteness did not at all imply that "a dozen wise men" would "do the thinking for all" (122), it is difficult to see how it could be otherwise.

The organizational measures that Lenin had proposed, so a counterargument might go, were necessary because of the oppressive political climate of czarist Russia. But after a successful proletarian revolution, all the hierarchies would be abolished, together with conspiratorial secrecy. But even Lenin had not subscribed to such an idyllic utopia. As he argued forcefully in his 1917 *State and Revolution*, the violent overthrow of capitalism would not result automatically in a classless society. On the contrary, to defend the benefits of revolution a new repressive mechanism would have to be established to replace the old state: the dictatorship of the proletariat. And under these conditions the Party would retain its traditional pedagogical mission "of being the teacher, guide, and leader of all the toiling and exploited in the task of building up their social life without the bourgeoisie and against the bourgeoisie."[16] Only later, much later, after people finally learned how to live without exploiting one another, would the state eventually wither away, ushering in the unsurpassable beatitude of Communism.

In the previous chapter I discussed the Marxist-Leninist philosophy of history in terms of romance: the proletariat's quest for identity culminating in its revolutionary ascent. But, as my present account suggests, political praxis has somewhat derailed this generic scheme. The Communist romance turned, in fact, into a never-ending story incapable of reaching the narrative resolution mandated by the genre. A happy ending is merely implied but never fully achieved. Let me explain what I mean by juxtaposing the consciousness-raising of the Russian proletariat to the myth that is supposed to be its mirror image: Adam and Eve's fall from grace. In the Old Testament it is tasting the fruit of knowledge that jettisons the couple into a class-divided world; in the class-divided world, by contrast, it is knowledge that is to propel the workers back into a classless

---

[15]   V. I. Lenin, *What Is to Be Done: Burning Questions of Our Movement*, trans. G. Hanna et al. (New York, 1969), p. 109.
[16]   V. I. Lenin, *State and Revolution* (New York, 1969), p. 24.

Eden. Yet their desire to know is never satiated. With the "forbidden fruit" dangling in front of them but effectively kept out of their reach by teachers, they will remain bound to a postlapsarian earth. The October Revolution was not a response of enlightened masses to the call of history but a successful strategic ploy by Party leadership. And afterwards, lo and behold, the state did not wither away at all. On the contrary, it grew stronger and stronger and stronger.

The centralization of power in the hands of the Party bureaucracy further deepened the gap between the knowledgeable and the ignorant. While the Party remained the leader to the masses, its rank and file began to require guidance of their own. Thus, like a set of Matryëshka dolls, the CC had become the guide to the Party, the Presidium the guide to the CC, and ultimately the general secretary—the omniscient Stalin—the bellwether of the entire flock. It was ultimately only he who could distinguish at every particular moment error from truth, rightist or leftist deviations from the Party line proper. Neither the ignorance of others nor their most secret thoughts would escape Comrade Stalin's gnostic gaze: a strong security apparatus made sure of it. And to justify the increase in the scope and power of this apparatus, Stalin amended Lenin's thoughts about the dictatorship of the proletariat with one important insight. After the revolution, he opined, class struggle would sharpen rather than abate. This was inevitable because the routed bourgeoisie would resort to any means at hand to stymie its ultimate end. Needless to say, class struggle did not cease to intensify until the Leader's untimely death in March 1953.

"The destruction of the most powerful bulwark," Lenin had predicted in his 1902 brochure, "not only of European, but (it may be said now) of Asiatic reaction, would make the Russian proletariat the vanguard of the international revolutionary proletariat" (29). As always, he was right, which explains Gottwald's visits to Moscow. And Gottwald was a quick learner, too. His 1951 remark about "grand"-style agents within the CPCS is a creative application to the Czechoslovak situation of Stalin's "hypothesis" about postrevolutionary class struggle. This instance of Gottwald's intellectual borrowing, however, should not mislead us about the other dimension of his attitude toward Stalin: like any other student, he too resented his junior status. In his memoirs Evžen Löbl mentions an episode that he witnessed in 1949 after his successful completion of trade negotiations in the United States and his return home. From the Prague airport (located very close to the Ruzyně prison where he eventually joined the rest of the Slánský gang), he was whisked by presidential limo to Prague Castle to be decorated by Gottwald himself (Beneš's successor since June 1948) with the highest Party order—the Golden Star of the February Victory. But, to his surprise, he was recalled to the president's office only two hours later to meet Bedřich Geminder, who had also returned that day from a state trip abroad. He had come from Moscow with disconcerting news: the Soviet comrades had serious reservations about Löbl's mission to the West and had warned Gottwald that the friendly face of Yankee imperialism was a mere ruse intended to divide and conquer the Socialist bloc. Gottwald's reaction to this message illustrates well the ambiguity that every disciple feels toward his ideal: "Stalin, that son of a bitch . . . who does he think he is, that he can treat me like his messenger boy? I am a worker—and who is he? He studied theology. *Theology*. I devoted my whole life to the workers' movement and to the Soviet Union. I am the first worker-president of Czechoslovakia. I will do what is best for the working class. I was the one who made up the slogan 'With the Soviet Union forever.' *With* the Soviet Union. The *two* of us. Czechoslovakia *and* the Soviet Union, partners. Together."[17]

Gottwald was speaking his mind because, Löbl tells us, he was thoroughly inebriated. Were he sober, he probably would have been more circumspect. His extensive experience with the Soviet lifestyle (he had spent World War II in Moscow in the Comintern Hotel Lux) must have taught him that nothing could be hidden from Comrade Stalin. This, perhaps, explains his strong reluctance to visit Russia after his Crimean sojourn of September 1948. He dared return only four years later as head of the CPCS delegation to the Seventeenth Congress of the Soviet Party (CPSU). Since this event took place just a month before the Slánský trial, he probably was reasonably confident that, by throwing his closest collaborator to the proverbial wolves on Stalin's orders, he had demonstrated beyond any reasonable doubt his absolute devotion to his teacher. And yet, according to Kaplan, Gottwald went to Moscow with another agenda in mind: he had discovered a hidden listening device in his living quarters and hoped to buttonhole Stalin about this matter. To his chagrin, Stalin did not grant him a private audience (222). But could you blame him for this? Would you invite to your house a guy who calls you an S.O.B. behind your back—and in front of a dirty "Zionist"?

If Gottwald secretly aspired to become teacher-like (for partnership implies equality), Stalin definitely wanted him to stay pupil-like. After all, the horse of Hegelian dialectics cannot carry more than one Absolute Spirit; and there were many who wanted to get into the saddle. Stalin's archrival, the scurrilous Trotsky, was finally eliminated in his Mexico exile, but another "spittle-licker of capitalism" rose prominently on the horizon. In the middle of the 1948 summer session Marshal Broz-Tito unexpectedly declared his graduation from the "Revolutionary Headquar-

---

17 Eugen Loebl, *My Mind on Trial* (New York, 1976), pp. 22–23.

ters High" and defiantly set up his own shop in Belgrade. If other disciples were to imitate him, the teacher-student ratio in Stalin's classes would drop precariously and put his job in jeopardy. (Such are the perils of an untenured position!) To avoid the humiliation of unemployment, Stalin had to discipline potential dropouts. And those who refused to listen to their master's voice (or were even just suspected of a hearing impairment) had to have their necks wrung—which, in a topsy-turvy manner, brings me back to the epigraph with which I started this chapter.

The application of revolutionary terror and the acquisition of this skill through learning conjoined in Gottwald's speech have more in common than meets the eye. Class societies, like classrooms, are hierarchical formations, social spaces where struggles for domination and subordination unfold. The Communist academy replicates the hegemonic organization of the outside world for the sole purpose of overthrowing it. There, students were supposed to learn to give capitalists cement galoshes so that the proletarians might slip into their Gucci loafers. But at the very moment when class justice triumphs the classroom hierarchy is imprinted upon the world: with the loss of a competitor, equally ferocious strife between masters and disciples replaces that which has just ended. If before the revolution a bourgeois could join the forces of progress as an educator of the masses, after the revolution—and here lies the crux of the matter—that dedicated Party member would find himself or herself in the enemy camp as soon as he or she seemed even a potential threat (whether real or merely perceived) to the newly established pecking order. And then nothing could save his or her neck. The anthropological principle of what René Girard calls "mimetic violence" fuels, it seems, the Marxist-Leninist project of social engineering.[18]

It is the human ability to imitate that, according to Girard, is the essential precondition for society and culture to exist. Yet, although Western thought since Plato has explored the topic of mimesis from different angles, one of its dimensions has been curiously neglected. The process of reproduction has been studied primarily on the semantic plane (model-replica correspondence), to the omission of its pragmatic level: what Girard calls "acquisitive mimesis." Our desire to possess a specific object, he holds, is motivated not solely by its capacity to satisfy our individual needs but rather by the fact that another desires the same object, and we simply emulate his or her behavior. Such "mimetic rivalry" is, naturally,

[18]   My presentation of René Girard's ideas which follows is distilled primarily from two of his texts: *Things Hidden since the Foundation of the World*, trans. S. Bann et al. (Stanford, 1987); and "Generative Scapegoating," in *Violent Origins*, ed. R. G. Hamerton-Kelly (Stanford, 1987), pp. 73–105.

highly divisive, and every society attempts to control it directly or indirectly. Taboos and prohibitions are the most obvious mechanisms of direct control. Rituals are oblique or mimetic strategies for managing competitive crises: resolution is achieved by reenacting them symbolically, without actual violence. Another symbolic possibility for conflict management is sacrifice: a surrogate victim is selected and ritually murdered in order to reconcile feuding parties. "Scapegoating" is the term generally invoked to designate this collective transference of guilt to an innocent member (or members) of a collectivity. Scapegoating, Girard suggests, is as old as humankind itself. All societies have violent beginnings; they all arose from processes of victimization, as can be gleaned from various originary myths across cultural boundaries. Mimetic rivalry is the initial impulse that pits everybody against everybody else in a chaotic strife that threatens the existence of all involved. At this critical moment centripetal forces might prevail: "acquisitive mimesis" might become "conflictual." That is to say, instead of one object of mutual desire dividing fellow beings into competitors, one common foe may unite them as allies. An appointed foe/victim—a mimetic substitute for all other victims—is punished collectively, this violent act in its unanimity yielding the glue necessary for social cohesion.

Successful scapegoating, Girard argues, must meet a number of conditions. One of them is the appropriate selection of victims. Preferably strangers to the community that will eventually persecute them, they might bear a special mark which sets them apart. Their evil character, however, should not be immediately obvious. Only scrutiny will reveal a criminal nature causing harm to the community (the syndrome of the "evil eye" —the casting of a spell or indiscreet watching—is the most frequent offense). Needless to say, the actual choice of scapegoat is arbitrary, and any link to the felony ascribed to him or her purely imaginary. But, according to Girard, these are necessary procedures because scapegoating is not a conscious activity in the sense that its participants are aware of its functioning. Victimizers not only perceive their sacrifice as guilty, but also see themselves as victims of an omnipotent villain whose nefarious activities are truly dangerous to them. And since any evidence will always be only tangential when juxtaposed to a direct confession, an ideal scapegoat will freely admit all his or her misdeeds. In the best of all of possible scenarios, the guilt is objective and the offender ignorant of his or her crime (like Oedipus of his incest). Neither may the miscreant be blamed for intending evil, nor may the community be blamed for punishing his or her acts in the only way conceivable.

The effacement of the surrogate victim (fire, according to Girard, is the preferred instrument), witnessed by the community or carried out by a contamination-proof sacrifice specialist, brings the scapegoating cycle almost to its end. The caveat "almost" is necessary, however, because the remnants of the offering (as the last trace of a collective crime) still have mythical relevance. They must be concealed; a tomb is erected specifically for hiding the remains of human sacrifice. Yet, as we have seen, scapegoating is a Janus-like pursuit with two faces looking in opposite directions, one aggressive (killing a human being) and one conciliatory (stopping random violence). If the latter prevails, the deceased victim is rehabilitated as the group's hero and the tomb becomes a place of worship. If, however, malevolence carries the day, the tomb is either destroyed or not built at all, and the remains are hidden in a curious double concealment of the original murder.

This general outline of scapegoating is, obviously, very sketchy, and each instance of surrogate victimization adds to this skeleton its own flesh and blood. But there are some historical commonalities in this "generative" process which Girard points out. Relevant for my discussion is his remark that the more recent the event of scapegoating, the more difficult it is to maintain the necessary delusion of the guilt of the victims and the nature of their crimes. In the Slánský case, the entire state propaganda machine and its agents abroad were mobilized to vilify the accused.[19] But it was precisely the intensity of this campaign and of the language used which rendered virtually impossible the subsequent positive transfiguration of Slánský and his cohorts. The murder was concealed for many years, and the final rehabilitation of the victims did not make heroes of them. Rather, they were used as pawns in the 1968 intra-Party fight between reformist and conservative Communists (the latter deeply implicated in the crime and its later cover-up).

To unravel all the threads spun into the rope with which Slánský and his confederates were hanged is a difficult if not an impossible task. Social forces and purely personal ambitions, naive zeal and a cunning scheming

[19]   The magnitude of this campaign can be gleaned from the sheer quantity of printed copies of Gottwald's speech (mentioned in note 9) made available. According to Václav Brabec, about 4.5 million copies were put into circulation, a respectable number for a country of 14 million. See "Vztah KSČ a veřejnosti k politickým procesům na počátku padesátých let," *Revue dějin socialismu*, no. 9 (1969), 372; "The Relationship of the CPCS and the Public to the Political Trials of the Early Fifties," *Radio Free Europe Czechoslovak Press Survey*, no. 2275 (244), November 25, 1969, p. 14. Quotations are taken, with some alterations, from this translation. Further references will be given in the text; the first number in parentheses refers to the Czech original and the second to the English translation. For the extension of this propaganda war to the shores of the New World, see, e.g., Louis Harap's pamphlet *The Truth about the Prague Trial* (New York, 1953), which purports to show that "the convicted members of the Slánský group, when confronted with evidence, documents and witnesses, confessed to involvement under the auspices of the United States intelligence in a conspiracy to damage and ultimately to overturn the Czechoslovak people's democracy" (p. 30).

intertwine in it to such an extent that they cannot be completely separated. But the main strands from which this strange text(ile) was woven can be identified. In his 1946 synaxary *On the Great Work and Life of Comrade Gottwald*, Slánský had devoted special attention to the speech delivered by his hero in October of that year. In it, according to the hagiographer, Gottwald "demonstrated that the means by which the Soviet Union reached Socialism are not the only ones possible. There is another road toward socialism which does not lead through the dictatorship of the proletariat and the Soviet political system."[20] Without ever using the phrase "read my lips," the chairman of the CPCS apparently spoke of a "kinder and gentler," Czechoslovakia-specific way to a classless society, quite different from that taken by the Big Brother to the East.

And, if we trust Löbl's story, he might even have meant it. From a purely pragmatic perspective, this would make perfect sense: as a developed country with an industrial plant virtually untouched by World War II, Czechoslovakia could have been the prime benefactor of the postwar economic boom which enriched the West Europeans. But then, all the benefits of schoolbusing Gottwald to Moscow would have been wasted, so Stalin had to say *nyet*. And, "wise pupil of Stalin" (521; 588), according to the felicitous locution of Jaroslav Urválek, chief prosecutor at the conspiracy trial, Gottwald knew better than to contradict his teacher. It later became crystal clear that the idea of attaining Socialism in Czechoslovakia through different means than the USSR was a red herring; Slánský had put it into Gottwald's mouth just to misrepresent him. Crushed by the preponderance of evidence, he admitted as much in his last plea to the court: "I hid behind Titoist parlance about the special road to socialism but was preparing a fascist dictatorship. I used dirty Trotskyite methods, the methods of duplicity, deception and cheating, intrigues" (541; 607). But I am perhaps getting ahead of myself.

The first Czechoslovak attempt to slip out of the Russian bear's hug dates to 1947, when the government agreed to participate in the U.S.-sponsored Marshall Plan, which was intended to stimulate war-ravaged European economies. Perceptibly irked by this "breach of trust," the Soviets nixed the project and the embarrassed Czechoslovak government hastily pulled out of it. But even after the Communist takeover, economic ties with the West were maintained to a considerable degree. The list of charges against the economic experts belonging to the "Conspiracy Center" (Fischl, Frejka, Löbl, and Margolius) illustrates their entrepreneurship in seeking lucrative hard currency markets for domestic goods. Thus, "even for the last year of the Five-Year Plan, i.e. 1953," Frejka told the

---

[20]   Rudolf Slánský, *O velikém životě a díle soudruha Gottwalda* (Prague, 1946), p. 26.

prosecutor, "we agreed that . . . the Western share of Czechoslovak foreign trade would be almost 60% of the total" (248; 276). Not only did the Soviets want a much larger quota of Czechoslovakia's industrial output but, more important, they also demanded the wholesale reorientation of its production from consumer goods to coal and steel. This decision was motivated above all by Stalin's strategies: the enormous numerical superiority of the Soviet forces on the Continent offered him a window of opportunity to dispatch the Red Army to the rest of Europe, thereby annexing it to the Communist bloc. In early 1951 Slánský and Čepička (as minister of defense) attended a supersecret meeting in Moscow, chaired by the Generalissimo himself, which was the initial coordination of this military operation between the USSR and its satellites.[21] Based on the experience of World War II, Soviet military planners believed that a massive deployment of tanks on the battlefield was the key to victory. Czechoslovak heavy industry was to become one of the major suppliers of armor for the future war, and it was beefed up accordingly.

The restructuring of foreign trade and industrial production initiated by the Communist government caused enormous dislocations in the Czechoslovak economy and brought considerable hardship to the population. After a period of relative improvement in general prosperity, we read in a report by Václav Brabec that the end of 1950 marked a dramatic drop in the standard of living. The cost of cereals and baked goods increased, to be followed in February 1951 by a second round of increases, combined with the rationing of basic food items. Consumer taxes were raised in July, making not only food but also industrial products more expensive; potatoes were rationed in October, and Christmas bonuses were abolished for most workers at the same time (378; 22). And, though in his report to the CPCS Central Committee of February 1951 (from which I quoted earlier), Klement Gottwald, armed with exact statistical data, proved beyond any reasonable doubt that the average citizen was living better then than under the yoke of the capitalists, some less class-conscious malcontents remained unconvinced.

The exposure of saboteurs and wreckers in the highest Party and governmental offices provided tangible evidence that the partial economic setbacks did not originate in the Socialist system per se but came from outside—the roguery of bourgeois hirelings. The Slánský gang was charged with (among other things) misdeeds that seriously jeopardized

---

[21]   About the Moscow meeting, see Karel Kaplan, *Mocní a bezmocní* (Toronto, 1989), pp. 201–4, who interviewed Čepička twice in 1968. For more speculative treatments of the connections between Stalin's war plans and the Slánský trial, see, e.g., Josef Belda's review of the Czech edition of Arthur London's *On Trial*, in *Revue dějin socialismu*, no. 9 (1969), 768; and Karel Bartošek, "Politické procesy v Československu 1948–1954: K analýze jedné či více mytologií," *150 000 slov: Texty odjinud*, no. 10 (1985), 44–45.

the welfare of the country: willfully distorting, as planners, the growth of vital industry and mismanaging investment; illegally compensating foreign capitalists for property that had been nationalized in 1948; ruining foreign trade by charging artificially low prices for exports to the West and the opposite for those going East; and, last but not least, leaking secret economic information to hostile intelligence services. Was it not, Party propagandists never tired of repeating, proof of the great viability of Socialism that despite all of this havoc the Czechoslovak economy continued to grow? As Urválek energetically put it: "The conspirators caused our homeland enormous losses worth billions. And yet we are victoriously fulfilling the Five-Year Plan and constructing a new, beautiful life for ourselves and future generations of this land. Against a handful of conspirators stands the unshakable effort of the masses. . . . A great boulder has been removed from our path—a path toward the further peaceful building of our beautiful homeland" (524; 589). Some people simply have a way with words!

While the scapegoating of the "conspirators" for economic crimes was carried out with great publicity, their punishment included yet another agenda that was only hinted at. The presence of Karel Šváb among the defendants would seem at first glance a strange anomaly, given his Aryan and proletarian background. But, like everything else in this trial, it was not accidental: he was included as a representative of the security sector. A personification of the symbiosis between Party and state security, Šváb was an excellent choice. A specialist in detecting enemies within the Party ranks, he was eventually appointed to the Ministry of State Security (established according to the Soviet model in 1950) to supervise its political correctness. The major charge against Šváb and his immediate boss Slánský (who from 1949 was shadow Minister of the Interior to Václav Nosek, considered unreliable by his comrades for having spent the war years in London) was that they had covered up the crimes of the group, thus preventing its timely exposure. But, occasionally, another felony—the persecution of innocent people—came to the fore. When asked by Urválek whether Slánský had instructed him how to conduct the security business, Šváb volunteered the following: "He advised me to read and learn from the book of the former French prefect Foucher [sic]. . . . In his book Foucher—as 'an expert'—depicts an endless series of devious scheming, plotting, planting of agents provocateurs, staging of trials to compromise and remove uncomfortable people, the latter even by murder. . . . It was clear that Slánský was suggesting that I do the same" (442; 495).[22] Was

---

[22]   The misspelling of Joseph Fouché's name gives rise to a curious pun. The Czech *fušer* (derived from the German der *Pfuscher*) signifies a sloppy craftsman performing his job outside regular hours primarily for fast money.

this—an allusion to staged trials within a staged trial—a case of what Russian formalists used to call "laying bare devices"? Most likely not. But within the charged atmosphere of the early 1950s, this revelation had a special ring. It signaled to the victims of the terror who considered themselves blameless (and who would not?) that perhaps their suffering was inflicted not by the CPCS as such but by evil Slánskýites, and that now (since the culprits had been apprehended) justice would take its course.

It did, but in a completely unanticipated way. Stalin and Gottwald outlived the conspirators by only three months. And with their departure the shiny façade of Communist jurisprudence began to crack. Beria was condemned for suspending the rule of law (if only in a few instances) and he was shot, together with some of his most notorious henchmen. By 1956 it was clear that any further cover-up of what had transpired was untenable; Nikita Khrushchev's secret speech at the Twentieth Congress of the CPSU revealed to the delegates the tip of the iceberg of the atrocities committed by their Party (or, more precisely, by Stalin, who became a convenient scapegoat for all legal grievances).

The situation in Prague, however, was more convoluted. The leaders of the Party who succeeded Gottwald, also as presidents of the Republic (Antonín Zápotocký from 1953 to 1957, and Antonín Novotný until 1968), were actively involved in the prosecution of their comrades and, thus, quite reluctant to have the past opened to independent inspection. But since a critical revision of recent history was taking place throughout the Communist bloc (the show trials in various countries were to some degree interconnected), they had to act somehow.[23] Party-appointed commissions (there were about four of them) gradually chipped away most of the crimes with which the "conspirators" had been originally charged. Thus, in a curious twist, the abuse of Socialist justice eventually became an indictment preventing their full rehabilitation. Slánský was declared the Czechoslovak Beria—an evil genius who had for personal gain perverted due process to become, paradoxically, a victim of his own scheming. Even in 1963, when a new report critical of the trial was debated at a Central Committee meeting, Novotný, we are told, recycled the Fouché story as proof of Slánský's perfidy and the ultimate justification for his hanging.[24] Meta-scapegoating is perhaps the most fitting label for the double bum rap that Slánský got from his comrades.

But there is yet another scapegoating function—very specific to the Communist movement—which the Slánský trial fulfilled. When the edi-

---

[23]   The linkage among the trials of all the leading Communist leaders in the satellite states is well documented in George H. Hodos's study *Show Trials: Stalinist Purges in Eastern Europe, 1948–1954* (New York, 1987).

[24]   Jiří Pelikán, ed., *The Czechoslovak Political Trials, 1950–1954: The Suppressed Report of the Dubček Government's Commission of Inquiry* (Stanford, 1971), p. 234.

tor in chief of *Rudé právo*, Josef Guttmann, was expelled from the Party in 1933, F. X. Šalda commented sarcastically: "That a revolution, like Saturn, devours its own sons has been known to observers for a long time. . . . If things continue this way we will soon experience the very elevated spectacle of the last Czechoslovak Communist facing a mirror—so that there are two of him—and purging himself from the Party as a Babbitt, a petit bourgeois, and a skunk."[25] This syndrome of self-hatred can perhaps best be subsumed under the Girardian category of "evil twin." By recognizing in another member of the movement his or her own likeness, a radical revolutionary might easily ascribe to this comrade all his or her feelings of inadequacy and doubt stemming, as I argued earlier, from the nonproletarian background characteristic of the majority of prominent Communists, however deep their bourgeois upbringing might have been buried.[26] Through such negative identification, self-loathing is transferred to the appointed double, who turns from an ally into an "evil twin" —a dangerous enemy who must be destroyed at any cost. To remain effective, however, these hidden underpinnings of scapegoating should not be revealed. Animus must be projected onto an ideological plane, the pathology of this process described in terms of vitality, the victimizer's weakness presented as might. This is especially important if the victimization is as visible as the Slánský trial was. "What we should feel after the exposure of Slánský's treason," the garrulous president of the Czechoslovak Academy, Zdeněk Nejedlý, instructed the bewildered listeners of his regular radio broadcasts devoted to the case, "is admiration for how strong and undamaged the Party remained in this affair. The capitalist world tackled the Party with all the evil of which it is capable or could even think of. And it used all its tricks. But it failed; it lost this game and the Party triumphed."[27]

A prudent selection of surrogate victims, as I wrote earlier, is an essential precondition to felicitous scapegoating. In this respect the organizers of the Slánský trial fared relatively well, despite several obstacles in their way. First of all, some of the chosen victims, refused to play the role of confessed criminals, despite the considerable physical and mental pressure exerted by dedicated security personnel. They selfishly saved their

[25] *Šaldův zápisník*, no. 6 (1933–34), 172.

[26] The ego split of a Communist intellectual was brilliantly expressed in the concluding distich of S. K. Neumann's 1923 poem "About the Battlefield within Ourselves" : "let the heart moan and the brain burst/let us smash him within ourselves, let us smash him—the bourgeois." You win some, you lose some, one might comment on this internal struggle, for in 1929 Neumann joined six other writers protesting against Gottwald's new leadership and was expelled from the CPCS. But he eventually succeeded in purging himself of his despised alter ego to become the model poet of Czechoslovak Socialist Realism.

[27] Zdeněk Nejedlý, *K procesu s protistátním spikleneckým centrem: Čtyři projevy v Československém rozhlase* (Prague, 1953), p. 21. Further references will be given in the text.

own necks but did not make it to the big show. The second problem was the frequent shift in casting, owing to political considerations. In early 1950 the producers wanted Vladimír Clementis in the lead role. But by the end of that year Otto Šling had become the star designate. To secure a good group of actors for supporting roles, about fifty high Party and government officials were apprehended in a wave of arrests lasting from January 27 to February 16, 1951 (authorized by, among others, Slánský). Not until July of that year did Stalin intimate to Gottwald that Slánský was not the optimal general secretary and should be reassigned to a different role (the deputy premiership)—which happened amidst all the fanfare celebrating Slánský's fiftieth birthday on July 31. Finally, on November 24, Slánský was arrested and the final cast completed.

Given the high positions of all the defendants in the Communist and state establishments and their long-term membership in the Party (Margolius was the only one who had joined after the war), their criminal involvement against a cause to which they had dedicated their lives was completely unsuspected and sent a deep shock wave through the entire society. But the accused were to some extent different from the community they had governed/harmed, and the prosecution was never reticent about driving this point home. For example, Urválek questioned Geminder on his educational background (he had studied in German schools):

PROSECUTOR: And you never learned to speak Czech properly, not even in 1946 when you returned to Czechoslovakia and assumed a responsible function within the apparatus of the CPCS.
GEMINDER: No, I have not learned how to speak Czech well.
PROSECUTOR: Which language have you mastered completely?
GEMINDER: German.
PROSECUTOR: Do you know German really well?
GEMINDER: I have not spoken German for a while but I know that language.
PROSECUTOR: Do you know German in the same way you know Czech?
GEMINDER: Yes.
PROSECUTOR: So you do not know any language well. You are a typical cosmopolite. And as such you insinuated yourself into the CPCS. (110; 122)

Geminder's case was perhaps extreme in the sense that his Czech was nonnative enough to set him recognizably apart from the local population.[28] But those wishing to ostracize will hear a foreign accent even where

[28] Strangely enough, the foreignness of Germinder's speech is completely lost in the transcript of the trial. But it is quite detectable in his last letter to Gottwald, written on the eve of his execution, reprinted in Kaplan, "Poslední dopisy," pp. 154–55. The English transla-

there is none. Ivan Olbracht's keen ear, for example, detected that "though [the Slánskýites] give their depositions in Czech, Czech is not the native tongue for most of them."[29] This impression may have been influenced, at least in part, by the indictment, which referred to eleven of the defendants as "of Jewish origin" (Frank and Šváb were listed as Czechs, and Clementis as a Slovak). Or perhaps Olbracht's ear was accustomed to such subtle phonic nuances from his own home, since his mother was Jewish.

All this is just another way of saying that the label "cosmopolite" was not an objective linguistic category. Instead, like Derridean *différance*, it inscribed a radical alterity onto those physically excluded from societal closure. As such, it was neither a word nor a concept but a set of marks in a signifying chain informed by the vagaries of the context. Let me amplify. "Cosmopolite," first of all, was never meant as a *simple* substitution for "Jew." The Communist movement has always prided itself on being the only true champion of racial equality, and it would have been quite awkward to change that tune at the time. So bourgeois propaganda was faulted for having invented the anti-Semitic canard about the trial. To distract attention from its own racism, Nejedlý charged in a radio broadcast just three days after the execution of the defendants, "the imperialist world orchestrated an entire campaign to prove anti-Semitism in Czechoslovakia. . . . Nobody," he continued, "could wish national self-determination for the Jewish people more than we. But this should not confuse us in reacting to Zionism, when this movement has become a servant of the United States" (16). Thus, it was the shibboleth "Zionist" that the prosecution used to refer to the "cosmopolites of Jewish origin," making ethnicity merely a concomitant (to use the parlance of structuralist linguistics), not a distinctive, feature of their profound alienation from the Czech and Slovak people. *Dictum sapienti sat est.*

If all Zionists were by definition cosmopolites, not all cosmopolites were necessarily Zionists. Even a son or a daughter of the Czech and Slovak nations could become a stranger to his or her ethnos. An extended stay abroad might erect an impenetrable barrier between a formerly reliable comrade and the fatherland/motherland, making him or her hopelessly *déraciné*. At this point, however, it is necessary to draw a firm line between "bourgeois cosmopolitism" and "proletarian internationalism." This fundamental distinction had, it seems, a geographic basis. Living in the Soviet Union for perhaps most of one's life would never have abrogated the bond with distant compatriots; on the contrary, it could only

---

tion of the letter, published in "Appendix A" of Kaplan's book *Report on the Murder*, once again obliterates this important stylistic feature.
[29] Olbracht, "Konec zrácův," p. 2.

have strengthened it. Going West, however, even on an internationalist mission, almost inevitably would have led to estrangement. Czechoslovak Interbrigadists—the Communist volunteers fighting on the Republican side during the Spanish civil war—learned this lesson the hard way, as did émigrés who, like Clementis, lived in England during the Second World War or, like London or Šling, even married Westerners.

Clementis's case is especially intriguing. In his political praxis this former minister of foreign affairs managed to bridge the seeming antinomies of "cosmopolitism" and "nationalism." From his student years, the prosecution argued, Clementis had advocated the breakup of Czechoslovakia and the creation of an independent Slovak state. In so doing, however, "he was not concerned with securing self-determination for Slovakia," Urválek insisted in his concluding speech. "What mattered to Clementis, and with him to other Slovak bourgeois nationalists, was to serve their masters, the American imperialists, and on their behalf to advance the positions of the Slovak bourgeoisie. Slovak separatism, according to Clementis . . . was but the surrender of Slovakia to American imperialists" (502; 563). The two remaining ethnic Czechs had excluded themselves from their tribe, the prosecution suggested, by their shameful collaboration with the Nazis. As political detainees in Buchenwald and Sachsenhausen, they had been involved in the prisoners' self-administration of these concentration camps, torturing their fellow inmates (Frank's name allegedly had been included on an international list of wanted war criminals). It was Slánský's knowledge of their heinous past, admitted during cross-examination, that had made them a pliable tool in his hands and, by extension, in the hands of their new foreign bosses.

With such backgrounds, it should not come as a surprise that the welfare of the Czechoslovak working masses was not what motivated the Slánskýites' behavior. In collusion with foreign powers, they conspired to overthrow the government of Czechoslovakia, thereby undermining the nation's prosperity and stripping it of its military security (at least five hostile espionage services were supposed to have been involved in this plot), or so the prosecution charged. Besides these major felonies the defendants were accused of a plethora of "lesser" crimes. The leader of the ring—Rudolf Slánský—for example, had connived with Gottwald's personal physician to maltreat the chairman so that Slánský might eventually usurp his office. And this had not been Slánský's first homicidal attempt against a prominent Party functionary, witnesses testified. During the Slovak anti-Nazi uprising in 1944, his malevolent negligence had caused the death of the National Hero Jan Šverma, whose vigilant presence in the Tatra Mountains had previously thwarted many of the villainous plans of his murderer. In addition, the conspirators allegedly had endangered the life of yet another National Hero, Julius Fučík. Reicin, a Gestapo agent after 1939 (despite, or perhaps because of, his Jewish origins), had several times betrayed to the Nazis the whereabouts of this intrepid resistance fighter, who escaped arrest only because of his guerrilla prowess. The "unexpected" testimony of his widow, Gusta (who had read the indictment in the newspapers and had felt compelled to help class justice triumph)—a combination of facts as she remembered them and an eloquent reading from her husband's *Reportage* crowned with the obligatory warning, "People, I liked you. Watch!"—had, according to journalistic accounts, a powerful emotional impact on the audience.[30] After this devastating oratory, the disgraced Reicin might have considered himself lucky just to be hanged.

If you are having serious trouble believing all this, you begin to understand how important it was for the prosecution to make the accused confess their crimes. And confess they did—which obviously made some doubting Thomases wonder what had led them to do so with such a vengeance. But the sage Nejedlý clarified it all:

> Some explained it by saying that the accused were given special pills or drugs, though I think that neither a chemist nor a doctor, even one with the most unbridled imagination, could dream up a pill with such mysterious effects. . . . But we should not think either that they were forced into it by beatings or some other violence. That is the method of the capitalist police. . . . Not a beating, but crushing evidence, a matter of facts, this is the method of the working class here as everywhere else. . . . Furthermore, we should not forget the surroundings where the investigation and the trial took place. It is not a capitalistically false but a communistically truthful milieu. Thus, here even the most callous person, after just a brief encounter with this better world, assesses the consequences of his behavior differently from a person used to lying and betraying himself and others in the so-called better society of the capitalist world. (22–23)

Nejedly's explanation, if we take him seriously for a change, is wrong for a simple reason. The willingness of a leading Communist to confess to the most outrageous crimes, so fascinating to outside observers of such trials, cannot be reduced to a single direct cause. Cold, hunger, sleep deprivation, beatings, false promises, fake executions, appeals to Party loyalty, and various combinations thereof were used, the survivors tell us, against

---

[30] See especially H. Sajnerová, "Fučík je s námi," *Rudé právo*, November 26, 1952, p. 1. By testifying against Reicin, Fučíková, one might quip, repaid him in kind, for Reicin (together with Šverma) had been a witness at her wedding to Julius in 1938.

all of them. But their accounts of what had made them ultimately agree to incriminate themselves and others in imaginary crimes are not uniform. For Löbl it was a matter of gradual demoralization, the leveling of all values. London, by contrast, had not been able to escape the double bind of his predicament: "In such conditions," he wrote in 1968, "it is not only impossible for a Communist to prove his innocence but it presents him with a grotesque conscience problem: if you agree to 'confess,' in the Party's eyes you enter the path of your redemption. But if you refuse to sign because you are innocent you are a hardened culprit who must be mercilessly liquidated."[31] In a move closely resembling Dostoyevsky's famous response to the dilemma of deciding between Christ and the Truth, London, a good Communist, could not but choose the Party over Justice.

Slánský's case provides another variation on the theme of "voluntary" confession. Although he himself could not write about his prison experience, his thoughts from Ruzyně were, in a curious way, preserved for posterity. If politics makes strange bedfellows in the United States, in Eastern Europe it makes strange cellmates. Bohumil Benda (a minor Party functionary arrested as a Yugoslav spy at Slánský's orders during an earlier purge) was planted in Slánský's cell by interrogators in early 1952 to monitor this VIP (Very Important Prisoner). On January 28 he recorded for his bosses the following musings of Slánský (reproduced in Kaplan's book): "The crimes I've been accused of are so great and of such a character that you can't even imagine them. My investigation," the former general secretary confided to Benda, "is a matter of time. I still feel, for example, that I did not commit some of the crimes I'm being accused of; but it is likely that interrogators will manage to persuade me, perhaps as early as tomorrow, that I in fact did commit them. The thing is, I have to sort it out for myself" (173). He continued in this vein for another three days, while being prodded by Benda to confess and be done with it, until his unsuccessful suicide attempt of January 31, which marked the beginning of his surrender.

The logic of Slánský's utterance may seem strange. Culpability, he was saying, is a matter of persuasion, of authorizing a fiction. And he appears to have been almost eager to be persuaded. But why? The fear of fallibility, like an invisible Damoclean sword, always hung above the head of every Communist. I mentioned earlier some sources of this transcendental guilt: an inability to engender a truly proletarian consciousness owing to bourgeois origins; ignorance of the goals pursued by the Party at a par-

---

[31]   Arthur London, *On Trial*, trans. A. Hamilton (London, 1968), p. 161. For a discussion of this phenomenon, see Hannah Arendt, *The Origins of Totalitarianism: New Edition with Added Prefaces* (New York, 1973), pp. 472–74.

ticular moment because of restricted information; and so on. To compensate, the Communist movement invented the compulsory ritual of "constructive" self-criticism through which a "sinner" (the analogy with the Catholic sacrament of penance is obvious) publicly acknowledged wrongdoing and asked his or her comrades for forgiveness. Slánský himself had done this in 1935, when, during Gottwald's stay in Moscow, he (and Šverma) steered the CPCS and were accused of straying, if ever so slightly, from the Comintern-prescribed course. He performed similar public self-flagellation in 1951 after being demoted from the post of general secretary. And he was ready to do it again. In his letter to Gottwald two days after his arrest Slánský wrote: "I know I bear a heavy responsibility for errors, above all in personnel policies, because I was short-sighted and trusted bad people, I grossly neglected vigilance, I was flighty, and was inconsistent in . . . ideology. I have committed many other grave errors in organizational work, and these have harmed the Party. But never, ever did I harm the Party consciously" (Kaplan, 161). This time, however, forgiveness was not forthcoming. The sinner was to be burned at the stake.

Like Slánský, all the accused were more than willing to admit to Party representatives political failings of various kinds—with the important caveat that these were just lapses and not intentional crimes. Thus, interrogations usually began with detainees being asked to provide critical accounts of their past. Since such statements, as a rule, were found not sufficiently candid, the remorseful victims volunteered additional examples of blunders they had committed. But at this point some mistakes began to be interpreted not as accidents but as willful misdeeds, and "unacknowledged" crimes were woven into the narrative (corroborated by face-to-face confrontations with fellow conspirators who had already confessed to them). By eliminating in their minds any distinction between error and intention, fact and fiction, victims were "persuaded" to accept legal responsibility for confessions concocted by interrogators and, ultimately, to internalize them through thorough memorization. Earlier I mentioned the myth of Oedipus and argued that it was this hero's subjective innocence that made it easier for him to admit his crime. Modern scapegoating is, obviously, much less merciful: it demands that Oedipus acknowledge publicly not only that he knew all about the maternal side of his family but, even more, that he actually raped Jocasta.

The meticulous staging paid off, and all the defendants behaved as expected during the trial. To judge from the records, Ludvík Frejka was the most convincing performer. Not only did his son write an open letter to the court demanding the death penalty for his father, but also his wife refused to see him before his execution. London comes in a close second: in an open letter his wife asked the court to punish the traitors justly. It was only André Simone who, according to his old friend Arthur Koestler, attempted to transmit to those who knew him an encrypted message asserting his innocence. In urging the court to send him to the gallows, Simone concluded his deposition: "The only good service that I can still render is to be a warning memento to those whose origins, character, and temperament could tempt them to take the same hellish path which I took. The sterner the punishment, the greater the warning" (229; 254). Koestler was able to detect in this passage a paraphrase of the last speech by the veteran Communist Rubashov in his own novel *The Darkness at Noon*—the victim of a political trial fashioned after Bukharin's famous case: "The phrasing by Otto [Simone's autonym was Otto Katz] of his last statement was clearly intended as a camouflaged message, to indicate that he, too, had been brought to confess to crimes as imaginary as Bukharin's and Rubashov's." Whether the world chose not to listen, as Koestler claims, or whether it was too cryptic, as I believe, Simone's "last message was like a scribbled SOS in a bottle washed ashore by the sea, and left to bob among the driftwood, unnoticed by the crowd."[32]

If their public appearances before the court were well directed and rehearsed, it is perhaps the defendants' last letters, written during the fateful night of December 2 just before their executions, which serve as more reliable indicators of their private thoughts. But since even this correspondence could not have been regarded by the authors as truly private or privileged (indeed, some families did not receive their letters until ten

---

[32]   Arthur Koestler, *The Invisible Writing* (New York, 1954), p. 405; for a mini-portrait of André Simone (Otto Katz), see pp. 209–12. More recently Josef Škvorecký raised two interesting questions concerning Simone's desperate words and Koestler's reaction to them ("Z deníku spisovatele [36]," *Literární noviny*, July 14, 1994, p. 14). First of all, Škvorecký claims that Simone's utterance as reproduced in the trials' official transcript (from which I am quoting) and Koestler's rendition of it are markedly different. From this he surmises that, since Koestler heard Simone's speech through the BBC Monitoring Service, there must be a discrepancy between Simone's authentic words broadcast over the radio and their printed version which might have been subsequently censored by the authorities. This, however, is not the case. Koestler's version—"I . . . belong to the gallows. The only service I can still render is to serve as a warning example to all who, by origin or character, are in danger of following the same path to hell. The sterner the punishment . . ."—does not, in my opinion, differ significantly from the quotation I have given. The same is true of Simone's words as they appear in the *Proceedings of the Trial of Slánský et al. in Prague, Czechoslovakia, November 20–27, 1952, as Broadcast by the Czechoslovak Home Service*, an obscure text that bears neither the name of a publisher nor any date or place of its publication and which I obtained from the Niagara University Library: "Such . . . belongs to the gallows. The only service I can still render is to warn all who by origin or character are in danger of following the same path to hell. The sterner the punishment . . ." (p. 116). But Škvorecký is correct on the second point: that, more than Rubashov's last speech, Simone's idea about the utility of his death resembles an assertion made in Koestler's novel by the interrogator Gletkin and later repeated by Rubashov during one of his depositions.

years later), one might suspect that these epistles too were written with strategic objectives in mind (such as ensuring good treatment for relatives in the future). How else can one understand, for example, Margolius's prison eulogy, embedded in a letter to his wife:

> This time in detention has been a great education for me even though, unfortunately, it came too late. All the personnel with whom I have been in contact, wardens and interrogators, have behaved wonderfully toward me. I was their enemy but they always saw in me a human being who was not born an enemy but became one under the influence of class relations. Only here have I fully recognized the futility of my previous petit bourgeois life in contrast to the strength and purposefulness of the working class building a new life. (266)

Unless, of course, Margolis is emulating the good soldier Švejk's discursive strategy that performs rather than asserts.

Leaving aside this and similar imponderables, we find that the ten correspondents (Slánský refused to participate in this epistolary exercise) seem to fall into three categories: those who wrote to both their families and Gottwald (Clementis, Reicin, Simone, Šling, Šváb); those who wrote only to their families (Fischl, Frank, Margolius); and those who addressed Gottwald alone (Frejka, whose family had renounced him, and Geminder, who had none). The choice of addressees reflected, it seems, the author's attitude toward his guilt. The first group (except for Reicin) unequivocally denied having committed the crimes with which they were charged: "I understood from the very beginning the political necessity of the sentence passed on me. But I had nothing to do with Slánský's conspiracy" (Clementis; 251); "I was never a conspirator, a member of Slánský's anti-state center" (Simone; 272); "I truthfully declare before my execution that I have never been a spy" (Šling; 279); "Before my arrest I was not aware of any conspiracy and I did not know Slánský's true intentions. If I spoke [differently] in court I did so because I considered it my duty and a political necessity" (Šváb; 282). The latter two, however, admitted culpability of a different kind: Šling blamed himself for having succumbed to Slánský during the interrogations in 1950 and for accepting false charges, Šváb for not recognizing Slánský's true face in time. Both agreed that these failings were serious enough to warrant their death penalties. Reicin's acceptance of the verdict appeared in the context of his petition to Gottwald—"I realize that the criminal activity for which I am justly condemned has resulted in my family losing any entitlement to a pension" (269)—and he asked the magnanimous Leader to restore this benefit. The purely pecuniary nature of Reicin's request suggests to me that what little obeisance he paid to

those who condemned him was motivated more by practical considera-
tion than by any moral imperative.

By contrast, the two defendants who sent their last letters only to
Gottwald played the role of justly sentenced felons to the last moment: "I
only wish it to be believed that if I had not fallen into Slánský's hands I
would not have ended up on the platform of betrayal and crime. But I am
alone responsible for my deeds. . . . I will pay for it with the death sentence correctly given me" (Geminder; 263); "I write you above all to ask
forgiveness for having deceived you so many times . . . I beg you in my
last hour to believe that subjectively I did not wish to deceive you. I know
that subjective wishes are not important, only objective deeds and, thus,
nothing I write now can diminish my monstrous guilt" (Frejka; 260–61).
Of the remaining three correspondents, Fischl and Frank more or less
avoided the issue of guilt in their letters or treated it in an abstract manner. The tone of Margolius's epistle was close to that of Frejka's and Geminder's, though, as I pointed out earlier, this, to some degree, might
have been motivated by regard for his family.

So they were hanged on that freezing morning of December 3 soon after
they finished their letters, their remains cremated on the spot and, as if to
complete the Girardian script on scapegoating, their ashes deliberately
dispersed in a desperate attempt to obliterate the last traces of collective
murder. But can this be done? Can the past be completely erased and replaced by a surrogate? Let us return, for the last time, to Kundera's story
of that wonderful day, February 25, 1948, when Klement Gottwald told
his fellow Czechoslovaks that social utopia was at hand.

> Gottwald was flanked by his comrades, with Clementis standing next to
> him. There were snow flurries, it was cold, and Gottwald was bareheaded.
> The solicitous Clementis took off his own fur cap and set it on Gottwald's
> head.
>
> The Party propaganda section put out hundreds of thousands of copies
> of a photograph of that balcony with Gottwald, a fur cap on his head and
> comrades at his side, speaking to the nation. On that balcony the history of
> Communist Czechoslovakia was born. Every child knew the photograph
> from posters, schoolbooks, and museums.
>
> Four years later Clementis was charged with treason and hanged. The
> propaganda section immediately airbrushed him out of history and, obvi-
> ously, out of all the photographs as well. Ever since, Gottwald has stood on
> that balcony alone. Where Clementis once stood, there is only bare palace
> wall. All that remains of Clementis is the cap on Gottwald's head. (9; 3)

Gottwald, Kundera's apocrypha suggests, was not a good student of
Hegel after all, for he missed a crucial point about history which the mas-

ter dialectician forever reiterated: negation of the past is never a simple act of annihilation but rather one of sublation, a double play of canceling through preservation. Perhaps. But it is more likely that Gottwald's attitude toward the past was a case of dialectics turned pathology, the repression of a shameful memory, the avoidance of responsibility for the murder of his comrades. A synecdochic remnant of the presence of absence, an index of an event that has never happened, a retentive fold on the airbrushed surface of instituted oblivion, Clementis's cap is a powerful symbol of the censored yet indelible trauma that haunted the Communists throughout their uneasy reign over Czechoslovakia.

I began this chapter by drawing attention to the strange relationship between the first- and second-person pronouns in Communist discourse. These linguistic forms are the essential markers of a conversational turn taking which facilitates every process in a communicative transaction between two (or more) interlocutors. It is Bakhtin and his circle who are generally credited with bringing to the fore the dialogic nature of language. A speech act, according to these theoreticians, is never an isolated event but a link in a communicative chain: a response (from a specific ideological perspective) to what was said before and, at the same time, a prefiguration of a future replica. "Ultimately," as the modern Bakhtinologists put it, "dialogue means communication between simultaneous differences."[33] This insight should be seminal, it seems, for the study of a political trial, the poetics of which, intuitively speaking, ought to be at least as polyphonic as Dostoyevsky's. What a charged setting: ideological enemies locked in a face-to-face exchange, a plethora of witnesses adding further voices to the heteroglossia, and independent observers (the judges) trying to interpret partial, contradictory information! The 1933 Leipzig trial of Georgi Dimitrov and three other Bulgarian Communists accused by the Nazis of setting fire to the Reichstag, about which André Simone produced two books, was precisely such a drama attracting the world's attention.[34]
    Yet the pronominal confusion of which I spoke earlier obliterates the explicitly dialogic context of the Slánský trial. Its discourse is virtually devoid of communicative differences: the prosecution, the accused, their attorneys, as well as media commentators all used the same language to such an extent that their utterances (with deictics modified) could easily be interchanged. True, all these interlocutors came from the same ideolog-

---

[33] Katerina Clark and Michael Holquist, *Mikhail Bakhtin* (Cambridge, Mass., 1984), p. 9.
[34] *The Brown Book of the Hitler Terror and the Burning of the Reichstag* (London, 1933); and *The Reichstag Fire Trial: The Second Brown Book of the Hitler Terror* (London, 1934). Although the first volume was authored by the World Committee for the Victims of German Fascism and the second was anonymous, according to Koestler (*The Invisible Writing*), both were written and/or edited by Simone.

ical milieu, were steeped in the same Party lingo, shared the same hierarchy of values. But this unison of voices is characteristic not only of trials of leading Communists. A cursory glimpse at the proceedings of the *Trial against the Vatican Agents in Czechoslovakia* (prominent members of the Catholic establishment) from the early 1950s yields a similar picture,[35] which is somewhat bizarre, to say the least.

The category "political trial" which I have been using rather cavalierly so far needs, it seems, further nuancing. There is obviously a great dissimilarity between, let us say, the trials of Dimitrov, the Chicago Seven, and the Slánskýites. Whereas the first might be considered truly dialogical in the Bakhtinian sense, the second appears so only formally insofar as it involved profound differences (but very little communication), while the third was more or less monological with no discernible differences among the interlocutors and the ex-communication of fourteen Communists as its primary goal.[36] Confessional trials, as the third subgenre is sometimes called, are unlike other types of political trials because they are functions of a very specific ideology that by its very essence is nondialogical.

To explain this, I must go back to Lenin—whose name gave this intellectual strain its appellation. I begin (in dialectic fashion) with a disclaimer. Leninism, according to its self-assessment, is not an ideology at all, or at least not in the ordinary sense of the word. This denial, of course, does not mean much because no ideology, owing to its own blindness, can recognize itself as what it truly is: a "false consciousness," a distorted worldview concealing specific group interests. Yet if all ideologies are "software for minds," to metaphorize my situation as I write this, programs for homogenizing input-output processes among members of a particular collectivity, we should not see them as identical, mixing Apples with IBMs (Apple OS with MS DOS, to be precise). And Leninism is not even that but more like an owner's manual for a computer. There are several reasons why Lenin believed that his doctrine transcended the narrow confines of prejudice characteristic of all ideologies. First, Marx's narrative about the progress of humankind was not just his story but History: not a fiction promulgating narrow, partisan interests but the Truth, the Absolute logic of the passage from the past to the future. Second, proletarians were significantly different from the other classes, whether aris-

---

[35]   *Proces proti vatikánským agentům v Československu: Biskup Zela a společníci* (Prague, 1950).
[36]   It is difficult to render here succinctly the carnivalesque ambiance that permeated the trial of the Chicago Seven. Leaving aside the antics performed in the courtroom by the defendants themselves, I believe it suffices to mention that even their attorney, William Kunstler, was cited by Judge Julius Hoffman twenty-four times in contempt of court and was sentenced to forty-eight months and thirteen days for his "antiestablishment" behavior. For details, see *The Tales of Hoffman*, ed. Mark L. Lavine et al. (New York, 1970).

tocracy or bourgeoisie, that had spearheaded progress on earlier occasions. Whereas a minority of humankind for its own sake had initiated all previous revolutions, the workers' revolution would, for the first time, put a majority in control. And, finally, by abolishing all private property, the ultimate revolution would effectively and forever eliminate the cardinal cause of exploitation, thus bringing history to its happy end. Obviously only an unreconstructed reactionary could fail to see that the class interests of the workers coincide fully with the interests of humankind in general and call Leninism an ideology.

In a less partisan tone, one could describe Marxism-Leninism as a bird with two wings. On one side, it is a meta-ideology: a critique of all other existing ideologies from a higher, omniscient position. This presumption of superiority (stylistically reflected in the derisive tone with which Marx and Lenin treated their opponents) made any meaningful dialogue among Communists and non-Communists impossible from the very beginning. The street is clearly marked "one way," for no exchange of ideas is possible between two parties if one is a priori correct and the other always wrong. But critical theory is only one wing, so to speak, of, the phoenix of revolution. To soar high, it must be supported as well by its other extremity: a specific social praxis. Rational persuasion does not seem the most effective method for rectifying a well-entrenched, self-serving bourgeois *Weltanschauung* alienated from Reason by economic interests. The closing of the age of ideologies requires above all the eradication of unjust material conditions from which these collective myths draw their mephitic juices. Thus, Marxism-Leninism is also a well-defined prescript for political action—class warfare aimed at a radical and total transformation of society. The scope and severity of the struggle that it launches leaves no room for talking to the enemy. The bourgeoisie cannot be merely pacified (as Social Democrats believed) but must be destroyed. It is either our necks or theirs, to paraphrase Gottwald. *Tertium non datur.* And insofar as Leninism is concerned, the stress is definitely on action: the reconstruction of an economic basis, not the deconstruction of alien ideological superstructures.

But, as I argued earlier, the leader of the Russian Bolsheviks had his own way of accomplishing this. Eschewing a deterministic conception of social change (whereby a less fecund mode of production is automatically displaced by a more efficient one), Lenin emphasized the mental preconditions of this process. A proletarian revolution, he declared, is a function of the working class's self-consciousness. And here comes the rub. How might one convey highly abstract ideas about the philosophy of history to a mass of none too well educated people concerned above all with their immediate material needs? To achieve their desired effects, the tenets of

Marxism-Leninism had to be considerably simplified, illustrated by concrete, comprehensible examples, and spoon-fed to the targeted audience. The "scientific worldview" had to be made palatable to popular taste. Thus the art of political propaganda was born.[37] The indoctrination of workers is, it is easy to see, a two-pronged task. It involves, on the one hand, filling the minds of a large segment of the population with the right stuff. But, on the other hand, this activity also has its negative aspect: the prevention of the wrong stuff from impregnating the untrained intellects of proletarians and sinking its pernicious roots there. In Chapter 3 I treated extensively the positive dimension of Communist propaganda. Julius Fučík's *Reportage: Written from the Gallows* was very much a book that provided common citizens with a powerful role model to emulate. And with the author safely dead, nobody had to worry any longer that he might eventually succumb to some ideological deviation, that his shining image would have to be whitewashed.

It is the preventive measures taken by the Party apparatchiks intended to ward off what they termed "ideological diversion" that require elucidation. The image of an "iron curtain" invoked by Churchill after World War II captured the popular fancy because it vividly rendered the severity of measures imposed by the ruling Communist Parties of Eastern Europe to check the human outflow from and the informational inflow to the countries over which they had established their control. But these are only the most obvious mechanisms of negative mind control—effective but insufficient in and of themselves. As a revolutionary movement, Communism never denied that it had powerful enemies: the uncrushed bourgeoisie abroad and its "fifth column" at home. And these could not be completely ignored by Party propagandists. While the question was how to familiarize the workers with this evil without running the risk of confusing them, of polluting their minds with reactionary ideologies, it could be presented not as such, at face value, but only after being defanged, neutralized, and cast in a politically correct light. Like the weakened germ of a dangerous disease, hostile ideologies were administered to the proletarian body as an innocuous pathogen in order to boost its natural immunity against them.

This medical metaphor, however, does not do full justice to the com-

---

[37] I am using the word "propaganda" here in its general sense. Lenin himself differentiated between propaganda and agitation. Avoiding the pitfalls of the bourgeois metaphysics of presence which always treated *gramma* as a mere degenerate form of *phoné*, he wrote, "the propagandist operates chiefly by means of the *printed* word; the agitator by means of the *spoken* word," and he considered these two activities complementary (*What Is to Be Done*, p. 67).

plex state of affairs in Communist societies after the successful revolution outlined earlier. Even if, by an unexpected stroke of luck, the proletarian movement was without any true foes, some would have to be invented so that Communists could justify in perpetuity their "educational mission"—a one-party political system guaranteeing them total hegemony. And, at the same time, class struggle turning into a classroom brawl, ever new agents of the bourgeoisie had to be generated from within the Party ranks to provide grist for the mill of ongoing scapegoating meant to discourage any potential threats to Stalin's one-man rule. Thus, the most heterogeneous ideological deviations (whether leftist or rightist) were concocted by Party propagandists, ventriloquized by them through the mouths of preselected victims, and vigorously repudiated by the very same people who had conceived of them in the first place. Within such a soliloquy there could hardly have been any communicative difference, any traces of a dialogue at all.

After this digression it perhaps becomes clear what distinguishes the "confessional trial" subgenre from all other political trials. The trial is not a quest for justice (however skewed) but an exercise in propaganda. As a tool of mind control it serves a very specific function: to present the evil as the necessary counterpart of the good. Let us return once more to the genre of romance with its black and white vision of the world. If the biographies of the Communist heroes, very much like Christian hagiographies, depict superhuman perfection, confessional trials portray subhuman depravity. They are *demonographies*: compendia of personal traits, social behavior, and ideological attitudes that, according to the criteria of the period, are reprehensible beyond the pale. But the impersonators of these negative characteristics are put on public display in a very particular way. The enemies of the people are vanquished foes, shamefacedly confessing to all their crimes and begging the judges for the sternest punishment. So framed, the evil is harnessed in the service of the good, turned into a vivid example of the fact that the Party has the resolve and the resources to apprehend and destroy without mercy all who would try to oppose it, regardless of social status.

With their inherent monologism devoid of dramatic tension and their ritualized repetitiveness, the speeches of confessional trials do not make especially sizzling texts. But then, thrill or entertainment is not their primary function, as the Slánský trial clearly indicates. There were very few people who at the time of the hearings were fully familiar with what transpired in court. The audience was constantly changed so that as many delegations of workers and farmers as possible would have a chance to catch a glimpse of the miscreants admitting their guilt. The rest of the population had to rely on radio broadcasts and reports in the daily news, which conveyed the proceedings in a highly condensed and one-sided form. And the full transcript of the trial published about a year later is an utterly indigestible book, crammed with so many names, dates, and particulars that I myself had a hard time finishing it and remembering all the details.

But does this matter? Definitely not. Confessional trials, a literary critic might observe, are like Chekhov's plays: the real action takes place not on stage but off. Or, put more radically, such trials are not texts in the sense that it is their inherent structural properties that count, but rather pretexts for generating public discourse: a uniform condemnation of the accused. Even a cursory glimpse at the Czechoslovak press starting November 21, 1952, reveals the enormous scope of this campaign. And if the language of the trial itself is rather trite, the essays, letters, and resolutions denouncing the fourteen defendants are quite flamboyant, a plethora of metaphors, hyperboles, allusions, and more or less imaginative circumlocutions for the death penalty.

The printed materials, though quite visible, represent only a small portion of this condemnatory avalanche. Václav Brabec, who in the mid-1960s had the rare opportunity to probe the archives of the CPCS Central Committee in order to assess public reaction to the political trials of the previous decade, volunteered the following information concerning the Slánský case:

In a few days (from November 20 to December 2, 1952), according to the record of the central administrative department of the CPCS, 8,250 resolutions, letters, and telegrams were sent to the CC and the State Court—not only from the rank and file of the Party, factory meetings, and offices, but also from the leadership of other political parties and organizations, and even from Pioneer organizations [the Communist equivalent of the Scout movement] and school children. In most cases they express "hatred," "the highest degree of indignation," "satisfaction" that at last the conspiratorial band was charged, and they requested the highest punishment for all accused. Thousands of death sentences were passed at mass rallies at factories, offices, and other establishments, most of them before the trial ended and the defendants were convicted. The most radical voices demanded: "Let's not waste time and shoot them like cats," . . . "they must be all hanged or we will go to the streets," . . . "a new February [the month of the Communist revolution in Czechoslovakia] has come—let's take machine guns and get them." . . . There were even cases of outright hysteria. Reports about public reactions to the trial contained the following depictions: "When Slánský's name was mentioned women cried and screamed that he was a murderer, and that he wanted to kill our beloved comrade Gottwald and they exacted as retribution that Slánský be hanged," . . . "rage drove people to extremes and some demanded that the accused conspirators be tortured," . . . "a worker . . . wept and shouted: 'one death is not enough for these traitors, they should be flayed.' " Even if we take into account that the approval of the trial was promoted by all the means of mass manipulation, it is obvious that large groups in all strata of society actually identified with the trial and some of them were ready to accept violation of the elementary principles of jurisprudence and humanity. (368; 8–9)

It is not the staggering quantity of responses or the depth of emotions expressed that strikes me in Brabec's report. Instead, I am intrigued by the curious linkage of words and actions that it illustrates. Public utterances in a Communist society, it seems, exhibit strong anticipatory power, an uncanny ability to foreshadow future events. This can be easily attributed to the monological nature of the Marxist-Leninist discourse, discussed earlier. By obliterating all communicative differences, it in fact collapsed, among other things, the interval between linguistic cause and effect. Slánský and his comrades were sentenced, so to speak, by the very first sentence publicly announcing their arrest.

I am not the first one to observe this curious etiology inherent in totalitarian discourse. In *The Art of the Novel*, Milan Kundera, for example, recounts a story (from the novel of yet another Czech writer in exile, Josef Škvorecký) in which the official word carries an analogous predictive force.[38] It concerns an engineer who goes to London for a professional meeting. But after his return to Prague he reads to his astonishment a report in *Rudé právo* about a Czech engineer who, during a conference in London, slandered his Socialist homeland and defected to the West. Kundera recounts all the official institutions that the poor fellow visits to point out that the incriminating news item is totally incorrect and that he is back in Prague. Although he is always assured that he has nothing to worry about, he does worry. And not in vain, it seems: "He soon realizes that all of a sudden he's being closely watched, that his telephone is tapped, and that he's being followed in the street. He sleeps poorly and has nightmares until, unable to bear the pressure any longer, he takes a lot of real risks to leave the country illegally. And so he actually becomes an émigré."[39]

---

[38] Josef Škvorecký, *Příběh inženýra lidských duší*, vol. 2 (Toronto, 1977), pp. 41–48, 56–60; *The Engineer of Human Souls: An Entertainment on the Old Themes of Life, Women, Fate, Dreams, the Working Class, Secret Agents, Love, and Death*, trans. P. Wilson (New York, 1984), pp. 301–6, 311–14.
[39] Milan Kundera, *The Art of the Novel*, trans. L. Asher (New York, 1988), p. 100. Further references will be given in the text.

Kundera calls his story "Kafkan," which brings me obliquely to the beginning of this chapter where I used a similar expression to characterize the irrational turn of Czechoslovak justice after the February victory. This label, however (and Kundera himself is quick to point this out as well), is too vague to be used analytically. Its further refinement is required. Most commonly it refers to a grotesque, alienating situation existing in a real world that in some way resembles the chimerical universe of Kafka's prose. From this observation, then, it is only a small step to crediting the Prague writer with the gift of clairvoyance, of depicting in his works social pathologies that were yet to come. Thus, defying the words of Jesus, Kafka did become a prophet with honor in his homeland, for in the 1950s many Czech readers drew in their minds a precariously close parallel between his fiction and the Stalinist system in which they lived. The philosopher Alexej Kusák during the famous Kafka conference at Liblice Castle in May 1963 expressed this view most pregnantly. It was Kafka's creative method, Kusák argued, his brilliant ability to typify, that enabled the writer to recognize once and for all that if "social relations were made opaque and institutionalized power made absolute, absurd situations in which the innocent are accused of crimes they never committed will be generated on a daily basis." And to drive his point home, he continued, "*The Trial*, word[s] that have after all stigmatized our reality for twelve years, is for me the pillar of Kafka's oeuvre, of its epistemology . . . an elementary probe into the social reality of the modern world."[40]

Kusák's interpretive strategy, it must be emphasized, was not motivated by purely hermeneutic concerns. In April 1963, just a month before the Liblice conference, a plenary session of the CPCS Central Committee was convened to deliberate a report commissioned in the fall of 1962 to reassess the political trials of the leading Party functionaries of the previous decade. Although in its candor the meeting surpassed previous discussions of this delicate theme, it fell short of clearing fully the names of those who had been executed. This was to be expected because, as I suggested before, in the early 1960s the top Party leadership was still chock-full of those with blood on their hands. In this politically charged atmosphere it was not surprising that the organizer of the conference and the leading Czech Kafkologist, Eduard Goldstücker, should vehemently reject his junior colleague's ingenious foray into reader-oriented criticism. Kafka can be correctly understood, he declared authoritatively, only within the social context of his origin and not against a background of what transpired much later. Goldstücker should have known—and not only as a student of Kafka. To wit,

[40]   Alexej Kusák, "Poznámky k marxistické interpretaci Franze Kafky," *Franz Kafka: Liblická konference, 1963*, ed. E. Goldstücker et al. (Prague, 1963), pp. 174–75. For an abbreviated translation, "On the Marxist Interpretation of Franz Kafka," see *Franz Kafka: An Anthology of Marxist Criticism*, ed. K. Hughes (Hanover, N. H., 1981), pp. 95–103.

he was one of the government witnesses against Slánský during the first day of the trial, and in a subsequent trial of his own he himself was given a life sentence. So if not even Goldstücker could see any similarity between the predicament of the Slánskýites and that of Josef K., who could?

Levity aside, this example is sufficient to illustrate how shaky the ground is on which content-oriented mimesis is usually built. "Resemblances," a famous Russian author put it deftly, "are the shadows of differences. Different people see different similarities and similar differences." Thus, to call the Slánský trial Kafkaesque is above all, I would argue, a case of poetic justice, or, more precisely, an instance of a particular use of language that is also characteristic of the Prague writer's poetics.

The peculiar power of words to prefigure later events, of which the story of the Czech engineer is such a telling specimen, was analyzed by Clayton Koelb in his insightful study *Kafka's Rhetoric*. It was his profession, Koelb argues convincingly, that made Kafka the lawyer especially sensitive to the performative aspect of language, its capacity for having very real consequences. As a writer, however, he exploited this linguistic phenomenon in a very unusual fashion. The effects triggered by words in his fiction are highly unexpected, to say the least—hence the attribute "Kafkaesque" to which these disturbing narratives give rise. There are a number of ways in which utterances can inscribe themselves onto the future. At the tropological level, the figure of prolepsis, "an anticipatory imitation of the text to follow," is, according to Koelb, one of Kafka's favorite devices.[41] The opening sentence of *The Trial*, "Someone must have traduced Josef K., because without having done anything wrong he was arrested one fine morning," is a good example of a typically Kafkan exploitation of this figure of speech. In an authoritative voice it announces both the arrest of the protagonist and his innocence. But as the plot thickens, the subsequent narrative seems to contradict these facts. As in the trope of "forensic prolepsis," in which anticipated arguments are refuted in advance, or at least cast in an unfavorable light, the story undercuts the veracity of what was stated at the very outset. Though allegedly arrested, Josef K. is free to move about wherever he wishes, and though innocent, he is more than accommodating toward his executioners. "Kafka's prolepsis," Koelb sums up his observations, "usually works in this paradoxical and unsettling fashion. A statement whose meaning we have no reason to question is discovered to anticipate later discourse suggesting or requiring an entirely different interpretation. This use of prolepsis is a rhetorical construction . . . in that it not only produces a text readable in two conflicting ways but also actualizes both readings in the text" (33).

---

[41] Clayton Koelb, *Kafka's Rhetoric: The Passion of Reading* (Ithaca, N.Y., 1989), p. 31. Further references will be given in the text.

Intuitively speaking, prolepsis in the Slánský trial should have played no aporetic role at all. On the contrary, the opening should have been fully replicated by the closure. To this end meticulous care was taken by the organizers to ensure that there would be no discrepancies between what transpired in the courtroom and what was announced by the media at the outset of the trial. "Shortly before 0900 hours," reported the Czechoslovak radio broadcast on November 20, "the accused were brought into the courtroom. Representatives of the working people who filled the courtroom [looked] with disgust—even with deep contempt—at the faces of the accused, these imperialist mercenaries whose dirty plans were foiled in time!"[42] What they heard that morning probably met if not exceeded their expectations. "The Anger and Contempt of Our People Fall on the Heads of the High Traitors: Our Workers Demand a Just Punishment for the Traitors" read one of the headlines on the front page of *Rudé právo* the next morning. And, once again, as if not to frustrate the anticipation of the millions, justice was swift and merciless, nudged along the correct line by letters from righteous citizens.

Nothing, or virtually nothing, was allowed to disturb the smooth façade of this preorchestrated trial. And yet, despite all the detailed planning and careful rehearsing, or perhaps precisely because of it, the reports from undercover informants preserved in the Party archives indicate a certain disillusion with the trial among some oversuspicious Czechs and Slovaks. Václav Brabec, who in the 1960s scrutinized these unpublished records, wrote in his above-mentioned study:

> After the initial satisfaction [accompanied] by work pledges and resolutions a few days into the court proceedings, "a reversal of the opinion of workers" was recorded in number of places. Let us look at some of these statements: "Some say that the trial strikes them as well-prepared theatre" ; "when I listen to the broadcast of the trial it sounds as if all was written down or learned in advance. They don't even let the prosecutor finish and they spill everything out" . . . "a well-acted comedy, three rehearsals, and now it's easy as pie." . . . Perfect staging and the universality of the indictment had thus created the suspicion that something had gone awry. (379; 11)

The temporal gap between discourse and its proleptic anticipation, to reiterate Koelb's categories, turned into a semantic conflict not because (as in Kafka's story) the two contradicted each other but, paradoxically, because they fit only too well. And (again, as in *The Trial*) this conflict was capable

---

[42]   *Proceedings of the Trial of Slánský*, p. 1.

of generating simultaneously several antinomic readings of the Slánský trial. They can be sorted into a neat triad according to their increasing perplexity: from the prima facie acceptance of the crime and punishment as presented by the media; through a negation of such a simplistic misprision (the charges are phony and the "conspirators" innocent victims); to a dialectical sublation of these two interpretations, one that in recognizing the accused as not guilty of conspiring to overthrow the Communist government sees in them accomplices of the Stalinist terror who deserve their punishment, even if at the hands of equal criminals.[43] Different strokes for different folks—and vice versa.

The uncanny strangeness of Kafka's universe is generated, Koelb believes, by yet another tropological device that can be termed broadly the actualization of figures of speech. Standard linguistic competence includes, among other things, our ability to differentiate between literal and transferred meanings of words. We know that metaphors, for example, do not really mean what they say—or, to be more precise, they mean it in a special, indirect way. If I call somebody "a louse" I am perfectly aware that that person is not a real louse but that he or she merely resembles, in my opinion, that creature in a certain respect or capacity. But not in Kafka's texts. There a curse has the power of transforming the addressee into its own image. Gregor Samsa's rude awakening as "a gigantic insect" in "Metamorphosis" is precisely the product of this generative potential of figuration. "Kafka knew very well," Koelb argues, "what was ordinarily intended by the trope '*Du bist ein Ungeziefer*' when it was addressed to particular persons, but by ignoring that intention he found in it the possibility for a story" (16). Whether Kafka's awareness that figures of speech, despite their lexical obliqueness, can have direct existential consequences stems, as Koelb suggests, from his vulnerability to his father's verbal abuse is a matter of speculation. But even if so, he was able to sublimate

43   The third reading, some might recognize, is the one imputed by Hannah Arendt to Bertolt Brecht's famous comment about the Trotskyites charged in Moscow with crimes comparable to those of which the Slánskýites were accused in Prague some twenty years later: "The more innocent they are, the more they deserve to die" (*Men in Dark Times* [New York, 1968], p. 227). Along these lines, one should perhaps further differentiate between the defendants directly responsible for setting up the actual mechanism for this system of injustice (such as Reicin, Slánský, and Šváb) and those who, out of Party loyalty, "willingly" implicated others in imaginary crimes. The attitude of the latter is well encapsulated in Ludvík Frejka's final letter to Gottwald written just before the execution: "From that very moment [four days after his arrest] I, as a man faithful to the labor movement for more than thirty years—please believe me Mr. President—assumed honestly and mercilessly the objective attitude of the Czechoslovak workers, forcing myself to view all that I have done through the eyes of my interrogators. Accordingly, I provided all the evidence against myself. During the interrogations I felt that I helped to expose many things" (Kaplan, "Poslední dopisy," pp. 153–54).

this mental scar into a significant element of his poetics. It is instructive to compare the curses hurled by Kafka Senior at his good-for-nothing son with those used against the Slánskýites. They were called, among other things, "bedbugs literally gorged with human blood," "monsters of cloaca," "a dirty bunch of vipers," "a shameful tuber of betrayal which must be burned out to its root," and "a boil just cut out."[44] These figurative execrations, however, were not used merely to induce anxiety or to cause mental pain. Their purpose, it seems, was more sinister. By comparing the defendants to loathsome creatures or diseases, they paved the road for their subhuman treatment and the inevitability of their eventual physical destruction and extirpation.

While these particular imaginative curses suggested a certain course of future action, they were not actualized extralinguistically. But others, in a truly Kafkaesque manner, did indeed materialize. Most macabre on my list is Nikita Khrushchev's hyperbole from his speech at the Fifth Party Conference of the Moscow Region in June 1937: "Our Party . . . will mercilessly crush the gang of traitors and betrayers, will wipe off the face of the earth the entire Trotskyite-rightist carrion. . . . We will annihilate without a trace all our enemies to the last man and scatter their dust [prakh] to the winds."[45] This profoundly non-Christian locution has a distinctly biblical ring. It invokes not only the Old Testament's "In the sweat of thy face shalt thou eat bread, till thou return unto the ground; for out of it wast thou taken: for dust thou [art], and unto dust shalt thou return" (Genesis 3:19) but also the famous phrase from the Book of Common Prayer, "Earth to earth, ashes to ashes, dust to dust." If the Russian idiom pokoy prakhu is a rough equivalent to the English expression "R.I.P.," then the threat Nikita Sergeyevich was making to the despicable Trotskyites is crystal clear: they deserve neither to live nor to rest in peace.

But did he really mean it? I could perhaps point out that the dispersion of one's remains as a form of punishment reserved for the most hated political enemies was practiced in Russia as late as the seventeenth century. The corpse of a pretender to the Russian throne, Pseudo-Demetrius I (killed in 1606), the father of Russian historiography, venerable Karamzin, relays to us, was later exhumed and burned, "his ashes mixed with gunpowder, discharged from a gun," and "the wind scattered the villain's mortal remains."[46] One might wonder, together with the good soldier Švejk, "How are they going to put him together when the day of the Last

---

[44] The authors of these imaginative epithets are H. Sajnerová, Dominik Tatarka, Ivan Skála, Josef Urválek, and Zdeněk Nejedlý, respectively.

[45] *Pravda*, June 7, 1937, p. 2.

[46] Nikolai Karamzin, *Istoriya gosudarstva rossiyskago: Izdanie pyatoe v trekh knigakh* (St. Petersburg, 1843), bk. 3, vol. 11, p. 177.

Judgment comes?" But the idea of resurrection could have hardly been on the mind of Khrushchev—a dialectical materialist—when he was forewarned the enemies of the people about their inevitable fate. In Kafka's world, Koelb insists, a speaker's intentions must be ignored for a trope to materialize. So whatever end Khrushchev might have pursued in saying what he said, his image was eventually instantiated: the dust of Slánský and Company *was* scattered to the winds. "The comic is inseparable from the very essence of *Kafkan*," Kundera argues in *The Art of the Novel*. In this narrative universe the comic destroys the tragic and "thus deprives the victims of the only consolation they could hope for: the consolation to be found in the (real or supposed) grandeur of tragedy" (104–5). Appropriately, when the three policemen charged with scattering to the winds the dust of the eleven executed Slánskýites returned to their headquarters to report their ghastly mission accomplished, "the driver laughed that he had never before carried in his car fourteen people at once—three alive and eleven in a bag."[47]

The proleptic power of certain utterances, their ability to have consequences in the real world, may be approached from still another perspective: that of speech act theory. Ever since J. L. Austin's pathbreaking *How to Do Things with Words* appeared in the early 1960s, philosophers and linguists have paid close attention to the fact that locutions can have what the British philosopher termed a perlocutionary effect, that is, they can secure an extralinguistic result. Particularly relevant for my argument is Austin's concept of "an illocutionary act," that is, the use of language for a particular purpose. Let me explain. In uttering a string of lexical items ordered correctly according to relevant grammatical and semantic rules, I convey to the addressee more than an abstract linguistic meaning: I assert, promise, order, or threaten. Now, for such illocutionary acts to be felicitous, to have a particular upshot, they must conform to certain conventions. I can, for example, threaten to flunk my students but cannot tell them (alas!) that if they miss a deadline I will scatter their dust to the winds. Well, I can say it, but it would be understood as an empty threat, an infelicitous illocutionary act, one lacking conventional force.

Kafka's work, as Koelb shrewdly illustrates, abounds with such less than usual linguistic constructions. Some of his stories evolve entirely around quasi-illocutionary acts that bring about effects which are clearly illegitimate. An example is the short story "The Judgment," in which an irritated father, Bendemann, concludes a harangue addressed to his son Georg by saying, "I sentence you now to death by drowning!" And Georg, with an alacrity so sorely missing among young men today,

---

[47] Quoted according to Josefa Slánská, *Zpráva o mém muži* (Prague, 1990), p. 49.

obliges the patriarch immediately by jumping into the closest stream. "Although the father's words of 'sentencing' seem to lead directly to Georg's self-execution," Koelb observes, "we still cannot say for certain that a genuine illocutionary act of sentencing to death has taken place" (60). This is so because the father has no legal authority to condemn anybody, not even his son, to capital punishment; and Georg, for his part, need not submit to such cruel and unusual punishment. This patriarchal "judgment" clearly lacks illocutionary force but, strangely enough, carries the perlocutionary effect: the death by drowning of the sentenced son.

It is obvious that the status of illocutionary acts in confessional trials is more than dubious since these are not real legal proceedings but fictions, enactments of prior scripts. An inquiry by the prosecutor merely pretends to be this kind of a speech act because he knows the answers in advance, and the same is true of the replies of witnesses or defendants which do not purport to give any new information. The true objective behind these locutions, one might say, is not to gain or impart the knowledge relevant for deciding whether a crime has been committed, but rather to create a simulacrum of such an inquiry. So, instead of cutting through this thicket of murky intentions, I will limit my discussion to an utterance in the Slánský case whose similarity to Kafka's quasi-illocutions seems quite clear. On November 26, 1952, *Rudé právo* published the following excerpts from a letter to the State Court from Tomáš Frejka, a son of one of the defendants:

> I request for my father the ultimate punishment—the death penalty.
>
> Only now have I realized that this creature, which I cannot call a human being for he did not have in himself even a fragment of feeling or human dignity, was my greatest and most implacable enemy.
>
> I swear that wherever I work I will always work as a dedicated Communist, and I know that my hatred toward all of our enemies, especially those who directly wanted to destroy our ever richer and happier life, but above all my hatred toward my father, will always strengthen me in my struggle for the Communist future of our people.
>
> I request that this letter be presented to my father or, if possible, that I tell him myself.

In its tenor, as any true connoisseur of Kafka must clearly recognize, this text resembles to some degree Franz's never-sent letter to his father. And a Freudian critic would delight in fathoming the depth of the oedipal complex among the Jewish families of Central Europe that these two epistles unabashedly exhibit. A student of confessional trials must note, however, that such public patriarch-baiting has been a standard feature of this genre ever since the Shakhty case, during which the Soviet papers printed a letter from the son of one of the defendants—Kirill Kolodub—demanding "a stern punishment for his father-wrecker."[48] And it is the peculiar relation of perlocution to illocution that makes these filial letters akin to Kafka's "The Judgment." Earlier I pointed out a certain infelicity in Bendemann's act of sentencing his son to death. The younger Frejka, by contrast, seems well aware of the limitations of his power and instead asks the court to pass the ultimate sentence. But does this endow his illocutionary act with greater conventional force? Not at all. Though related to the defendant, young Frejka is not a party to the trial, does not know all the evidence, and so his request for sentencing is totally out of place—only with the caveat that it was granted and the father executed. Once again, an illocution that does not meet its felicity conditions succeeds in securing an effect.

The importance of illocutionary acts in our transactions of everyday life can hardly be overestimated. They anchor our linguistic behavior to social reality because only through them can our words affect the world around us. Because of this power these acts have their ethical dimension: speakers can be held responsible for what they say. So we might be perceived as liars if our assertions are deemed insincere, as thieves if our claims illegitimate, or as impostors if our commands unauthoritative. Quasi-illocutions, however, present a moralist with a difficult case: where to assign the onus of responsibility for infelicitous speech acts with existential consequences. Kafka's stories, for instance, often take a paradoxical turn when hapless victims assume guilt for their unearned ordeal—whence Josef K.'s feeling of immortal shame as the executioner's knife twists in his heart.

Not surprisingly, the issue of responsibility for confessional trials seems equally perplexing. Was it not the man demanding in 1937 that the Trotskyite-rightist carrion be wiped off the face of the earth who, some nineteen years later, condemned the unjust prosecution of innocent Party members by Stalin? And can Khrushchev's vivid hyperbole, or, more to the point, Tomáš Frejka's infelicitous request concerning his father, be judged as incitement to murder. By whom? His fellow countrymen, who themselves passed innumerable resolutions to the same effect? Or those few who knew better but for more than good reasons did not dare speak up?[49] Yes, unlike poor Abraham, one could perhaps find ten righteous

---

[48]   "Syn Andreya Koloduba trebuet surovogo nakazaniya dlya otca-vreditelya," *Pravda*, May 25, 1928, p. 5.

[49]   As far as I was able to find out, it was only Karel Kreibich, a founding member of the CPCS, a longtime functionary of the Comintern, and from 1950 the Czechoslovak ambassador to Moscow, who, in his letter to the Central Committee of December 12, 1952, protested against the blatantly anti-Semitic nature of the Slánský trial. He was recalled

persons within this Czechoslovak Sodom, but would they be willing to serve on a jury? As far as criminal justice is concerned, only a handful of the most brutal Czechoslovak policemen were brought to justice in the mid-1950s, charged with "using unlawful interrogatory methods," duly sentenced, and quickly released, while some of those against whom these methods were applied remained behind bars.

So who was responsible? Well, nobody it seems. When the dust settled and the body count was complete, everybody was excused. Over two million Czechoslovak Communists (not a negligible number for a country of about 14 million) were allegedly kept at bay by those in charge, and most of the leadership apparently trusted blindly in the security apparatus managed by seasoned Soviet experts, or so the story goes.[50] The debilitated Gottwald (suffering the belated consequences of untreated syphilis), scared for his own well-being if not his life, took to the bottle. And those who approved the final verdict that he presented at the Politburo meeting convened on the penultimate day of the trial pointed at the sentencing judges, who in turn argued that, since the accused had confessed to all the charges, they had no other choice. With everybody passing the buck, blame was eventually fixed on those who were unable to defend themselves anymore. The evil Slánský, who had started the whole business, ended up hoist with his own petard. And though the intervening years have brought to the surface more and more facts, they also have made legal retribution more and more difficult. Justice delayed . . .

Poetics, however, is not ethics, and a critic should not play the role of Nemesis. What interests me here is not the morality of the story but the involvement of literature in it—or, to be more precise, its ability to bring out in artistic guise what was otherwise politically taboo: the psychopathological mechanism of guilt suppression and blame shifting that informed official discourse about the crimes of the Stalinist era in Czechoslovakia. Milan Kundera's first novel, *The Joke*, begun in 1961 and published in 1967, confronted head-on the nettlesome issue of redressing injustices of the not so distant past. It presents the private tragedy of a young Communist student, Ludvík Jahn, subjected to a humiliating prosecution in the

---

from his post but was not prosecuted, despite the fact that he continued his epistolary crusade. His wife, Charlotte, however, was expelled from the Party in October 1957 for the same activity. See Pelikán, *The Czechoslovak Political Trials, 1950–1954*, pp. 118–19, 205.

50   Karel Kaplan's *Mocní a bezmocní* provides composite psychohistorical portraits of all the main protagonists of this era. As a secretary of the Central Committee commission investigating the political trials of the previous decade, Kaplan had access to hitherto secret archives, and, even more significantly, was able to interview (officially and unofficially) all surviving participants. This study offers the most comprehensive information on how those involved in the Slánský trial assessed their personal responsibility for what happened.

early 1950s for an alleged ideological lapse, who a decade later attempts to avenge himself on the man he perceives as the main instigator of his suffering. Although Kundera's text is ostensibly about a single victim of the Stalinist terror, its political ramifications are much broader.

In passing I might point out that in a subtle way the novel calls attention to the Slánský trial as well. Small details dispersed throughout the book point unmistakably in that direction. The scandalous exclamation "Long live Trotsky!" which Ludvík writes on a postcard to the object of his affection is, for example, literally lifted from the mouth of Slánský, who apparently had cried it out in the 1920s at a street rally, and it was introduced at the trial by Urválek as incontestable proof of Slánský's long-term Trotskyism.[51] The figure of Alexej—Ludvík's fellow soldier and the son of a prominent Communist official arrested as a traitor—who publicly renounces his disgraced father and eventually commits suicide, brings to mind the ill-fated Tomáš Frejka. And the speech of Ludvík's chief accuser, Zemánek, quoting dramatically lengthy passages from Fučík's *Reportage*, clearly recapitulates the histrionics of Fučík's widow during her court deposition against Reicin, which I described earlier.

The picture of guilt and retribution that *The Joke* presents is bleak, to say the least. An old injustice can never be fully redressed, as the protagonist himself learns the hard way. What the novel further problematizes is the very possibility of a clear-cut distinction between victims and victimizers. In a country with a history as convoluted as Czechoslovakia's, such an opposition never remains meaningful for too long. Each new ideological turnabout effectively subverts the hitherto valid criteria for moral judgment, de facto reversing the roles of the two. Does this radical relativism imply surrender to the vicissitudes of history on Kundera's part, a simple and comfortable erasure of an inconvenient past—like the Communist Party propagandists' airbrushing from old photographs the images of the comrades who, according the most recent political reconfiguration, had lost their right to be there? This, of course, is merely a rhetorical question, for *The Joke*, as I will illustrate in the next chapter, is a sustained and conscious effort on the part of it its author to come to grips with the troublesome first half of his life.

[51]   Most likely it was the absurdity of this charge that caught Kundera's attention. It is utterly unclear when exactly Slánský saluted Trotsky. According to *Trial of the Leadership*, this information comes from a police protocol of October 11, 1927 (50; 56), so the incriminating statement had to have been made prior to that date. Karol Bacílek's *Poučenie z procesu*—an authoritative source given the fact that its author was then the minister of national security—dates this incident as far back as 1924 (p. 7). In any case, one should not forget that Trotsky was not expelled from the Bolshevik Party until October 23, 1927.

5

Ironies of History

The Joke by Milan Kundera

Nel mezzo del camin di nostra vita
mi ritrovai per una selva oscura
ché la diritta via era smarrita.

[In the middle of the journey of our life
I found myself within a dark wood
where the straight path was lost.]

—*The Divine Comedy of Dante Alighieri: Inferno*

Hegel remarks somewhere that all facts and personages of great importance in world history occur, as it were, twice. He forgot to add: the first
time as tragedy, the second as a joke.

—Karl Marx, *The Eighteenth Brumaire of Louis Bonaparte*

In his musings on the subject of history during interviews in the late
1980s, Milan Kundera repeatedly drew attention to the curious dyadic
quality that, according to him, informs this process. The evolution of the
novel, he claimed, consists of two halves with the hiatus between them oc-
curring somewhere at the beginning of the nineteenth century. The same
is true, he asserted elsewhere, of European music, in which the magisterial figure of Bach personifies the caesura articulating its development into
two distinct segments. But it is not only the supraindividual history of art
that, according to Kundera, exhibits such a bipartite structure. Human life
often breaks into two halves as well, and Kundera's own biography, or
that of Witold Gombrowicz, one of his favorite novelists, attests to this
fact. Kundera's understanding of history differs from the traditional pro-
gressivist view (of whatever provenance) which conceives of change as an

orderly, accretive process unfolding according to some preordained telos. There is a certain degree of discontinuity among the entities belonging to the same developmental series; the fabric of time is sundered in places. This, however, does not mean that the Czech novelist subscribes to the catastrophic model of history characteristic of modernist thinkers who shatter the past into a succession of disconnected states devoid of any overall coherence. By envisioning historical segments as halves, Kundera obviously wishes to suggest that their autonomy is merely relative, that they ought to be united somehow, that only together do they constitute the totality of history.

In these discussions and elsewhere Kundera addresses the most basic metaphysical issue of Western historiography: the problem of sameness and difference. How can something be considered self-identical if with the passage of time it has changed? For Kundera the solution to this riddle lies in the relationship between successive temporal segments. He describes it, first of all, in psychological terms. Like childhood, the first half is the source of all obsessions and traumas, which the second half (the age of maturity) strives to forget, repress. These attempts at obliterating the past, however, Kundera regards as unhealthy. Not only can the process of repression cause severe mental complexes, but also that which is repressed does not vanish from history. Rather, it remains there as a subversive potential, a hidden charge ready to explode. The relationship between the two halves also has its ethical aspect. For Kundera the rejection of the past is morally wrong, and he speaks of the necessity of paying old debts, of the "sin" of forgetting, and of historical "betrayal."[1]

---

1 "[In Kafka, Broch, Musil, Gombrowicz] there is no disdain for 'tradition,' but another choice of tradition: they are all fascinated by the novel preceding the nineteenth century. I call this era the first 'half-time' of the history of the novel. This era and its aesthetic were almost forgotten, obscured, during the nineteenth century. The 'betrayal' of this first half-time deprived the novel of its play essence (so striking in Rabelais, Cervantes, Sterne, Diderot) and diminished the role of what I call 'novelistic meditation.' " Lois Oppenheim, "Clarifications, Elucidations: An Interview with Milan Kundera," *Review of Contemporary Fiction*, no. 2 (1989), 8–9. "Between the Bach of *The Art of the Fugue* and the classical music that follows there is the greatest caesura that music has ever known. The average melomaniac of today still lives within the aesthetic created by Haydn, Mozart, and developed later by the Romantics. What preceded, he experiences as an archaism as foreign to him (though a little more agreeable to the ear) as the modernism of Boulez or Stockhausen. The forgotten past of the first 'half-time' acted on nineteenth-century music like a hidden charge, like a repression, like a complex. This is what bears witness to the greatness of Webern or of late Stravinsky. . . . The history of the novel, it seems to me, also knows this kind of division into two 'half-times.' Somewhere between Sterne and Laclos on one side and Scott and Balzac on the other, a radical change in aesthetics took place and the memory of the first half-time was concealed or repressed. When, in the fifties and sixties, the partisans of the so-called new novel criticize what they call the 'traditional novel,' what are they alluding to with the word 'traditional'? . . . One cannot dispute the nineteenth century and at the

This model of history is idiosyncratic enough to suggest that it might be related somehow to the existential experience of its author: Kundera's efforts to come to grips with his own traumatic youth. And indeed, the novelist's biography points directly to the source of his anxiety. "My generation," Kundera explained in an interview in 1967, "matured in the period of Stalinism." It was the ethical double bind of this period that stigmatized him for the rest of his life: "Stalinism . . . was based on a majestic humanistic movement which even amidst its Stalinist disease retained many of its original attitudes, ideas, slogans, words, and dreams. It was a tremendously confusing situation. Moral orientation became more than difficult if not impossible. . . . The danger of Stalinism for all virtues and ideals stems from the fact that while originally based on them it gradually perverted them into their opposite: love for humankind into cruelty toward humans, love for truth into denunciation, and so on."[2] This moral confusion created by Stalinism had a devastating effect on a good many of Kundera's generation. It made them behave in a manner they subsequently regretted, and it implicated them in crimes of which they were initially unaware. For them to connect the two halves of their lives requires an involved and painful process of reflecting about their shameful past and drawing from it disconcerting conclusions for their present conduct. *The Joke*, explores the possibilities available to the members of Kundera's cohort in this search, in what Kundera termed elsewhere their "stalking of the lost deed."[3]

According to the literary critic Lubomír Doležel, whose own life trajectory approximates Kundera's in many respects, "*The Joke* can be designated an *ideological novel*," for "the narrators of *The Joke* are representatives

---

same time participate in its greatest 'sin': in its forgetting of the half-time of Rabelais and Sterne." Milan Kundera, "On Criticism, Aesthetics, and Europe," ibid., pp. 14–15. "It is very interesting to see just how rooted we are in the first half of life, even if life's second half is filled with intense and moving experiences. Not only is there the question of experience (Gombrowicz did indeed have many important experiences in Argentina), but of obsessions, of traumatisms, which are inextricably tied to the first half of life—which includes childhood, adolescence and adulthood." Jordan Elgrably, "Conversations with Milan Kundera," *Salmagundi* 73 (Winter 1987), 10. Further references to this last source will be given in the text.

[2] Antonín J. Liehm, "Milan Kundera," in *Generace* (Cologne, 1988), p. 56; "Milan Kundera," in *The Politics of Culture*, trans. P. Kussi (New York, 1970), pp. 140–41. Quotations are taken, with some alterations, from Kussi's translation. Further references will be given in the text; the first number in parentheses refers to the Czech original and the second to the English translation.

[3] Milan Kundera, *Kniha smíchu a zapomnění* (Toronto, 1981), p. 15; *The Book of Laughter and Forgetting*, trans. M. H. Heim (Harmondsworth, 1980), p. 9. Quotations are taken, with some alterations, from Heim's translation. Further references will be given in the text; the first number in parentheses refers to the Czech original and the second to the English translation.

of various systems of 'false' ideologies-myths."[4] Let me proceed from this insightful remark and elaborate it in some detail. "Ideologies," according to Karl Mannheim's classical study on this subject, "are the situationally transcended ideas which never succeed *de facto* in the realization of their projected contents."[5] But, the Hungarian sociologist of knowledge argues, there are two fundamental ways in which such a deficiency can skew our worldview. There are, on the one hand, sets of collectively shared beliefs rooted in a given social situation to such an extent that they completely ignore all facts that could destabilize it, change the status quo. These mental constructs Mannheim calls ideologies proper. To them he juxtaposes another type of the collective unconscious driven by the opposite desire: to destroy or transform a given society. The utopian mentality, as he calls it, is "guided by wishful representation and the will to action" to such an extent that "it turns its back on everything which would shake its belief or paralyze its desire to change things" (40).

The respective worldviews of Kundera's novel's four narrators resemble, surprisingly closely, three forms of utopian mentality, which in Mannheim's terminology are the chiliasm of the Anabaptists, the conservative idea, and the Socialist-Communist utopia. These three modes of utopian thought differ from one another, Mannheim observes, in their peculiar perceptions of time or, more precisely, in their orientations toward specific segments of the temporal spectrum. The distinctive feature of chiliasm is its absolute presentness. Neither what has happened nor what will happen motivates the agents of this mentality, but only the atemporal Logos, the voice of God which speaks in their soul. "For the real chiliast," Mannheim writes, "the present becomes the breach through which what was previously inward bursts out suddenly, takes hold of the outer world and transforms it" (215). For the conservative utopianist the past is of cardinal importance. The present is legitimized only insofar as it has evolved organically from some prior existence. All historical configurations are connected because they are the embodiments of the spirit that unfolds through the collective creation of a community, whether tribe, nation, or state. Finally, the Socialist-Communist utopia is future oriented. It shares with the conservative idea the belief in historical determinism, but it sees the past not as a validation of the present but as the blueprint for the future. Furthermore, whereas for conservatives a spiritual force propels history, the Socialist mentality projects economy into this role.

The Christian character in *The Joke*, Kostka, fits the image of the chilias-

---

4 Lubomír Doležel, *Narrative Modes in Czech Literature* (Toronto, 1973), pp. 115–16. Further references will be given in the text.
5 Karl Mannheim, *Ideology and Utopia: An Introduction to the Sociology of Knowledge*, trans. L. Wirth et al. (London, 1936), p. 194. Further references will be given in the text.

tic type as Mannheim formulated it. Although the text furnishes no clues as to his actual religious denomination, Kostka's church, it seems, is the communion of those whom Christ rules with his Word. For his actions are governed not by customary social considerations but by the gospel alone. Thus, paradoxically, in the struggle between Party and Church, Kostka sides with the former. He sees its quest for social justice, though atheistic in appearance, as closer to Christ's message of love for "thy neighbor" than the benign neglect of the disadvantaged practiced by the organized church. But besides these minor involvements with the mundane concerns of the day, Kostka lives outside time, in *unio mystica* with God, his absolute presence. "The help religion offers," he explains, "is simple: Yield thyself up. Yield thyself up together with the burden under which thou stumblest. This is the greatest relief, to live, giving yourself." And "to yield oneself up," he continues, "means to lay aside one's past life. To remove it out of one's soul."[6] The same holds true, Kostka maintains, for the future. Hearing Jesus' words (Matthew 6:34), "Take therefore no thought for the morrow: for the morrow shall take thought for the things of itself" (209; 213), he leaves his prestigious academic position to assume a menial job at a state farm.

If in *The Joke* Kostka personifies chiliastic utopianism, it is the character of the folkorist Jaroslav who embodies the conservative idea. He derives the meaning of his existence not from the divine presence but from the bond with the spirit of his people, that "age-old tradition which got hold of man after man and pulled him into its sweet stream. In this stream everybody became like everybody else and merged into humankind" (143; 146). Moravian folklore is for Jaroslav the medium through which the past projects itself into the present. The most prominent manifestation of this legacy in the novel is the Pentecostal ritual known as "the Ride of the Kings"—a festive procession of male equestrians in female dresses leading a blindfolded and muted "king"—that reenacts, according to some, the flight of the defeated Hungarian King Matthias Corvinus through southern Moravia in 1469. For a true conservative mentality, however, the continuity of a tradition limited to a mere five hundred years is just a flash in the pan. Hence Jaroslav's quasi-scholarly foray into the history of Moravian folk music (omitted from the first English edition of the novel) which links it to ancient Greece and the mystical jubilation of Dionysus. And whereas Kostka supports the Communists because of their affinity with the purported values of Christianity, Jaroslav's mem-

---

6   Milan Kundera, *Žert* (Prague, 1967), pp. 218–19; *The Joke: Definitive Version Revised by the Author* (New York, 1992), p. 228. Quotations are taken, with some alterations, from this translation. Further references will be given in the text; the first number in parentheses refers to the Czech original and the second to the English translation.

bership in the Party is a function of its massive support of folklore as a desirable alternative to decadent bourgeois art.

The Socialist-Communist utopia is represented in Kundera's novel by two protagonists, Helena and Ludvík. One reason for this doubling, I believe, rests in the fact that these characters illustrate two different motivations for embracing Marxist-Leninist doctrine: an intellectual and an emotive one. Ludvík's utopia is axiomatic, governed by the internal logic of Marxism as a totalizing system of knowledge. In this respect Ludvík is similar to the other two male narrators. Helena's utopia, by contrast, as a response to her sexual drive, is far less rational. She says: "I'm not ashamed of the way I am, I can't be other than what I've always been, till I was eighteen all I knew was being cooped up in a convent, two years in a TB sanatorium, another two years catching up on the schooling I'd missed, I didn't even go to dancing lessons; all I knew was the tidy apartment of tidy Pilsen citizens and schoolwork, schoolwork; real life was beyond seven walls. Then in '49 when I arrived in Prague it was suddenly a miracle, a happiness which I'll never forget" (19; 15–16).

Helena identifies the social revolution with her sexual liberation. Her *Weltanschauung* was formed by an orgiastic experience during the May First demonstration where she fell in love, and by the Party's intervention that delivered her coy partner into matrimony. The world for which Helena fights in the name of Communism has ever since been one of full and requited love. Although Ludvík too had initially drifted toward the Party for personal reasons (a negation of his bourgeois background), his Communist utopia had far more global ramifications than Helena's. It was linked, he recollects later, "to an altogether idealistic illusion that we were inaugurating the era of humankind when man (every man) would neither be *outside* history, *nor under the heel* of history, but would direct and create it" (72; 71). Ludvík's disquisition on the renaissance of folk music in Socialist Moravia presented before his old friends just after the Communist coup captures in a nutshell the basic tenets of the Marxist mentality with its peculiar perception of time. As Jaroslav, a witness to this event, sums it up: "[Ludvík] had an air all the Communists had at that time. As if he'd made a secret pact with the future and had the right to act in its name" (136; 139).

But there is yet another, more significant reason for the existence in *The Joke* of two characters who subscribe to the same type of utopian mentality. Helena is a captive of the *Weltanschauung* she adopted in her youth, unable to go beyond its limits, to change the mental filter through which she processes social reality. In this respect she is quite similar to Kostka and Jaroslav, whose worldviews are equally singular and unitary, though each in its own particular way. Ludvík, by comparison, represents a skeptical, post-utopianist attitude. An ill-conceived joke—a postcard blaspheming some of the most cherished Communist ideals intended to shock the girl of his dreams but fallen inadvertently into the wrong hands—cost Ludvík not only his Party card but his student status as well. From being a member of the elite, he overnight became a social pariah: a private in a penal battalion and a miner in the Ostrava coal-pits. This sobering experience helped him to recognize not only the limitations of his own belief system but also the relativity of all ideological constructs. Thus, as Doležel argues cogently, in the novel "Ludvík is assigned the role of destroying not only his own myth but also of contributing substantially to the destruction of other characters' myths" as well (119).

Applying Kundera's image of history as an essentially bipartite process to the biographies of his four protagonists, one finds that it is only Ludvík whose existence seems truly historical. The lives of the others are prehistorical, consisting solely of first halves. Even as the gap between their beliefs and reality increases, they are unwilling to reflect on the past from a new perspective and desperately cling to their original identities. Helena's words, repeated several times throughout the text, "I don't want my life to split down the middle, I want it to remain whole from beginning to end" (25; 22), illustrate this "ideological" aversion to adjusting one's existence to new circumstances. "One's destiny," Ludvík meditates as the novel closes, "is often complete long before death, the moment of its end need not coincide with the moment of death" (292; 317). And though it is only Jaroslav to whom he refers, his observation pertains equally to Helena and Kostka.

In *The Joke*, an unwillingness to scrutinize one's past critically is considered a fatal weakness, and those afflicted by it are symbolically sentenced to death as their respective utopias collapse. Helena attempts suicide and leaves town in disgrace with a man she does not love. Kostka commits a mortal sin and loses his contact with God; he is unable to recognize God's voice in the polyphony he suddenly hears. Jaroslav suffers a crippling heart attack that will forever prevent him from playing with his band. We part with these damaged beings convinced that they will be unable to construct anything positive from the shambles of their lives. Ludvík's fate is different because he was able to shed his youthful vision of utopia relatively early in his career. In the penal battalion to which he was sent for punishment, he "realized that the line tying [him] to the Party and its members had hopelessly slipped through [his] fingers" (53; 52). At this moment the decisive rupture in his biography occurrs and the second half of Ludvík's life begins.

Yet, as I argued earlier, what interests Kundera is not merely the articulation of history into distinct segments but rather their connection, the recuperation of the past from the present perspective. Thus, one must ask, what is the relation between the two halves of Ludvík's biography? How does he manage to incorporate his traumatic experience into his subsequent behavior? The story of Ludvík's life unfolds according to the principle of inversion. An innocent joke turns into a personal tragedy that then transforms his infatuation with the Marxist utopia into revulsion and his former friends into enemies. Accordingly, the only connection between the two halves of his personal history is purely negative. In Ludvík's words: "And . . . the main bond with which I've wanted to tie myself with the past which hypnotized me was revenge" (270; 293). The entire motivation for his present actions is the desire to avenge himself upon those who punished him unjustly. The Czech word *litost* best describes this unsettled mental state. "What is *litost*?" Kundera asks in *The Book of Laughter and Forgetting*. It is a word "with no exact translation into any other language. It designates a feeling as infinite as an open accordion, a feeling that is the synthesis of many others: grief, sympathy, remorse, and an indefinable longing. . . . Under certain circumstances, however, it can have a very narrow meaning, a meaning as definite, precise, and sharp as a well-honed cutting edge. I have never found an equivalent in other languages for this sense of the word either, though I do not see how anyone can understand the human soul without it" (130; 121).

The semantic mystery of the word *litost*, which Kundera puts on display, has a solid lexicological basis. This noun is a homonym that shelters two highly incompatible meanings: the feeling of pity or grief on the one hand and the state of fury or ferocity, on the other. Curiously, this freak of semantics grasps perfectly the peculiar psychic mechanism that intrigues Kundera: self-pity vented as aggression. As he explains: "*Litost* works like a two-stroke engine. First comes a feeling of torment, then the desire for revenge" (132; 122). Ludvík's story in *The Joke* parallels the sequence of mental states in *litost* as Kundera outlines it. Unjust dismissal from the Party and the university indelibly scars his psyche, and the subsequent social discrimination to which he is exposed only adds insult to injury. With a bruised ego, he seeks to settle accounts with the culprits who derailed the first half of his life. An accidental meeting with the wife of his chief inquisitor, Zemánek, provides him with a welcome opportunity. He seduces her and during their sexual encounter treats her sadistically. But the principle of inversion strikes again. Ludvík's revenge turns into another joke, and instead of getting even with the villain, he merely hurts innocent bystanders. *Litost*, the novel suggests, is not the best mental state for accessing one's past. It is another form of "false consciousness," of a distorted worldview that, in contrast to its collective counterpart, is strictly individual.

Earlier I quoted Mannheim's definition of ideologies as "the situationally transcendent ideas which never succeed *de facto* in the realization of their projected contents." Utopias, then, are "futurist" schemes that, in the name of a particular certitude, aim to transform the world. Ludvík's drive to correct earlier wrongs is the mirror image of the utopianist undertaking. It substitutes for the myth of transcendental Truth that of transcendental Justice and strives to project it onto the past. With the same tenacity with which Helena, Jaroslav, and Kostka hold to their ideals until time renders the gap between their utopias and reality untenable, Ludvík holds to his belief that a former injustice can be rectified—until the outcome of his action proves him wrong. The intervening fifteen years have altered everything. Those who once had punished him for his ideological deviation are now thinking very much like him, and his carefully crafted plan is transformed into a mockery of itself. "When postponed," Ludvík realizes, "vengeance turns into something deceptive, a personal religion, a myth detached more and more from the lives of the participants. . . . [T]oday a different Jahn faces a different Zemánek and the blow . . . which I dealt today, after all these years is an unintelligible blow, and because of its unintelligibility it assumes completely different, alien, unintended meanings, it becomes something else than I had in mind, it can turn in many directions and I cannot control it and even less justify it" (270; 293). Thus, Ludvík's quest for justice becomes as illusory as his earlier quest for a better world.

With this experience, history appears to Ludvík a series of jokes, an endless irony over which he has no command, which transforms each of his deeds into something different. The past cannot be recouped because it is never the same. Protean to the point of incomprehensibility, history appears a frustrating enigma which ought to be purged from memory: "All that has been done, has been done and cannot be undone. . . . [N]obody can redeem an injustice which has happened but all will be forgotten" (271; 294). This recognition breaks the tenuous link that held together the two halves of Ludvík's biography. Yielding to blissful oblivion, he imagines himself falling into the timeless chasm that has suddenly opened in his life: "I felt myself falling . . . down into depths of years, the depths of centuries, fathomless depths (where love is love and pain is pain), and I told myself with astonishment that my only home was this very descent, the searching, longing fall, and I abandoned myself to it, feeling its sweet vertigo" (291; 316).

It would be facile, however, to interpret *The Joke* merely as a novel about delayed justice. Ludvík is much more that just a luckless victim of Czechoslovak Communism. The image of vertigo employed in the foregoing passage is crucial to an understanding of the hidden dimension of this character. Referring to *The Unbearable Lightness of Being*, Kundera unraveled for an interviewer his metaphoric usage of the word: "Vertigo [is] the intoxication of the weak. Aware of his weakness, man decides to give in rather than stand up to it. He is drunk with weakness, wishes to grow even weaker, wishes to fall down in the middle of the main square in front of everybody, wishes to be down, lower than down."[7] This figurative interpretation of vertigo suggests that Ludvík's sudden desire to dissociate himself from his past is a sign of mental frailty, a form of suicidal urge.

The source of this foible, however, is not immediately obvious from the text. To pinpoint it let me return once more to the notion of *lítost*. The similarity between *lítost* and the utopian mentality of which I spoke does not end with the fact that both are forms of false consciousness. More important, they are manifestations of wishful thinking, the manipulation of reality according to the needs of a group or an individual who projects them. The source of Ludvík's weakness, I would argue, is the repressed aspect of his personal history, that part of his previous life that the feeling of self-pity censors. Throughout the novel Ludvík portrays himself, above all, as a victim of the Marxist-Leninist utopia, the avenger of the injustice to which he was subjected. What comes out only rarely in the text, however, is the fact that as a former Party member, he was involved in the abuses of power that occurred after the Communist takeover. This suppressed guilt emerges in *The Joke* only occasionally in Ludvík's internal dialogues between his two selves—the victim and the victimizer. "Very often in my reminiscences," he reflects, "I return to that lecture hall where a hundred people raised their hands, giving the order for my life to be fractured. . . . Since then whenever meeting new men or women who might become my friends or lovers I project them back to that time, to that hall and ask myself whether they would have raised their hands: no one has ever passed that test." But now the second voice chimes in:

> Perhaps it was cruel of me to submit the people I met to such severe scrutiny. . . . Say I did it for one purpose only: to elevate myself above all others in my moral complacency. But to accuse me of conceit wouldn't really be justified; true, I've never myself voted for anyone's destruction, but I knew well that this is a rather problematic merit because I was deprived of the right to raise my hand sufficiently early. I've tried for a long time to convince myself at least that if in similar situations I wouldn't have raised my hand, but I'm honest enough to laugh at myself: would I've been the only one not to raise his hand? Am I the one just man? Alas, I found no guarantee within myself that I'd been better than others. (76–77; 76–77)

The logic of this utterance is quite revealing of Ludvík's ambiguous attitude toward his past. He steadfastly denies any complicity in Stalinist

[7] Christian Salmon, "Conversation with Milan Kundera on the Art of the Novel," trans. L. Asher, *Salmagundi* 73 (Winter 1987), 126.

crimes because he never raised his hand to condemn anyone. Yet the feeling of guilt hovers in the air. He never had to decide anyone's fate, but if push came to shove he would have behaved like the rest of his comrades.

The guilt exists because Ludvík's hands are not altogether clean, as another of his inner dialogues reveals:

> If asked by various commissions, I could list dozens of reasons why I became a Communist, but what enchanted me the most about this movement, even intoxicated me, was the *steering-wheel of history* in whose proximity . . . I found myself. For in those days we actually did decide the fate of people and events; especially at the universities: among the faculty were very few Communists then and, therefore, in those early years, Communist students governed the universities, they themselves deciding academic appointments, educational reform, the curriculum. (71–72; 71)

It was therefore Ludvík himself who, in concert with others, participated in the purges after the 1948 coup: firing professors who did not fit the new ideological mold, thereby in the name of the highest humanistic principles ruining their lives. This is a responsibility, however, that Ludvík is not willing to face. He is eager to paint himself as a victim of Communism, not as one of its promoters. This status furnishes him with the moral high ground for his vendetta. Only after his attempt at avenging himself turns him into a victimizer does another connection between his past and present begin to dawn on him. Running away from the place of his unsuccessful revenge, Ludvík realizes that "every time I tried to redress the wrongs done me I ended wronging others. I was chasing away these thoughts because I had known what they were telling me for a long time" (285; 310). This old knowledge, never revealed in the text, is Ludvík's suppressed guilt: the fact that both his Marxist-Leninist quest for social justice and his later action intended to redress a personal injury resulted in similar injustices. But Ludvík is too weak to admit his complicity in the wrongs of the Stalinist era. Unable to stand up to his past, he "becomes drunk" with weakness and in a "delicious vertigo" yields to a comforting historical amnesia.

So far we have seen that none of the characters from *The Joke* manage to come to terms with his or her own history, to connect somehow the two halves of his or her life. Some are unable to transcend the utopias of their youths; others, unwilling to confront the shameful memory of the past, recoil from it. But is there any way out of this dilemma for the members of the Kundera generation who matured in the perplexing era of Stalinism and who were more or less willingly implicated in its misdeeds? In writing his novel, Kundera provided one possible answer to this question. In his interview with the Czech novelist, Alain Finkielkraut pointed out what he considered Kundera's greatest contribution to the critique of the Communist utopia. "In your novel *Life Is Elsewhere*, you speak of Stalinism as if it were an era where 'the poet reigned along with the executioner.' If the New Philosophers find the roots of the Gulag in Fichte and Hegel, you yourself find them in poetry."[8]

Kundera's discovery of a latent affiliation between lyricism and totalitarianism is no doubt connected to his own biography, which, it is worth mentioning, exhibits some points of contact with the life of his hero, Ludvík. Like him, Kundera joined the Party in 1948 only to be expelled some two years later for a joke—a parody of a poem by the leading coryphaeus of Socialist Realism, Vítězslav Nezval. But in contrast to Ludvík's career, Kundera's rebounded rather quickly. As early as 1953 he managed to publish the collection *Man—a Vast Garden*, a book very much attuned to the ideological ambiance of the time, and then two years later *The Last May*, another tendentious poetic composition about the Communist hero of the anti-Nazi resistance Julius Fučík. It was his next book of poems, *Monologues* (1957), which heralded the transition in Kundera's creative career. In its verse form it was a continuation of his earlier poetic output, but in its deliberately antilyric mode it hinted at the subsequent stage of Kundera's writerly trajectory, the shift from poetry to prose. In the late 1950s Kundera produced his first short story, the embryo of his next collection, *Laughable Loves*, and abandoned verse, never to return to it again. "My life," he recollected for Jordan Elgrably in *Salmagundi* some quarter century later, "took flight with the first story for *Laughable Loves*. This was my Opus 1. Everything I'd written prior to it can be considered prehistory" (8). But even the short story did not satisfy Kundera entirely. In 1961 he published a scholarly monograph about the Czech avant-gardist Vladislav Vančura, *The Art of the Novel*, and it was in this latter genre that the footloose author finally found his artistic home. *The Joke*, begun in 1961 and finished in 1965, was his first novel.

The dichotomy between verse and prose, the lyric and the novel, is for Kundera more than a matter of form. These modes of writing represent for him two incompatible mentalities, two opposite attitudes toward the self, others, and the surrounding world. The lyric, Kundera claims, is unreflexive, emotive. It is a direct self-expression of the poet who through empathy strives to merge his ego with the audience's collective spirit. "In rhyme and rhythm," Kundera puts it in one of his novels, "resides a cer-

---

[8]   Alain Finkielkraut, "Milan Kundera Interview," trans. S. Huston, *Cross Currents: A Yearbook of Central European Culture* 1 (1982), 22. Further references will be given in the text.

tain magic power. If a woman *weary of breath* has *gone to her death*, dying becomes harmoniously integrated into the cosmic order. . . . Through poetry, man realizes his agreement with existence, and rhyme and rhythm are the crudest means of gaining consent."[9] To the poetic yearning for an all-embracing unity Kundera juxtaposes the prosaic awareness of an all-pervasive difference: "An anti-poetic posture grows out of the conviction that between what we think about ourselves and what we actually are there exists an infinite distance, just as there is an infinite distance between what we wish things were and what they are, or between what we think they are and what they are. To apprehend this distance, this abyss, means to destroy the poetic illusion. This is also the essence of the art of irony. And irony is the perspective of the novel."[10] This explains Kundera's argument that there exists a close affinity between social utopianism and the lyric. Both correspond to the deep-seated human need for stability, predictability, harmony. They create a totalizing universe of discourse closed to critical scrutiny. The former does so through a quasi-rational argument that reduces the complexity of the world to a simple formula whose self-evidence is beyond doubt, the latter through a poetic pathos to which we yield joyfully. It was during the Stalinst period, Kundera intimates in his interview with Finkielkraut, when this latent kinship became manifest. "The totalitarianism of the '50's was not just oppression alone. It was not by means of its execution posts that it attracted the masses, the young, the intelligentsia. It was by its smile. We tend to forget this today; we are ashamed of this. We no longer say: the bloody totalitarianism of the '50's had a poetry that we succumbed to. If we blame it on the Gulag, we feel pardoned. If we speak of the poetry of totalitarianism we remain implicated in the scandal" (23).

This condensed statement provides, I believe, a key for interpreting Kundera's attitude toward his own past. The word he chose to designate Communist totalitarianism has powerful connotations. Marcel Detienne reminds us of the curious

"machine" hidden in the Greek *skandalon*: the deadfall of a trap in which bait has been placed. . . . But the site of the scandal, its own space, is made up of a dual motion, repulsion and attraction. One points the finger, one becomes outraged, one makes a scene in order to eloign, to put a distance be-

---

[9] Milan Kundera, *Život je jinde* (Toronto, 1979), p. 231; *Life Is Elsewhere*, trans. P. Kussi (Harmondsworth, 1980), p. 193. Quotations are taken, with some alterations, from Kussi's translation. Further references will be given in the text; the first number in parentheses refers to the Czech original and the second to the English translation.

[10] Quoted from Antonín J. Liehm, "Milan Kundera: A Czech Writer," in *Czech Literature since 1955: A Symposium*, ed. W. E. Harkins et al. (New York, 1980), p. 49.

tween oneself and others, between oneself—in the eyes of others—and that very thing by which one is in danger of being attracted, seduced, or trapped. Like a double bind whose hieroglyph would be one hand cutting off the other.[11]

Thus, for Kundera the scandal of Stalinism is not merely the barbed wire around the Gulag—the steel jaws that crushed its victims—but also the allure of the lyricism that made the masses voluntarily enter its snare. Moral opprobrium of this period might comfortably distance us from it; yet it trivializes what happened, obliterates what should be remembered, mutilates the past. We cannot, Kundera argues, walk away from the *skandalon* of Stalinism in disgust but must return to it and explore it from within, fully and responsibly.

Thus, it is clear that Kundera's animus toward the lyric has its roots in his personal history. "My own youth (the lyric age)," he confessed to Antonín J. Liehm the very same year *The Joke* appeared, "my lyric activity and interests coincide with the worst season of the Stalinist years" (60; 145). To put it more bluntly, in an era when "the poet reigned along with the executioner," he played a less than innocent role. Kundera's awakening coincided with the first serious crisis of the Communist movement in 1956, and after that he was among the most vociferous critics of totalitarianism in Czechoslovak politics and culture. But how could he respond to his own past, the first half of his biography implicated in the blunders of the very same period that he now decried? The figure of Ludvík suggests some possible reactions: a feeling of *lítost*, a suppression of guilt, amnesia. Kundera, however, rejected the quiet fatalism of his hero's resignation that history is the master ironist playing jokes on him. Taking up the challenge of facing his past, he turned the joke on history. He returned to his "lyric age" and reinscribed it ironically, from a novelistic perspective.

The figure of the joke thrives on the essential ambiguity of language. It highlights the fact that words can mean something other than what they say. Ludvík, for example, hails Trotsky, but what he really wants is to get his reluctant girlfriend into bed. The hidden agenda of Kundera's own joke is to expose the dialogue between the two halves of his life, between the poet and the prosaist. The fictional universe that the novel projects obscures the ongoing polemics between the views its author held in the 1950s and those he holds now. We must not overlook the fact that *The Joke* reiterates a number of motifs and themes that occurred previously in Kundera's poetry: a strong affection for one's native place and childhood friends, the redeeming power of love, and the celebration of spontaneity

---

[11] Marcel Detienne, *The Creation of Mythology*, trans. M. Cook (Chicago, 1986), pp. 13–14.

to mention just a few. But while in his poems these lyrical clichés are presented at face value, as expressions of eternal ideals, in *The Joke* they become novelistic material. They are examined from different perspectives, unsentimentally dissected, debunked. It suffices to compare two passages, the first from the beginning of *The Joke*:

> So here I was, home again after all these years. Standing in the main square (which I had crossed countless times as a child, as a boy, as a young man), I felt no emotion whatsoever; all I could think was that the flat space, with the spire of the town hall ... had engraved an irrevocable ugliness on its face.... But I had been deceiving myself: what I had called indifference was in fact rancor.... [T]he mission that had brought me here [was] so cynical and low as to mock any suspicion that I was returning here out of some sentimental attachment to things past. (7; 3)

with Kundera's "From the Verses about Brno" :

> But it's my city, when I was small,
> when I was small and used to walk barefoot.
>
> And now, wherever I am, suddenly somewhere from below
> from inside my bosom a bell starts clinking:
> with a touching, childish, doleful voice
> my city calls me back.
>
> And I'll return, even if I were
> in black Africa or near the Kurils.

to appreciate the magnitude of this change of heart.[12]

Rather than piling up more such examples, I will illustrate my thesis using one detail from *The Joke*: the figure of the Czechoslovak National Hero Julius Fučík who, as several reviewers of the novel noticed, occupies a rather conspicous position in the text.[13] Earlier I wrote that Kundera joined the chorus of Fučík glorifiers in 1955 with *The Last May*, an imaginative amplification of a small episode from the Fučík *Reportage* to which I referred in Chapter 3: Julius's "temptation on the mountain" by the Gestapo Commissar Böhm which, according to *Reportage*, occurred one summer evening in 1942 on the hill near Hradčany Castle. Kundera, it

---

[12]   Milan Kundera, "Z veršů o Brně," *Nový život: Měsíčník pro soudobou literaturu a kritiku*, no. 10 (1953), 1164.
[13]   See, e.g., Jiří Opelík, "Kunderovo 'hoře z rozumu,' " *Literární noviny*, June 10, 1967, p. 5.

must be stressed, took certain liberties with his original source. For reasons that I will explain shortly, he shifted the time of this encounter to spring. Also, the story of *The Last May* unfolds on the terrace of a specific restaurant on Petřín, the hill in Prague next to Hradčany, an establishment never mentioned in Fučík's *Reportage*. True, during the summer of 1942 Fučík enjoyed an occasional glass of beer in Böhm's company at a pub in the Prague suburb of Bráník. Such sojourns were apparently an element in the game of deception that Julius played with the Gestapo: bait for his captors to make them believe that he still had contacts with the underground resistance.[14] The jejune locale and the equally uninspiring choice of drink, however, ill suited Kundera's lyrical temper. In his poem the biblical encounter between Julius and the Tempter takes place in a garden restaurant overlooking Prague with wine as the beverage of choice. It is where Böhm, under Kundera's direction, takes his stubborn captive amidst the fragrant beauty of the blossoming spring in hopes that a sudden exposure to nubile nature will undermine Fučík's resolve and inspire him to trade his life for Party secrets.

Within the context of Czech poetry, *The Last May* might be seen as a creative dialogue with another poet who eulogized Fučík—Konstantin Biebl—with whom Kundera felt a special affinity. Whereas Biebl's "Julius Fučík in Prison" begins with "Fučík enters the prison" and focuses on the physical torture the hero had to endure there, Kundera's poem, instead, concludes this way (" . . . and the gates of Pankrác closed behind him") while it opens with Julius's apparent release ("The dark cells have opened, / the Pankrác gates have opened, / and the prisoner came out").[15] The thirty pages or so that separate the first line from the last describe the mental torment to which this abrupt transfer subjects Fučík, debilitated by prolonged sensory deprivation and physical abuse.

Biebl's composition, however, is not the only subtext for *The Last May*. More important, its title is an unmistakable allusion to the most famous Czech Romantic poem, Karel Hynek Mácha's *May* (1836). The two compositions are linked, above all, thematically. Mácha's protagonist, the robber Vilém, is the victim of the very same predicament in which Fučík is trapped: at the height of spring this condemned felon awaits his imminent execution. Through such an analogy Kundera is able to draw a distinction between two existential stances, two attitudes toward *thanatos*. For

[14] Julius Fučík, *Reportáž, psaná na oprátce: První úplné, kritické a komentované vydání* (Prague, 1995), p. 59; *Notes from the Gallows* (New York, 1948), p. 67.
[15] Konstantin Biebl, "Julius Fučík ve vězení," in *Dílo: Bez obav 1940—1945*, vol. 4 (Prague, 1953), p. 27. Milan Kundera, *Poslední máj: Báseň* (Prague, 1955), pp. 7, 39. Subsequent references to the latter source will be given in the text. For Kundera's relationship with Biebl, see Finkielkraut, "Milan Kundera Interview," pp. 23–24.

Vilém—bereft of any transcendental ideals—death is the ultimate horror, the gate to the void and nothingness, and the buoyant nature of May only reminds him how cruel his punishment is. For the Communist Fučík, the herald of historical optimism, death is merely a personal sacrifice, a contribution to the final victory of the collective Cause outside of which life is meaningless. In an indirect dialogue with Vilém (Böhm being his understudy in Kundera's poem), he asserts:

> Those who live for their own life alone,
> for themselves, for their fleeting journey,
> live like a vain meteorite,
> falling into the darkness to perish. (25)

And as in *The Joke*, in *The Last May* too folklore plays an important role. It is a folk-song about another robber—Jánošík, the legendary "redistributor" of wealth in the Slovak Tatra Mountains—which nourishes Fučík's strength to deflect Böhm's temptation:

> After the death of a fighter his life
> changes into a fire on the mountains.
> And even a small droplet of betrayal
> would extinguish this bonfire.
> So, am I to dissolve myself in darkness?
> Am I to betray? Am I to become a suicide? (29)

These rhetorical questions are non-aporetic, for Julius, incited by Jánošík's example, answers them with stoic ease:

> Shoot me! Well!
> But after I fall to the ground,
> the hands of friends
> will lift my battle-ax [*valaška*].
> The fight will not cease! (32)

Even Mother Nature cannot remain indifferent to heroism, so noble, so eloquent, and, spoiling Böhm's fiendish design, becomes Fučík's ally. So, "embraced by the tender gaze of the entire universe" (35), the invigorated Julius joyously marches back to his cell to face certain death.

In the next decade, though, Kundera's attitude toward Fučík changed considerably. In Chapter 3 I argued that through its heavy-duty use by Party propagandists, the image of this resistance martyr became one of the most palpable emblems of the Stalinist era. And this is how Kundera presents him in *The Joke*. Julius, first of all, participates, if only symbolically, in Ludvík's prosecution. During the fatal meeting resulting in his expulsion from the Party and the school, chief prosecutor Zemánek dramatically juxtaposes Ludvík's postcard to the girl he wants to impress equating "optimism" with "the opium of the people" (36; 34) to a well-orchestrated medley of the most memorable passages from Fučík's *Reportage*, whose unbridled pathos makes Ludvík's joke look particularly perfidious.[16] Furthermore, this kangaroo court takes place in a classroom prominently adorned with the official portrait of Fučík. And the narrator, recounting the event from the distance of a decade or so, does not fail to draw attention to the idolized falsity of this quasi-icon, "almost girlish, effervescent, pure, and so beautiful that perhaps those who knew Fučík personally preferred this noble drawing to their memory of a real face" (188; 191).

The Joke, however, does considerably more than just tarnish Julius's image by linking it to the Stalinist terror. More important, it launches a full-fledged attack against the entire heroic cult of Fučík, which *The Last May* helped to build. Infuriated by the patent absurdity of a pseudo-Moravian folk song about this resistance martyr performed by Jaroslav's band, Ludvík speaks his mind. The author of *Reportage*, he charges, "though far from famous [at the time], considered it of the utmost importance to inform the world of what he thought, felt and experienced in prison, of what he conveyed to and recommended for humankind. He scribbled it out on small scraps of paper, risking the lives of people who smuggled them out of prison and kept them safe." Contrary to the Party *doxa*, Ludvík insists, jolting Jaroslav, that Fučík wrote *Reportage* not out of inner strength but rather out of "his weakness. Because to be brave in solitude, without witnesses, without the reward of others' approbation, in front of just oneself, that would take great pride and strength. Fučík needed the help of an audience. In the solitude of his cell he created at least a fictitious audience for himself. He needed to be seen! To draw

---

[16] Ludvík's reply to his accusers asking him reproachfully what the martyrs of the anti-Nazi resistance might have thought of his blasphemous message is another instance of the interaction between Kundera's early poetry and *The Joke*. Instead of paying mandatory obeisance to the victims of Nazism and committing a public auto-da-fé that might have saved his skin, Ludvík charges his persecutors with lacking of a sense of humor. These dead comrades, he retorts angrily, "weren't petty, to be sure. If they had read my postcard, they might have even laughed" (190; 191). These words are a distinct echo of Kundera's apostrophe to the dead Communist poet Biebl (who committed suicide in 1951), "You, Konstantin, Had Never Believed," from the "Polemical Verses" section of his collection *Man—a Vast Garden*, in which the author rebukes "those gloomy priests/who closed themselves into Marxism as if a cold castle" ("Vy jste, Konstantine, nikdy neuvěřil," in *Člověk zahrada širá* [Prague, 1953], p. 49).

strength from applause! At least a fictitious applause! To turn the prison into a stage and make his lot bearable by not only living it, but also by exhibiting it, performing it! To adore himself in the beauty of his own words and gestures" (152; 156).

This novelistic reinterpretation of Fučík, quite sacrilegious to Kundera's compatriots in the mid-1960s, renders the larger-than-life hero of *The Last May* a pitiful exhibitionist insecure of his identity, a laughable representative of what Kundera termed in his interview with Antonín Liehm " 'the lyrical age' . . . when man is still an enigma to himself" and "others are for him the mirrors in which he seeks his own significance and value" (58; 142). The narcissism of *Reportage* makes Julius, in Kundera's eyes, a close relative to Jaromil, the immature poet/police informer of *Life Is Elsewhere*, whose lyrics are the product of a similar self-obsession. This kinship is further underscored by the poet's name, which, whether intentionally or by chance, harks back to Mácha's and Kundera's songs of May. For not only is the name Jaromil a male counterpart of Jarmila—robber Vilém's femme fatale—but also, in its literal sense (and the English version of *Life Is Elsewhere* highlights this etymology, which is obvious to Czech readers), it means *"he who loves the spring"* as well as *"he who is beloved by the spring"* (17; 7), characteristics of Fučík in *The Last May*.

The irony of Kundera's treatment of his own poetry in *The Joke* rests in his ability to subvert the past through its preservation. It is neither repeated nor denied but reinscribed, voided of its lyrical appeal and rendered different. Despite their scandalous origin, or, rather, precisely because of it, these texts served Kundera as the perfect object for his "meditative investigation" of the old myth—the Communist utopia—to which he once subscribed. As he himself summed it up conversing with Liehm in 1967: "What we've lived through in the last thirty years wasn't a piece of cake but all these experiences are great capital for art. The story of this nation between Fascism, democracy, Stalinism, and Socialism contains in itself all the essentials that make the twentieth century the twentieth century. It enables us to ask perhaps more fundamental questions and create perhaps more meaningful myths than those who have not lived through this whole political anabasis" (63; 148).

But may the break with one's past be as ironic as Kundera's interview suggests? Can one detach oneself so fully from deep-seated old beliefs, rendering them just "engaging" artistic material? I am not entirely sure. Prague Spring, which *The Joke* helped to inaugurate, might prove this point. Clio is a fickle lady, indeed, who can prance not only back and forth but sideways as well. To trace her whimsical dance through recent Czechoslovak history, let me return to Gottwald's 1929 parliamentary speech with which I opened the previous chapter. His wonderful plan for "a proletarian state, for a state of workers, for a state of peasants" yielded rather unexpected results some twenty years later. Soon after turning the local bourgeoisie into dead meat, Czechoslovak Communists with break-neck speed managed to kill more of their comrades than all the other People's Democracies combined. One need not be a rocket scientist to reckon that wringing necks might not be the optimal path toward Social-ist utopia. The best and brightest in the Party realized this, too, and in 1968, when the reformist wing finally took over the CPCS's helm, soul-searching discussions about what went amiss began in earnest. Yet, like their fictional counterpart Ludvík Jahn, Czechoslovak Communists were incapable of stepping over their own shadow. True, they were more than eager to redress the grievances of their wronged comrades (partially as a lever to dislodge former Party bosses), but they felt somewhat queasy about extending the same courtesy to persecuted foes. It was abundantly clear to Dubček et al. that a systematic review of all legal wrongdoing since 1948 would seriously jeopardize the legitimacy of Communist rule. Theirs was a revolutionary party always ready to break a few eggs to make an omelette for the hungry. This culinary preparation, however, in-cluded such unpalatable measures as trying political opponents on con-cocted charges, brutally harassing suspected enemies, and, occasionally, even old-fashioned murder. Deep down they knew that what had hap-pened to Slánský and other comrades was merely the tip of the iceberg in an ocean of injustice.

The reformist leadership had, it seems, two roads to choose from—ei-ther to condemn repressive past practices in toto, thus ceasing to be a Communist Party in the Leninist sense, or to continue "the dictatorship of the proletariat" while softening somewhat the methods of political repres-sion. It opted, instead, for a third path whose advantage and drawback was that it did not exist. Dubček's group stirred things up enough to alarm Kremlin hard-liners. But they never found enough courage to break completely with their Soviet teachers. Perched uncomfortably between the rock of representational democracy and the hard place of totalitarian-ism, they waffled and wavered until others stepped in to put them out of their agony. "Death wish" might be the most appropriate label for such self-defeating behavior. Turning a blind eye to all signs of impending mil-itary intervention, the Presidium of the Party (as if abandoning itself to "sweet vertigo") passively waited for the armadas of the Warsaw Pact to cross the Czechoslovak borders, until they were apprehended en masse at Central Committee headquarters and were shackled and shipped to Moscow, where, with a single dissenting voice, they voluntarily signed their own death warrant. And then the searching, longing fall: a tearful Dubček reading over the radio to a stupefied population the text of an agreement authorizing the "temporary" stationing of Soviet troops in Czechoslovakia; the accelerating pull of gravity (reformists sheepishly vacating one office after another); the first purges of those who mistook "brotherly help" for military invasion; down, down, lower than down, until "Socialism with a human face" turned into one with gooseflesh.

Amidst this breathtaking tailspin, almost exactly forty-one years after Gottwald's speech that had started it all—on December 19, 1969, to be precise—Milan Kundera once more returned to the Marxist-Leninist utopia of his youth. But this time he saw it from an altogether different perspective: not as an unattainable folly whose pursuit caused considerable suffering to all involved whether voluntarily or otherwise, but as a viable social program that at last had come to its full fruition, if only for a while. In his winter notes about Prague Spring, Kundera declared: "The attempt to create finally (and for the first time in its world history) Socialism without an omnipotent secret police, with freedom of the written and spoken word, with public opinion that is heard and with politics supported by it, with a freely developing modern culture and with people who had lost their fear, this was an attempt by which the Czechs and Slovaks for the first time since the end of the Middle Ages stood again in the center of world history and addressed their challenge to the world." This lofty language, so unbecoming to a weathered ironist of Kundera's caliber, gushing with enthusiasm about the "hitherto fallow democratic potential of the Socialist project," does not seem to square well with the pointedly anti-ideological tenor of *The Joke*.[17]

Conceivably I am misconstruing the purport of Kundera's essay "The Czech Lot," reading it out of its original context. Addressed to the population of a recently invaded country with a divided leadership, but without control fully in Russian hands, this essay pursued altogether different goals than propping up the chimera of a classless society: to boost sinking public morale, to throw support behind the beleaguered Dubček and the political program he represented, to strike a spark of hope in the rapidly encroaching darkness of Soviet night. But even if so, I am not the originator of this misprision. It flowed from the pen of a Czech playwright, Kundera's junior by seven years, whose polemical jab at "The Czech Lot"— coming from a markedly opposed ideological matrix—yielded a far more sobering view of Prague Spring's alleged historical merits:

> Indeed, if we try to convince ourselves that the country that wished to introduce freedom of expression—something that is commonplace in the majority of the civilized world—and which wanted to check the arbitrariness

17   Milan Kundera, "Český úděl," *Listy*, December 19, 1968, p. 5.

of the secret police, stood, because of this, in the center of world history, we cannot, in all seriousness, become but smug Pharisees, ludicrous in their provincial messianism! Freedom and legality are the first preconditions of a normally and soundly functioning social organism, and if some state attempts to reinstate them, after years of their absence, it does not do anything historically unfathomable but simply tries to correct its own abnormalities, simply *normalizing* itself. . . . And if a particular system declares itself Socialistic, this provides not an excuse for human oppression and societal decay in it but, on the contrary, an indictment. So, its bid to eliminate injustice cannot be—from the vantage point of human history—but a bid to eliminate nonsense that it itself has laboriously heaped up before. It seems to me that we should be ashamed of this necessity of purifying ourselves rather than boasting about it as our far-reaching historical contribution.[18]

Who was this chrysostomic gentleman so gallantly defending old-fashioned civil values in those tempestuous times? The one and only, incomparable Václav Havel—the hero of my next chapter.

[18]   Václav Havel, "Český úděl?" *Tvář*, no. 2 (1969), p. 33.

6

Cops or Robbers

The Beggar's Opera by Václav Havel

[Gay's] *Comedy* contains likewise a *Satyre*, which, it doth by no means affect the present Age, yet might have been useful in the former and may
possibly be so in Ages to come. I mean where the Author takes occasion
of comparing those *common Robbers to Robbers of the Publick;* and their
several Stratagems of betraying, undermining, and hanging each other,
to the several Arts of *Politicians* in times of Corruption."

—Jonathan Swift, *Intelligencer*, no. 3

For anybody interested in the social ramifications of literature, *The Beggar's Opera* by John Gay and its numerous adaptations provide an optimal
topic of research. Throughout its more than 250-year history this work has
negotiated the gulf between the subversive and the sublime, between politics and poetics. From the very beginning the play was surrounded by
controversy. Its London premiere on January 29, 1728, caused considerable sensation. According to William Schultz, who gathered a wealth of
evidence about its earliest reception, "Contemporary comments on *The
Beggar's Opera* indicate that in its own day the piece was considered by
some an attack upon the government in general and by many an attack
upon the administration of Sir Robert Walpole in particular."[1] William
Empson, perhaps the most astute student of the play, seconds such an
"unambiguous" reading: "The main joke is not against the characters of
the play at all, nor does any one in the discussion about its morality seem
to have taken it as against the appalling penal code and prison system; the
main thing is the political attack and the principles behind it."[2] The pro-

[1] William Schultz, *Gay's "Beggar's Opera": Its Content, History, and Influence* (New Haven,
1923), p. 179. Further references will be given in the text.
[2] William Empson, *"The Beggar's Opera:* Mock-Pastoral as the Cult of Independence," in
Some Versions of Pastoral (London, 1935), p. 195. Further references will be given in the text.

duction of the play in fact led to some unpleasant consequences for the author, Schultz tells us. "Gay was soon afterwards deprived of his lodgings at Whitehall, which he had occupied for several years, and . . . his letters were read by the post office" (191). More important, his sequel to the *Beggar's Opera*, *Polly*, which was ready for production in late 1728, was banned by the Whig government, resentful at the thought of serving yet again as the butt of jokes. As a result, Gay's friends felt it necessary to deflect the political reading of the play, stressing instead its artistic nature, which, by definition, transcends the historical moment of its birth. Swift's eloquent "Vindication of Mr. Gay and the Beggar's Opera" which serves as this chapter's epigraph is a fine example of such an interpretive strategy. And his words, it turned out, were prophetic ones for the history of the play's reception, as I will illustrate.

Yet, aside from scandal and rancor in government ranks, the consequences of Gay's satirical comparison of British high society to the underworld were highly unexpected. Rather than alienating the upper classes or polarizing British society along class lines, the play's ultimate effect was to promulgate a national reconciliation. This happened, Empson is quick to point out, because the irony of *The Beggar's Opera* was deflected through a double irony, which he termed "Comic Primness." "In full Comic Primness," he explained this curious turning of a poetic trope upon itself, "the enjoyer gets the joke at both levels—both that which accepts and that which revolts against the conventions that the speaker adopts primly" (211). This contradiction cannot be resolved, but leads to the "comfortable" conclusion that social conventions are definitely false, but that's the way of the world. "Comic primness," Kenneth Burke expounds this concept, "is an attitude characterizing a member of the privileged class who somewhat questions the state of affairs whereby he enjoys his privileges; but after all, he does enjoy them, and so in the last analysis he resigns himself to the dubious condition, in a state of ironic complexity that is apologetic, but not abnegatory."[3] Prime Minister Robert Walpole himself initiated this attitude toward the play's message on the night of the premiere. According to an eyewitness account quoted by Schultz, after a song that most of the audience perceived as directed against Walpole, they "threw their eyes on the stage-box where the Minister was sitting and loudly *encored* it. Sir Robert saw this stroke instantly, and saw it with good humor and discretion: for no sooner was the song finished than he encored it a second time himself, joined in the general applause, and by this means brought the audience into so much good humor with him, that they gave him a general huzzah from all parts of the house" (186).

[3]   Kenneth Burke, *A Rhetoric of Motives* (Berkeley, 1969), p. 126.

There is one more reason, Empson argues, why Gay's play promoted belief in a common human lot: its genre. The pastoral (drawing a parallel between "low" and "refined" people) and the heroic (whose central character represents the whole nation) were the traditional literary mechanisms for expressing national unity. *The Beggar's Opera*, Empson illustrates convincingly, is an ironic subversion of these literary conventions; yet, in a curious twist, its social impact was very much the same.

> Clearly, it is important for a nation with a strong class system to have an art-form that not merely evades but breaks through it, that makes the classes feel part of a larger unity or simply at home with each other. This may be done in odd ways, and as well by mockery as admiration. The half-conscious purpose behind the magical ideas of heroic and pastoral was being finally secured by *The Beggar's Opera* when the mob roared its applause both against and with the applause of Walpole. (199)

A popular quip that began to circulate in London soon after the premiere—"this play made *Rich* very *Gay* and *Gay* very *Rich*"—grasped, it seems, the final settlement between British high society and its caustic satirist.

After its phenomenal success on the English stage, at about midcentury *The Beggar's Opera* began its march around the globe. Two hundred years after its premiere, in 1928 Brecht's adaptation of the play was produced in Berlin, establishing the play's canonic interpretation for our time. For Brecht the message of his *Dreigroschenoper* was above all political: an exposé of the false bourgeois ethics of the Weimar Republic. Citing his reasons for reviving Gay's text, he wrote in 1929: "Just like two hundred years ago we have a social order in which virtually all levels, albeit in a wide variety of ways, pay respect to moral principles not by leading a moral life but by living off morality."[4] To drive the point home, Brecht updated the original play in many ways, most significantly by shifting the action to Victorian London, which he considered the perfect embodiment of all bourgeois values. In this way, he believed, "the play would be more easily transported to Berlin than if set [in the period] in which Gay had (of necessity) had to locate it."[5] And commenting in the same conversation on the social impact of *The Threepenny Opera* in pre-Nazi Germany, Brecht listed as one of its most successful results "the fact that the top stratum of the bourgeoisie was made to laugh at its own absurdity. Having once

---

[4] Bertolt Brecht, "On *The Threepenny Opera*," in *Plays, Poetry, and Prose: The Collected Plays*, vol. 2, pt. 2, ed. and trans. R. Manheim et al. (London, 1979), p. 90.
[5] "Transcript from a Conversation between Brecht and Giorgio Strehler on 25 October 1955," ibid., p. 101. Further references will be given in the text.

laughed at certain attitudes, it would never again be possible for these particular representatives of the bourgeoisie to adopt them" (102).

Those who did not like his Marxist *Weltanschauung* yet appreciated his work on purely aesthetic grounds, however, did not share Brecht's own conception of the play. The editors of the most comprehensive English edition of Brecht's oeuvre, for example, insist that the author was deliberately reading into his play an ideological stance that was not there originally: "The trouble here is not only that when Brecht actually wrote his share of [*The Threepenny Opera*] he was only beginning to explore Marxism and had barely begun to relate to the class struggle . . . but that the issue was subsequently confused by Brecht's writing all his own notes and interpretations *after* adopting a more committed position in 1929." They continue, "Part of the common overestimation of the play's social purpose and impact is due most probably to the intense dislike felt for it by the German nationalist reaction which began gaining ground within a year of the premiere."[6] Some of Brecht's contemporaries also took a rather dim view of the playwright's social involvement. They saw him, at best, as politically ineffectual and, at worse, as counterproductive. In an essay significantly titled "The Poet Bertolt Brecht," Hannah Arendt revealed her preference for his aesthetics quite bluntly: "Every time Brecht wanted to create a direct political effect he fumbled. He could never break through the boundaries within which a poet is constrained, despite all his political-aesthetic argumentation. Always he only bore witness. . . . But this testimony remains poetically valid, even if it reveals itself as politically obsolete."[7]

In her book on totalitarianism, Arendt's analysis of why Brecht's play failed politically is particularly instructive if juxtaposed to the social impact of Gay's play in eighteenth-century England. Brecht's didactic attempt at reforming the German bourgeoisie by showing it a grotesque picture of its behavior was received in a way not unlike what Empson termed "Comic Primness." Like the British upper classes, the German bourgeoisie laughed at its own absurdities while at the same time seeing them as the follies of the world. "The theme song in the play, '*Erst kommt das Fressen, dann kommt die Moral*,' was greeted with fanatic applause by exactly everybody," Arendt tells us. "The bourgeoisie applauded because it had been fooled by its own hypocrisy for so long that it had grown tired of the tension and found deep wisdom in the expression of the banality by which it lived. . . . The effect of the work was exactly the opposite of what

6   Ralph Manheim and John Villet, "Introduction," ibid., pp. xiv–xv.
7   Quoted from *Brecht: A Collection of Critical Essays*, ed. P. Demetz (Englewood Cliffs, N.J., 1962), p. 45.

Brecht sought by it. The bourgeoisie could no longer be shocked; it welcomed the exposure of its hidden philosophy, whose popularity proved that they had been right all along."[8]

This, however, exhausts the similarity between the receptions of Gay's and Brecht's plays by their respective societies. The fanatic applause in Berlin was quite unlike that in London, where "the mob roared its applause both against and with applause of Walpole." In militarily defeated and economically ravished Germany, the lower and higher classes perceived the *Dreigroschenoper* in two different ways, Arendt insists. Its "irony was somewhat lost when respectable businessmen in the audience considered [the equation between themselves and gangsters] a deep insight into the ways of the world and when the mob welcomed it as an artistic sanction of gangsterism" (335). The lesson that the extreme right seems to have drawn from the play is quite simple. If the humanist ethics that the bourgeoisie displays so ostentatiously is nothing but a façade behind which life is governed by the law of the jungle, then pulling down this hollow shell and establishing society according to the principle that might is right appears only reasonable. Thus, in a historical irony that is truly Kunderaesque, Brecht with his Marxist critique of capitalist society, Arendt suggests, turned into the harbinger of the Nazi takeover.

The next twist in the long history of adaptations of *The Beggar's Opera* to different political contexts, and the one that interests me here, took place in a godforsaken Prague suburb called Horní Počernice on November 1, 1975. That Saturday evening, in the local House of Culture, an amateur group staged the premiere of Václav Havel's version of Gay's play. The invited audience numbered about three hundred people. By Western standards this event was definitely small potatoes: a nonprofessional production on the periphery of Prague without advertising a program, or even reviews in the papers the next day. For Kafka's hometown, however, this was the event of the year: a public performance of a play by a well-known author who, because of his nonconformist stance after the Soviet invasion of 1968, had been banned from the Czechoslovak stage. The question most likely preoccupying those who attended the premiere was whether the permission to produce *The Beggar's Opera* should be attributed to the ignorance and ineptitude of the local authorities, or whether the Czechoslovak government, under the spell of the Helsinki Agreement, had benevolently decided to overlook an action with such limited political fallout.

This charade was further complicated by the fact that Havel's adapta-

---

[8]   Hannah Arendt, *The Origins of Totalitarianism: New Edition* (New York, 1973), p. 335. Further references will be given in the text.

tion of *The Beggar's Opera* (in contrast to Brecht's play) was not modernized and deliberately refrained from any direct reference to Czechoslovak reality. As Havel insisted, "In the text of my play there is nothing directed against our state, its social order, or public morality."[9] Thus, ten days after the premiere, a reporter for the West German weekly *Der Spiegel* who had scooped the story could write: "It is certain that the secret police were also present [at the premiere]; but, despite general expectations, neither the actors, author, nor viewers have yet been interrogated. The police censors," he predicted slyly, "will have to study the text of this new piece especially closely to find a legal handle on Havel."[10] Unfortunately, the German reporter, the product of a liberal bourgeois society, was proceeding from hermeneutic assumptions that do not obtain in a one-party state. No textual evidence was necessary in post-1968 Czechoslovakia to deal with a "difficult" writer, and in any event, the police were not particularly good at providing it. Mr. Bolotka, a character from Philip Roth's *Prague Orgy*, is close to the truth when he tells Zuckerman that in Czechoslovakia, "the police are like literary critics—of what little they see, they get most wrong anyway."[11] This is not to cast aspersions on the intelligence quotient of the Czechoslovak security establishment, though it must be said that the local population frequently did so.[12]

Rather, a political reading is a particular type of "misprision." It can be best characterized as the polar opposite of the "close" reading propounded by the New Critics. A political reading is a maximally "open" reading because it always interprets the text according to the contingencies of a particular social context. As a working hypothesis, one might claim that the more political a reading is, the less it respects such structural properties of the text as grammar, narrativity, or logic, and the more it relies on the vicissitudes of the concrete situation. Given the heterogeneity and fluidity of a situation, it is obvious that not even the police can account for all the ramifications a political reading might have.

The impetus toward "open" interpretation is especially strong in drama, for among all the literary genres it is the most context-bound. As a component of a theatrical performance, according to Havel's theoretical essay of 1968, "The Peculiarities of Theater," drama is political in its very essence. "Theater," Havel writes, "[is] an art predestined by its nature to

[9] Václav Havel, "Fakta o představení Žebrácké opery," in *O lidskou identitu: Úvahy, fejetony, prohlášení a rozhovory z let 1969–1979* (London, 1984), p. 174.
[10] "Wenige Schritte," *Der Spiegel*, November 10, 1975, p. 212.
[11] Philip Roth, *Zuckerman Bound: A Trilogy and Epilogue* (New York, 1985), p. 763.
[12] Consider, e.g., the great proliferation of "police jokes" in Czechoslovakia in the 1970s. Here is my favorite: "Why do policemen in Prague always walk in threes? Because one knows how to read, another how to write, and the third has to watch them fuckin' intellectuals."

be a concentrated expression of its time because of the collective nature of its reception. . . . [It functions] as a specific organism incorporated into the social milieu and bound to it in an osmotic process. [It is thus] always hypersensitive to the political and social problems of its time."[13] In moments of political crisis, like that which occurred in Czechoslovakia after the Soviet invasion of 1968, the interaction between theater and society becomes especially palpable. It is important to remember that after Alexander Dubček's downfall, the most pressing objective of the new Party leadership was to "normalize" Czechoslovakia, that is, to mold it according to the political model of the Soviet Union. The chief sin attributed to Dubček was his abidicating power to the people. This claim constitutes the first point of a document approved at the plenary session of the Central Committee of the Czechoslovak Communist Party in December 1970, which became the ideological cornerstone of "normalization": "In 1968 the CPCS gradually ceased to be the directive center of the Socialist order. Under the sludge of revisionism it lost the character of a Marxist-Leninist Party, and this loss prevented it from exercising its leadership role in society. By negating the principles of democratic centralism, the Party has gradually lost the capacity for action."[14] To regain this precious capability, the first step under Gustáv Husák's leadership was to disenfranchise most of the native population, concentrating power in the hands of a tiny number of trusted cadres, the so-called "healthy kernel" of the CPCS.

This return to "normalcy" affected the relationship between theater and politics in two complementary ways. If Prague Spring had transformed Czechoslovak citizens from passive objects to active subjects in political life, the opposite occurred in 1969. By eliminating from the decision-making process any trace of popular participation, the Communist leaders transformed the people into an audience of a spectacle. Politics became theater. It is precisely this theatrical metaphor that Milan Šimečka, the most astute observer of the "normalization process," uses to open his pamphlet *The Restoration of Order*. In 1968, he comments:

> People suddenly began to perceive politicans . . . as human beings instead of cardboard cut-outs always spouting the same old platitudes. All of a sudden, people could see them cry. Fatigue, moral dilemmas and human weakness were there on their faces for all to see (thanks, of course, to television). Almost in a single moment public life came into existence and many people, for the first time in their lives, began to view politics as the work of

[13]   Václav Havel, "Zvláštnosti divadla," *Divadlo*, April 19, 1968, p. 18.
[14]   *Poučení z krizového vývoje ve straně a společnosti po XIII. sjezdu KSČ: Rezoluce k aktuálním otázkám jednoty strany* (Prague, 1971), p. 22.

human beings instead of a tedious, infinitely boring, inaccessible and anonymous annoyance coming from somewhere on high. Even the first phase of the restoration of order took place on the fully lit stage. People remembered the actors and knew their roles all too well. Therefore it was with a certain eagerness that they watched how they would act in a completely new play with a completely new director. I think I can state without exaggeration that for the people here post-1970 events certainly did not appear as an abstract process of "strengthening the leading role of the Party, removing the right-wing elements, purging Czechoslovak culture, deepening cooperation between socialist states," but rather as a historical drama with live characters. It was a play about betrayal, love and hate, about sacrifice and deception, greatness and baseness, revenge and fall, about money, envy, and in fact everything that is splendidly human. I do not wish to conceal the fact that I myself viewed the historical events primarily in that manner, and only in that fashion did they fascinate me.[15]

The second effect that Czechoslovak "normalization" exerted on the social function of theater was a direct result of that just mentioned. If the elimination of the citizenry from the decision-making process rendered politics theater, by the same token theater turned political. This is not to say that by some oversight Party censors failed to control what was performed on the Czechoslovak stage. Rather, their efforts were frustrated by an unpredictable human factor: the spontaneous reactions of theatergoers. To provide just one example, there is a famous aria in Smetana's *Bartered Bride* in which the singer urges other characters to tear up a "certain agreement." Whenever this aria was sung in the composer's homeland after August 1968, the audience always burst into frenetic applause. The source of their delight was obvious to everyone. For the viewers the words referred not to the premarital contract so crucial to the plot of the opera's libretto, but to what was on their minds at the moment: the Czechoslovak-Soviet agreement of 1968, which stipulated the "temporary" stationing of the Red Army on Czechoslovak soil. Through this contextualized "misreading," the viewers as a collectivity exercised a right denied to them outside the theater: to voice publicly their attitude toward the puppet government which, in collusion with a foreign power, had usurped control over their lands.

This hermeneutic strategy of Czechoslovak theatergoers, of course, enraged local authorities, who, after the scandalous premiere of Brecht's *Mother Courage* at the Prague National Theater in October 1970, issued a

---

[15] Milan Šimečka, *The Restoration of Order: The Normalization of Czechoslovakia*, trans. A. G. Brain (London, 1984), p. 17.

series of directives to correct such unseemly behavior.[16] But at the same time, these "liberties with the text" perplexed foreign visitors, totally unprepared for such blatant contextualization of theatrical classics. Giving vivid testimony to this effect is a story told by the Shakespearean actor Ian McKellen, who in 1969 traveled around Europe with a production of *Richard II*. "The costumes," he says, "were of the actual period of Richard II but the scenery was minimal because it was a touring production. On the whole we concentrated on the humanity of the characters rather than their political nature. We thought of the political factions as a family, Richard II as a man with cousins and uncles and other relatives, and I think it was in that sense that we looked at the politics in it." The Prague performance, however, turned into something completely unexpected:

> When I came to the speech where Richard II returns from Ireland to discover that his nation has been overrun by his cousin Bolingbroke, and he kneels down on the earth and asks the stones and the nettles and the insects to help him in his helpless state against the armies who had invaded his land, I could hear something I had never heard before, nor since, which was a whole audience apparently weeping. It shakes me now to think about it, because in that instant I realized that the audience were crying for themselves. They recognized in Richard II their own predicament of only six months previously when their neighbors and as it were their cousins had invaded their land and all they had were sticks and stones to throw at the tanks.[17]

As my short digression into the curious symbiosis between theater and politics in "normalized" Czechoslovakia indicates, a lack of direct textual clues is not an obstacle for an audience to perceive a text as referring to their own current predicament. Needless to say, a play that compares "several Stratagems of betraying, undermining, and hanging each other, to the several Arts of *Politicians* in times of Corruption" was a perfect vehicle for antigovernment sentiment in post-1968 Czechoslovakia. And given the vast power that the authorities wielded in a country with all too many Czechs but no balances, it is also obvious that anybody even vaguely suspected of impugning the honor of the Socialist government would be dealt with quickly.

What, then, was the reason for the momentary hesitation witnessed by the reporter from *Der Spiegel*? In my opinion, Havel's *Beggar's Opera* put Party ideologues into an embarrassing double bind. Had they punished

---

[16]   For more details, see "Normalizace v Národním divadle," *Listy*, no. 1 (1971), 17–19.
[17]   John Barton, *Playing Shakespeare* (London, 1984), pp. 191–92.

the instigators of the "travesty," they would have affirmed de facto an un-flattering similarity between *Wahrheit und Dichtung* as suggested by the play. If, however, they had done nothing, the public would have taken their inaction as a sign of weakness, since no Czechoslovak would miss such an opportunity to draw an unfavorable analogy. Caught between two equally unpalatable options, the authorities reacted to the challenge of *The Beggar's Opera* in a fashion that might best be characterized as schizoid. On the covert, unofficial plane, the authorities employed the time-honored device of turning the victims into villains. Havel and his co-horts, according to rumors emanating from high places, had tainted the political climate and were the direct cause of further tightening of censor-ship. They had victimized the citizenry.[18] On the overt level, the Party or-dered the most prominent participants in Havel's premiere (whether ac-tors or viewers) to be fired from their jobs, but they instructed employers that the Počernice affair must not be mentioned as the cause of dismissal. Since Havel, as a self-employed writer, seemed immune to this measure, the police, for the sake of justice, revoked his driver's license.[19] By acting in this contradictory way, however, the authorities unwittingly affirmed the deep-seated political message of Havel's play.

For *The Beggar's Opera*, without doubt, is a representation of collective schizophrenia. This quasi-medical term has been used in many different ways, and so I would like to explain my understanding of it. Following Gregory Bateson, by schizophrenia I mean a particular communication disorder in which human intercourse tends to combine messages of dif-ferent logical types. To carry out meaningful exchange, participants must be able to distinguish between serious assertions and jokes, literal and fig-urative usages of language, statements about objects and statements about statements. But a schizophrenic is hopelessly lost in this game. He or she is incapable of logical typing, that is, of properly identifying the level of abstraction of an utterance; this deficiency renders the schizo-phrenic a contradictory and unpredictable communicant. The cause of the disorder, Bateson maintains, is repeated exposure to double bind situa-tions during one's formative years. An authority figure (usually a parent) confuses a child by issuing two incompatible injunctions. The first, on the primary level, induces certain behavior under the threat of punishment. The second, also enforced by punishment, requires, on a more abstract level, behavior that is opposite to that demanded by the first injunction. But can this vicious circle be broken somehow? According to Bateson only

[18] For Havel's reaction to these rumors, see "Fakta o představení Žebrácké opery," pp. 173–74 and 179.
[19] For more details, see "Horní Počernice všecko vystoupit," *Listy*, no. 2 (1976), 26–27; and "Společenská rubrika," ibid., p. 48.

by assuming a yet higher level of abstraction from which the contradictions permeating the double-binding discourse can be plainly seen.

An illustrative example of such a double bind which Bateson presents is a visit by a mother to her schizophrenic son in a mental hospital. "He was glad to see her and impulsively put his arm around her shoulders, whereupon she stiffened. He withdrew his arm and she asked, 'Don't you love me anymore?' He then blushed and she said, 'Dear, you must not be so easily embarrassed and afraid of your feelings.' " The "impossible dilemma" in which this exchange put the patient consisted, according to Bateson, of the following logical incongruities: "If I am to keep my tie to mother," the son reckons, "I must not show her that I love her, but if I do not show her that I love her, then I will lose her."[20] Being a schizophrenic, the son was unable to approach this "paradox" in a critical manner, and following the visit suffered a mental breakdown.

Although the causes of collective schizophrenia are social rather than strictly mental, its basic structure remains the same. It involves a hierarchical relation between two groups in which the ones with power coerce the powerless to act in a certain way, all the while insisting that the subjects of coercion are free or that the enforced behavior is good for them. At the same time, the powerless are prohibited from expressing their true feelings about this arrangement. The reaction of Czechoslovak authorities to Havel's play, their covert shifting of blame onto the victims and their overt pretense of innocence masking actual persecution, is, I believe, a manifestation of the schizophrenic communicative disorder that characterized Czechoslovak society in the not so distant past. What are the symptoms of this peculiar condition? At the most basic level we should observe that every public statement made in Czechoslovakia either by the government or by citizens was always two-leveled. Its true import rested not in what was said but in what was implied. Havel's 1978 essay "The Power of the Powerless" focuses sharply on this communicative duplicity. Why, the playwright asks, does an ordinary greengrocer put on display among his vegetables the sign "Proletarians of all lands, unite!" ? It is quite obvious that he does not do so because of an irresistible desire to impart this message to his customers arising from his political convictions. Like his colleagues, he has received the ready-made slogan from the central office with instructions to put it in a prominent place. His noncompliance with this instruction would cause him difficulties with his employer—he could be fired. Hence the implications of his action are,

[20]   Gregory Bateson, "Towards a Theory of Schizophrenia," in *Steps to an Ecology of Mind: Collected Essays in Anthropology, Psychiatry, Evolution, and Epistemology* (St. Albans, 1973), pp. 173–98. Further references will be given in the text.

according to Havel, quite simple. The slogan signifies that "I, greengrocer XYZ, live here and know what to do; I behave as I am expected; I am reliable and cannot be criticized; I am obedient and, therefore, have the right to a peaceful existence."[21]

Such a communicative strategy, however, requires further explanation. If the government, Havel argues, reversed the informational hierarchy and turned the meta-message into a primary utterance, things might become somewhat sticky: "If the greengrocer was ordered to display the slogan 'I am scared and, hence, I am totally obedient,' he would not relate to its semantic content in such a relaxed manner, though this content would fully coincide with the hidden meaning of the slogan. The grocer would most likely hesitate to display this unambiguous message about his denigration; he would be embarrassed, ashamed" (60–61; 133). Thus, to save face, the grocer's submission to the system is wrapped in an ideological garment. It is justified as service to the most worthy, progressive cause. In his argument, one might observe in passing, Havel returns to Marx's original understanding of ideology as a "false consciousness" employed to justify the ruling class's claim to power. In an ironic twist, however, he turns this concept against those who consider themselves heirs of the German philosopher—the CPCS. According to its own understanding of Marxism-Leninism, this doctrine is not an ideology at all but the Truth. It is not a political ploy but an exact scientific theory, the Communist propagandists were never tired of repeating, the embodiment of the universal logic of history. But such a de-ideologization of ideology, Havel is quick to point out, served a very specific purpose. It enabled the Party "to pretend that it pretends nothing." The grocer, it is true, "does not have to believe in all these mystifications. But he has to behave as if he believes them" (63; 136). To put this injunction negatively, vis-à-vis his government he must pretend not to pretend.

I use this negative formulation advisedly. In addition to an ideological justification for submissive behavior reserved for official occasions, Czechoslovak citizens usually offered another justification to their immediate circle of family and friends. This private justification, however, had to be concealed because it directly clashed with the Party's injunction. It claimed that what the greengrocer and his fellow citizens were really doing was pretending to pretend. For obvious reasons, everybody implicated in official structures must maintain the façade of pretense. But since

---

[21] Václav Havel, "Moc bezmocných," in *O lidskou identitu*, p. 60; "The Power of the Powerless," in *Open Letters: Selected Writings, 1965–1990*, trans. P. Wilson (New York, 1991), p. 133. Quotations are taken, with some alterations, from Wilson's translation. Further references will be given in the text; the first number in parentheses refers to the Czech original and the second to the English translation.

only a very few Czechoslovaks were willing to admit to their families or friends that they were cowards or scoundrels, they had to come up with a credible explanation for patent support of the regime. Thus, they declared to those they trusted that the signs of fear and obedience they displayed in public were just a strategic ploy to achieve ends quite contrary to government policy.

Here the gate for collective schizophrenia swings wide open. Since the boundaries between private and public spheres in a totalitarian society are never well defined, Czechoslovak citizens were with astonishing frequency forced to change the logical typing of their utterances. And it was never clear whether their meta-pretending was really a strategic device or merely another face-saving mechanism to cover actual submission. That is to say, one always had doubts in Czechoslovakia whether one was dealing with heroes or collaborators who, as Havel characterized them in his open letter to Husák of 1975, "have the peculiar ability to persuade themselves again and again and under any circumstances that their dirty work supposedly protects something, or that at least they prevent those who are worse than they are from taking over their positions."[22] Under such conditions it ceases to be possible to draw a clear-cut line between the oppressors and the oppressed. In a truly schizophrenic fashion, "everybody," to use Havel's assessment from his essay "The Power of the Powerless," "is [the system's] victim and support" (70; 144). The all-pervasive fear I am describing was the function of the state's near-absolute power over its citizens. Any human weakness including parental love might have been used as an instrument of blackmail: it was a common practice to hold children's futures hostage to the proper behavior of their parents. And since virtually everybody in Czechoslovakia was a civil servant, economic persecution of those who breached the boundaries of the permissible was limitless.

These coercive mechanisms, however, would have been virtually useless if the government had not had at its disposal the most feared tool of control: an omnipotent and omnipresent secret police. In his letter to Husák, Havel compared this organization to a monstrous spider whose invisible web permeated the entire social fabric. And, he continued, "though most of the people most of the time do not see this web with their own eyes and cannot touch it, even the commonest citizen knows very well of its existence. At any moment and at any place he or she counts on its silent presence and behaves accordingly: i.e., so that he might pass the test of its hidden eyes and ears" (23; 55). As Havel suggests, the effect of a

<hr/>

[22] Václav Havel, "Dopis Gustávu Husákovi," in *O lidskou identitu*, p. 24; "Dear Dr. Husák," in *Open Letters*, p. 55. Quotations are taken, with some alterations, from Wilson's translation. Further references will be given in the text; the first number in parentheses refers to the Czech original and the second to the English translation.

secret police on collective schizophrenia can hardly be overestimated. The agents of such an Orwellian force introduce another level to the game of deception. Those who by pretending to pretend violate the injunction against primary communicative duplicity find their match in those who pretend to pretend to pretend: the undercover police, the nameless heroes who with "clean hands, cool heads, and ardent hearts" expose a citizenry's true colors. Yet it must be stressed that the Czechoslovak secret police had a certain compassion for those whom it caught red-handed. They could atone for their unworthy behavior. Instead of facing criminal prosecution, they could join the crew and themselves become the "hidden eyes and ears" of the state.

Needless to say, it was in the interest of those holding power in Czechoslovakia to convince their subjects of the omniscience of the secret police. To fulfill this task the mass media of the 1970s launched an ambitious campaign to promulgate a new type of positive hero, the double agent who patently would abet the enemies of the state while, in reality, laboring on its behalf. The symbol of this undertaking is the shady figure of Jan Minařík, whose story was prominently disseminated by Czechoslovak propagandists in 1976 through all available channels. A putative captain of State Security, he left his homeland on a "secret mission" in 1968 and joined Radio Free Europe as a broadcaster, only to re-defect in 1975. His subordinate position at Radio Free Europe, the evidence furnished by his co-workers for his sudden return, and the forged nature of some of the materials he allegedly brought home all indicate that the story of this master spy presented by the Czechoslovak official media was to a considerable degree deception. True, one can never trust a double agent, but this one looks particularly untrustworthy.[23] Nevertheless, the reason for the media blitz is quite obvious: to increase communicative disorder among the population and in this way to dissuade it from quitting the primary game of pretending required by the government. To put it differently, if in this mental poker game the secret police claim to have a royal flush, who is willing to call their bluff? The case of "Captain" Minařík indicates that third-level pretending was not the limit for the deceptive games in post-1968 Czechoslovakia. Theoretically speaking, the lamination of levels of abstraction in intercourse is limitless. And the thicker it gets, the more difficult the logical typing of utterances becomes and the more schizophrenic the communication, until it ceases to make sense for anybody involved.

Let me now turn to the text of Havel's play. I shall not dwell on its title, although it is rather curious that the dramatis personae do not contain a

---

[23] For more details about this case, see "První a poslední role 'kapitána' Minaříka," *Listy*, no. 2 (1976), 7–8; and "Skandál v Římě," ibid., no. 4 (1976), 11.

single beggar, and there is no singing either. The plot centers on Macheath, the head of a criminal gang, and on two nuclear families, the Peachums and the Lockits, each composed of a father, a mother, and a daughter. The head of the first family, William Peachum, is also the leader of a criminal gang, whereas Bill Lockit is the chief of police. The antagonistic occupations of the two fathers do not prevent their daughters, Polly Peachum and Lucy Lockit, from being married simultaneously to Macheath. In addition to these main figures, two lesser characters, an independent pickpocket, Filch, and a prostitute, Jenny, are instrumental in the power game unfolding in the play, in which the protagonists attempt to gain control over one another. This cast of characters might suggest certain tensions. Lockit is a policeman, and hence a natural enemy of the two criminals, Macheath and Peachum. These two, however, though bound by their contempt for the law, are at the same time potential competitors with conflicting goals in mind. Finally, both Polly and Lucy are married to Macheath, which makes the entire situation quite muddy. Parental feelings, ethical norms, love, and jealousy all foster alliances too numerous to be accounted for.

The multiplicity of relations among the protagonists is rich enough to sustain a number of dramatic plots. But what makes Havel's version of *The Beggar's Opera* particularly intriguing is the totally duplicitous behavior of its characters. To achieve their ends they seduce or coerce the others, lie about the motivations for their actions, and constantly shift sides (or at least they say they do) as the power configuration changes. Whenever a character steps out of this behavioral pattern by acting spontaneously or by displaying genuine feelings and convictions, he or she is immediately victimized by the others. The play unfolds as a series of gradual revelations about each protagonist, and at each step the levels of pretending are multiplied so that, at the end, in a state of collective schizophrenia, the outcome is utterly unclear.

As the curtain rises, Peachum and his wife discuss the intimate relations between their daughter and Macheath. The father has specifically encouraged Polly to seduce the leader of the competing gang. This plan has succeeded, and Polly announces that she is already married to Macheath. Delighted, Peachum undertakes the next step. As he tells his daughter, her husband is a "rake and spineless cynic" who married her only to gain control over Peachum's business.[24] Appealing to her daughterly love, he urges her to betray her husband and use her new position to

---

[24] Václav Havel, *Žebrácká opera: Na téma Johna Gaye*, in *Hry 1970–1976: Z doby zakázanosti* (Toronto, 1977), p. 120. Further references will be given in the text. For their English translation I am indebted to Paul Wilson, whose kind help I am glad to acknowledge.

gather incriminating evidence that will send Macheath to the gallows. This scheme backfires, however, because Polly has fallen in love with Macheath and wishes nothing but a happy family life. When the incensed Peachum banishes her from his home, her mother suggests that the next plot against Macheath be more radical.

The homeless Polly goes to the robbers' tavern, the hangout of Macheath's gang, and urges her husband to flee immediately. Upon leaving her home she had listened behind the door and now worries that Macheath will be trapped. But to her dismay her husband is not at all sympathetic to her story. She should have known from the very beginning, he argues, that her father intended to use her against him: "You should have agreed with everything he said and promised to go along with him so he'd think that his plan was working. And then you'd simply feed him false information, which I would provide, and eventually we'd snare him in his own net. . . . But now you've spoiled everything!" (125). If Polly loves him, as she claims to, she will go home, make up with her parents, and enact the role he has outlined. Macheath is irresistible, and Polly departs for her parental home as a double agent with her husband's promise that during her absence he will be faithful to her.

Yet the very next female visitor to the tavern attracts Macheath's attention. This is the prostitute Jenny, who tells him that some five years ago he seduced her under false pretenses and then abandoned her. But since he was her first lover she has remained faithful to him and now has come to see him again. Macheath, who does not remember the event, is very much attracted to Jenny and promises to make up for his previous betrayal. But in the middle of the passionate scene that follows, Jenny screams for help and bailiffs enter the room. As becomes obvious, the lady is a decoy, and Macheath is arrested for attempted rape.

During his arraignment the police chief, Lockit, suggests to Macheath that his case is not as hopeless as it might seem. It is not the bribe sensibly offered by Macheath that interests him. Rather, he would like the criminal to become a police informer. Macheath, however, thinks he can get out of jail without resorting to such distasteful tactics. He is secretly married to Lockit's daughter, Lucy, and is banking on her help. Very soon, Lucy indeed appears in her husband's cell. After a somewhat awkward moment caused by Macheath's year-long absence from his wife, he succeeds in persuading Lucy that he planned "to make a lot more money on the quiet, a fortune so that we could move to the country and live together in complete happiness" (138). A rhapsodic description of the life in a manorhouse that he has imagined for both of them persuades Lucy to arrange his escape.

As the seasoned reader might suspect, Peachum, who is in cahoots with

Lockit, has engineered Macheath's arrest. The police chief helped Peachum nab the "seducer" of his daughter, but not out of kindness. Peachum's organization, it turns out, is nothing but Lockit's instrument for gathering information about the London underworld. And in the course of their conversation, Lockit questions Peachum about the duke of Gloucester's gold watch, which has recently been stolen. This is a touchy point, since Peachum assigned the theft to the pickpocket Filch as a tryout for his acceptance in the gang—this despite Lockit's explicit injunction against Peachum's hiring new staff. Lockit's ruffled feathers are smoothed, however, when Peachum presents him with a valuable necklace, which Lockit, after much persuasion, accepts.

At this point the situation seems clear: it is a typical case of a mutually profitable collaboration between the mob and the police. But the duke's watch has added another wrinkle to the story. Filch, who spoke to Macheath after his escape, has learned about Peachum's contacts with the police and is offended. He is an "honest" thief who finds "such trafficking with the enemy disgusting" (143). To appease him, Peachum tells Filch the truth about his police connections:

> Trafficking with the enemy? Perhaps it is. It's a thankless task, sir, but someone has to do it. What would become of the underworld if people like me didn't put their honor on the line each and every day by keeping the lines of communication open, something for which they will very probably never receive recognition? . . . Oh, it's terribly easy to cloister yourself away and cultivate your marvelous principles, but what sense does it make? Only this: to gratify the egotistical self-interest of those who do it. The real heroes of the underground today are a different breed altogether. They may not be constantly flaunting their fidelity to the pure code of honor among thieves, but they do modest, inconspicuous, and risky work in that no-man's-land between the underworld and the police, and they make a real contribution to our objective interests . . . they expand the range of our opportunities inch by inch, strengthen our security, provide us with important information, and, slowly, inconspicuously, with no claim to glory, they serve progress. (143)

Despite this eloquent justification of Peachum's behavior, Filch sticks to his moral principles, quits his job, is promptly arrested for the theft of the duke's gold watch, and dies on the gallows.

Meanwhile, the escaped Macheath heads toward the house of ill repute where Jenny works so that he might exact revenge against his Delilah. But her attraction is so strong that instead of punishing her he listens to her for a second time. Jenny explains that she does not work for the police at all.

She was coerced to entrap Macheath because her father was sentenced to death, and this was the only chance of obtaining clemency for him. "It was a terrible dilemma," she pleads with Macheath. "I felt that I had to refuse, because I couldn't bring myself to save one man from death by sending another to the gallows. In the end, however, I reckoned that you'd figure a way out of it but Father wouldn't. You'd have to know him; he is so helpless" (149–50). Touched, Macheath apologizes to Jenny for his black thoughts and consents to wait for her in a little chamber where she will join him at the earliest opportunity. There Lockit's agents apprehend him for the second time.

The action now switches to Peachum's household. Polly, as charged by her husband, divulges to her parents the content of her conversation with Macheath: how he told her to go home, ask for forgiveness, and, under the guise of a repentant daughter, spy on Peachum. This idea, she proclaims, is so repugnant to her that she has lost all her former affection for Macheath, and to get even with him she is willing to assume the role of a plant in her husband's organization. Fatherly feelings, it seems, are Peachum's Achilles' heel, for he eagerly accepts her confession and rushes to Lockit to ask him for Macheath's release.

After the initial misunderstanding caused by Macheath's escape and second arrest, Peachum presents his new plan to Lockit. Since Polly has volunteered to gather evidence against her husband, it would be advantageous to set Macheath free, and then, after all the details of his operation become known, to apprehend him with all his accomplices. But Lockit is skeptical. Why is Peachum so eager, he asks, to release a man whose arrest he so recently demanded? Is he trying to get hold of Macheath's property or to make Polly happy? Moreover, through an inmate planted in Filch's cell he has learned what Peachum told the pickpocket about his "trafficking with the enemy," and he demands an explanation. Such distrust offends Peachum: "Bill," he addresses the police chief:

> Have you any idea at all what it means to spend years fighting against the underworld while you're living in it and cultivating its confidence? . . . Struggling against crime while appearing to commit it? Do you have any inkling of what that means? Wearing two faces for so long? Leading a double life? Thinking in two different ways at once? . . . Constantly trying to fit into a world you condemn and to renounce a world to which you really belong? . . . It's all terribly simple, sitting here in your warm office . . . and handing down your simplistic judgments. But try going out into the midst of life, putting your honor on the line every day of the week by maintaining contacts for which you will probably never receive proper recognition, and undertaking modest and risky work in that dangerous no-man's-

land between the underworld and the police, fighting slowly, inconspicuously on the side of law and order without any expectation of fame. That is
a very different matter. (166–67).

Lockit is touched by Peachum's emotional outburst, and the two hatch
a stratagem. Peachum is let into Macheath's cell and tells him that if he
agrees to merge his gang with Peachum's and assume the position of
deputy, Peachum will prevail upon Lockit to release him. He can do so
because he is Lockit's informer. But this fact should not worry Macheath
because his collaboration with the police is merely a handy façade for his
criminal activities. "Why do you think I cooperate with the police?" he
asks Macheath. "Because I love the king? I am just doing what everyone
else is doing in one way or another: working for my own ends and cover-
ing my back at the same time" (172). The erstwhile competitors agree to
become allies.

No sooner does Peachum leave the cell than an unexpected visitor
comes to see Macheath. It is Jenny, who has decided to tell the man she
has already betrayed twice why she behaved in such an abominable manner. She has entrapped Macheath, she claims, not just because she works
for the police but because of her passionate love for him. "For a long
time," Jenny confessed, "I was not even aware of it, but the longer that fire
smoldered in my subconsciousness, the more violent the flames that rav-
aged my consciousness. I was beside myself, I walked about in a daze,
hating you and cursing you; my pride became helpless anger and then it
happened: I realized if I ever wanted to belong to myself again, I had to
destroy you. Yes, my humiliation could only be swept away by bloody
vengeance, in a kind of drastic act of self-affirmation. I had to kill you in
order to live" (176). The veracity of this story obviously has something to
do with Jenny's sex appeal, and the enamored Macheath accepts her explanation. He declares his love for Jenny and assures her that when he is
released, the two of them will run far away, "where no one will ever find
us, save for the birds and the stars" (177).

But alas, Macheath is not destined to enjoy this pastoral life. As Lockit
questions him, Macheath first denies the deal he made with Peachum and
then admits to it. Yet, as Lockit tells him, the deal is off anyway because
Macheath has acted in bad faith. He has accepted Peachum's proposal,
Lockit insists, "only so you could get out, take control through a counterfeit merger of the assets of both organizations, and then you would run off
with a certain lady to a place where no one would find you save for the
birds and the stars. . . . In other words, when you understood that
Peachum was double-crossing you when he said he was double-crossing
me, you decided to double-cross him. But luckily for us and unluckily for

you, you yourself were double-crossed shortly thereafter" (180). Since Peachum's plan has obviously been compromised, Lockit returns to his original proposition and asks Macheath to serve as his hidden eyes and ears in Peachum's gang. In a long monologue Macheath ponders the pros and cons of this offer:

> What if I were to turn that offer down? Those around me would understand it as an ostentatious expression of my own superiority and conceit. . . . Everyone would ask: where does he get the right to be so different from the rest of us . . . and to spit on that modicum of discipline without which no society can function properly? I would be seen as a pompous and arrogant exhibitionist, someone who wanted to play the conscience of the world. . . . And I can understand that: to reject totally the rules of the game this world offers may be the easier way, but it usually leads nowhere. It is far more difficult, and at the same time far more meaningful, to accept those rules, thus enabling one to communicate with those around one, and then to put that ability to work in the gradual struggle for better rules. In other words, the only truly dignified and manly solution to my dilemma is to turn and face life head-on, plunge bravely into its stormy waters, fear not the dirt and the obstacles life places in my way, and invest all my strength and all my skill in the struggle to make life better than it is. (182–83)

With these words, the chastened Macheath accepts Lockit's offer, which could not be refused.

At this stage of the play—and we are just a few minutes from the end—the gullible reader might discern a hint of optimism. The law, despite the somewhat dubious techniques it employs, has finally triumphed over the criminals. By striking separate secret deals with both gangsters, Lockit has divided them and turned them into pliable instruments of police control over the mob. Yet at this very moment another switch takes place that makes us wonder what has actually been transpiring throughout the play. After the now docile Macheath leaves the scene, the following conversation takes place between Mr. and Mrs. Lockit:

> LOCKIT: "Well, Mary, from this moment on, our organization has practically the entire underworld of London under its control."
> MRS. LOCKIT: "It took a bit of doing, didn't it?"
> LOCKIT:"Gaining control of the London police force was a piece of cake by comparison."
> MRS. LOCKIT:"I still find it strange, though, Bill. No one knows about our organization, yet everyone is working for it."
> LOCKIT:"They serve best who know not that they serve." (184)

We realize now that all the elaborate deceptions in which Lockit the police chief engaged were just partial plots in an overarching scheme devised by Lockit the gangster.

This sudden revelation changes our understanding of the play in another, more fundamental way. It is not simply our discovery that an additional layer of pretense has been added which shocks us, but the recognition that in the universe of discourse depicted by Havel there is no ultimate limit to the levels of deception generated. In light of this, Lockit's supposed triumph appears problematic, to say the least. It is derived solely from his knowledge of what the other characters do or say. But since in the schizophrenic world he inhabits every communication contains a multitude of logical levels without any key to correct ordering, his victory may well be a self-deception, an incorrect reading of the messages he receives. That cops might be robbers we learn at the end of the play. But we leave the text with the uneasy feeling that the opposite state of affairs—that robbers might be cops—is more than a possibility.

Is there escape from this paranoid deadlock? Although Havel's play remains silent on this point, its very existence challenges the status quo. Earlier I mentioned that, according to Bateson, the way out of a double bind is through a meta-statement that exposes the multilevel contradictions inherent in such a mental trap. Havel's text, which depicts the communication disorder of "normalized" Czechoslovakia, is a step in that direction. Let me explain what I mean by returning to Bateson. The act of playing, he insists, is the most rudimentary mechanism by which all living beings learn about the variety of logical types involved in their interactions. Playing by definition involves two levels, both an action and a qualifying signal of a higher order that frames it as play. Thus, in play there is an implicit assertion to the effect that "these actions in which we now engage do not denote what the actions for which they stand would denote."[25] This observation might sound trivial, but it has important consequences. By creating a fictional universe, play splits reality from its representation and opens the possibility of transcending the immediate givens of a situation, of reflecting about the world in a detached fashion.

Artistic creativity obviously has its roots in this *Spieltrieb*. But it is not simply playing—at least not for Havel. "Art," he argued cogently in his 1967 polemic against modernism, "The Vicious Circle," "is play that does everything possible not to be play; play which, just as it begins, 'spoils' play; play which always and ever betrays precisely what it proceeds from."[26] Like play, art thrives on the gap between reality and its represen-

25   Gregory Bateson, "A Theory of Play and Fantasy," in *Steps to an Ecology of Mind*, p. 152.
26   Václav Havel, "Začarovaný kruh," *Divadlo*, January 18, 1967, p. 3. Further references will be given in the text.

tation. Yet unlike free play it tends to recoil, it strives to close that gap. "Somewhere in this dialectical balance," Havel continues, "between unknown and knowledge, convention and its negation, play and non-play, lies the most intrinsic mystery of art. And it is one of its paradoxes that it is most true to itself when it reaches the extreme point of this paradox. Which is, obviously, the very point where art is maximally both—play and non-play, knowledge and mystery, regularity and chance, convention and its transcendence" (3–4).

The artistic process, Havel is suggesting, very much like the Batesonian double bind, derives its existence from the union of pairs of mutually incompatible requirements. Thus, not surprisingly, like a schizophrenic patient it can end up caught in the cul-de-sac of its own logical contradictions. This is, Havel insists, the predicament of modernism. Art of this period did everything possible to deny its ludic nature, to become lifelike. By radically violating every aesthetic norm, modernists struggled to escape the proverbial "ivory tower"—the symbol of their social isolation. Such an iconoclasm, however, led to unexpected results. "Perhaps every avant-garde movement," Havel muses,

> wished initially not only to transgress the existing "rules of play" but to abolish play as such—to cease to be art and merge with life—and perhaps each of them ceased to be art, indeed, and merged irrevocably with the banality of life. Or, contrary to its proclamations, it left behind ordinary artifacts that are yet displayed in galleries, printed by publishers, performed at concerts—next to all other art against which it originally rose as a total negation. So it appears that the significance of all modern avant-gardes lies where it should not have been at all: in art. Life—which these movements most intended to transform—has remained even more than before untouched by the poet's creative hand. (6–7)

To move out of the modernist impasse—and this is the gist of Havel's piece—art must draw a lesson from its previous fallacies. It can ill afford to turn a blind eye to the paradoxes that constitute art's very essence: one-sidedly pitting play against life and vice versa. This road has already been taken once, but in vain. Havel is resolute on this point. The artistic double bind, he argues in a way reminiscent of Bateson, can be overcome only by reflection, a conscious scrutiny of the contradictions underlying this human activity. "In my opinion, there is only one solution," the Czech playwright stakes out a postmodernist position of his own: "nothing more and nothing other than the genuine exploration and comprehension of the vicious circle within which we move. . . . Reaching the very bottom of our insecurity, helplessness, and impotence; doing what we have done hitherto but doing so authentically and consequently, without any self-mystification" (7). This is a rather minimalist program, to be sure, easily susceptible to delusions of its own. But Havel seems well aware of these shortcomings. "In spite of it all," he concludes his essay, "this, I think, is the only viable road. It would not make any sense if we tried to convince ourselves that it leads anywhere because we do not know that. Yet, if we know, nevertheless, that this is the only road left to us, we are obliged to take it" (9).

I quote extensively from Havel's programmatic statement because its logic suggests how to approach the political function of his version of Gay's drama. Neither a simple case of engaged art that from behind a thin aesthetic veneer advocates concrete social action, nor a self-absorbed play oblivious to the world outside, Havel's *Beggar's Opera* avoids these extremes to affect its audience in a very specific way. It is a playful representation of schizophrenia addressed to an audience for which this state of affairs was everyday reality. By communicating about a communication disorder, Havel theatrically reframes the double bind of those locked in the primary frame and offers his reframing to them for inspection. *The Beggar's Opera* is both an artistic meta-statement and a political gesture: an invitation to its audience to break out of their vicious schizophrenic circle by reflecting on their own behavior.

Mimicking Havel's skepticism toward his own artistic program, one might ask whether this was the only road to be taken at that moment. Since *The Beggar's Opera* premiere was as well its *dernière* (the security apparatus made sure of this), one could hardly suggest any direct social impact.[27] From a more general perspective, however, one might observe that 1976 represented a watershed in Czechoslovak political life. Just a year later Charter 77 was launched—a united dissident platform combining all the different ideological streams—whose signatories accepted the implicit invitation of Havel's play: to step out of a schizophrenic double bind and speak their minds freely, regardless of the consequences.

---

[27] Curiously enough, while banned at home, Havel's play never attracted much attention abroad, and its text has never been published in English. "Why this is so," the author mused in 1977, "is not clear to me. But the reasons must be deeper than those usually proffered: a universal Brecht cult in Western theatrical circles generating . . . shock and revulsion that anybody might dare touch a subject which the great B. B. has already touched once" ("Dovětek autora," in *Hry 1970–1976*, p. 308). As far as I am able to ascertain, the English-language premiere of the play was Michal Schonberg's production which took place on March 16, 17, and 18, 1977, staged by the students of the Scarborough College Drama Workshop at the University of Toronto.

Index